APACHE NIGHTMARE

APACHE NIGHTMARE

The Battle at Cibecue Creek

Charles Collins

University of Oklahoma Press : Norman

Also by Charles Collins

The Great Escape: The Apache Outbreak of 1881 (Tucson, 1994)

Library of Congress Cataloging-in-Publication Data

Collins, Charles, 1952–
    Apache nightmare : the battle at Cibecue Creek / Charles
Collins.
        p.   cm. — (The civilization of the American Indian series)
    Includes bibliographical references and index.
    ISBN 0-8061-3114-4 (cloth : alk. paper)
    1. Cibecue Creek (Ariz. : Creek), Battle of, 1881. 2. Cibecue
Apache Indians—Wars. 3. Cibecue Apache Indians—Government
relations. 4. Cibecue Apache Indians—Religion. 5. Nakaidoklini,
d. 1881—Influence. 6. Nakaidoklini, d. 1881—Death and burial.
I. Title. II. Series.
E83.88.C67 1999
973.8′4—dc21   98-31383
                                                                        CIP

The paper in this book meets the guidelines for permanence and durability of the Committee
on Production Guidelines for Book Longevity of the Council on Library Resources, Inc.∞

Copyright © 1999 by the University of Oklahoma Press, Norman, Publishing Division of the
University. All rights reserved. Manufactured in the U.S.A.

1 2 3 4 5 6 7 8 9 10

To my wife, Janet, and two children, Stephanie and Eric, and to my father, Charles Arthur Collins, Sr., who provided advice and technical assistance until his death shortly before this project was completed.

CONTENTS

ILLUSTRATIONS

Figures

Maps

PREFACE

One of my fondest childhood memories is of my father telling stories of the Apache and their confrontations with settlers and the U.S. Army. As we drove along the highways of Arizona and New Mexico he pointed out mountain ranges and places of historical interest. I imagined what it was like to live during those times and even participated in the events in my dreams. One trip was especially memorable.

In the mid-1960s my father took the family to Fort Apache. As we approached the fort he told us a story about an Apache medicine man who had lived on nearby Cibecue Creek. According to his story this medicine man was a charismatic individual who attracted many followers. He urged them to throw the white man out of Apache country. When the whites learned about this the military sent troops to the medicine man's camp to arrest him. While leaving his village after making the arrest hundreds of the medicine man's followers attacked the soldiers. The Indian scouts, who were working for the military, mutinied and joined the attackers. The medicine man tried to escape, but as he shouted to his followers, a soldier thrust a pistol barrel into his mouth and pulled the trigger. Before the soldiers retreated that night they checked to make sure the medicine man was dead. Finding him still alive, they crushed his head with an ax. The surviving soldiers made it back to Fort

Apache. The Apaches went on the warpath and killed settlers and soldiers throughout the region. The military managed to put down the uprising but never again trusted the Indian scouts.

My interest in the Cibecue affair increased in the late 1980s and early 1990s when I was working on the story of the 1881 Chiricahua outbreak. Since the Cibecue battle occurred a month before that outbreak, much of my research covered the Cibecue troubles. I soon learned that the soldiers who had been in the area at the time of the troubles and had written about them later in their lives had promulgated rumors as though they were facts. Portions of most scholarly accounts of the affair relied heavily on these rumors—which were often erroneous—and existing accounts did not consider the Apache's perspective, perhaps in part because little material had been found which presented their point of view. It was obvious that no one had written a thorough, balanced account. This is what I have set out to do.

In an effort to find all the firsthand material that exists on the Cibecue affair, I traveled to the National Archives in Washington, D.C., the U.S. Army Military History Institute, and the Arizona Historical Society and visited many Apache and military sites associated with the affair.

This story is reconstructed from many archival documents: military officers and Indian Bureau officials wrote many telegrams, letters, and reports during the affair; participants and people who lived near the event left memoirs; and the five newspaper correspondents who were sent to eastern Arizona to cover the affair wrote voluminously on the events as they unfolded. In addition, I found accounts of the troubles by contemporary Cibecue Apaches and by Apache scouts who participated in the mutiny. Interestingly, these accounts, which have never been published, do not suggest that the medicine man was instigating trouble with anyone.

Below is a brief summary of the facts that lay behind the story my father told me many years ago. The details presented in the following chapters will show the inaccuracies in his account.

In June 1881 a Cibecue Apache medicine man living on the White Mountain Indian Reservation in eastern Arizona claimed he could bring the dead back to life. Apaches flocked to him. As his following grew, rumors that he was instigating an uprising began to circulate. Nearby settlers, the military, and the reservation agent were worried.

On August 28, 1881, two cavalry troops left Fort Apache, Arizona, with a company of Indian scouts to arrest the medicine man, who was living about forty-five miles away, on Cibecue Creek. The trip to the creek and the arrest were uneventful. However, while the force was returning to the fort, the medicine man's followers attacked them. At the start of the fight the Indian scouts joined the attackers, marking the only wholesale mutiny of an Indian scout company in U.S. military history. More soldiers were killed in this fight than in any other in Arizona against Indians. The army's reaction to the battle was incredible. As Apaches accused Apaches of other bands of involvement, the army arrested the accused without considering the animosities and jealousies between the various tribes and bands on the reservation. This is the story of the fight, the events that led to it, and its aftermath.

ACKNOWLEDGMENTS

Many people helped with this endeavor. My father reviewed a late draft of the manuscript. The final draft was critiqued by Edwin Sweeney of Saint Charles, Missouri, who has written several important books and articles on Apache and military history; Dr. Joe Nicholas of Show Low, Arizona, who has a deep interest in Apache and military history and is researching the life of frontier military officer Charles B. Gatewood; and Sergio Macedo of Tahiti, who is developing an illustrated book on the Apaches. Marlene Bufkin of Tucson, Arizona, wife of the late Don Bufkin, provided permission to redraw one of Don's maps. Unless designated otherwise, all other maps herein were drawn by David Vandenberg of Tucson. James Walker of Scottsdale, Arizona, Richard Hirschberg of Chandler, Arizona, and my brother, Keith Collins, also of Chandler, helped with the fieldwork. Frank Chapman of Young, Arizona, took us to the site of the Middleton Ranch.

Ramon Riley, resource director for the White Mountain Apache Tribe, provided useful historical information. Mike Pilgrim, Richard Fusick, Mike Meier, Michael Musick, and DeAnne Blanton of the National Archives and Records Administration retrieved needed documents. Personnel at the U.S. Army Military History Institute at Carlisle Barracks, Pennsylvania, provided important papers. Riva Dean of the Arizona Historical Society helped to obtain archival information. Throughout my effort I used the libraries of the University of Arizona, the city of Tucson, and Fort Huachuca.

Without the support of these individuals and institutions, I could not have finished this project to my satisfaction. I am indebted to them all.

APACHE NIGHTMARE

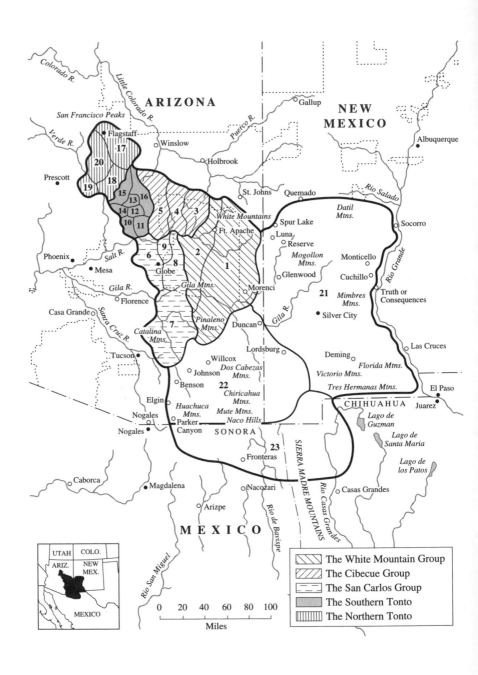

The White Mountain Group
The Cibecue Group
The San Carlos Group
The Southern Tonto
The Northern Tonto

Chiricahua and Western Apache territory, ca. 1850. The Chiricahua Apache were divided into three large bands (21, 22, and 23); and the Western Apache were divided into five separate groups (see map key), each of which was further divided into bands. The Chiricahua and Western Apache bands, numbered on the map, are as follows:

1. Eastern White Mountain Band
2. Western White Mountain Band
3. Carrizo Band
4. Cibecue Band
5. Canyon Creek Band
6. Pinal Band
7. Aravaipa Band
8. San Carlos Band
9. Apache Peaks Band
10. Mazatzal Band
11. First Semiband Southern Tonto
12. Second Semiband Southern Tonto
13. Third Semiband Southern Tonto
14. Fourth Semiband Southern Tonto
15. Fifth Semiband Southern Tonto
16. Sixth Semiband Southern Tonto
17. Mormon Lake Band
18. Fossil Creek Band
19. Bald Mountain Band
20. Oak Creek Band
21. Chiricahua Eastern Band
22. Chiricahua Central Band
23. Chiricahua Southern Band

Redrawn from map by Don Bufkin.

INTRODUCTION

The Cibecue Apache is one of five subtribal groups of the Western Apache; the others are the San Carlos, Northern Tonto, Southern Tonto, and White Mountain.[1] During prereservation times the territorial boundaries of each group were clearly defined. Each group considered itself distinct from the others, although their language was the same and there was some intermarriage.

Each subtribal group was composed of bands, each with its own territory. Each band consisted of numerous local groups made up of varying numbers of extended family groups. These local groups had their own farm sites and hunting localities. As most members of a local group were related by blood or marriage, they were highly cohesive and felt obligated to aid each other in every way possible.

At the subtribal group and band levels there were no leaders or political governments. Each local group was headed by a chief who directed its collective activities and its participation in activities with other local groups. Occasionally a chief of a local group was influential enough to represent two or more local groups for a particular cause or project.

The Western Apache also had a clan system. Members of the same clan lived scattered throughout various bands and local groups. Members of the same clan believed they were matrilineally related—that they were the descendants of a group of ancestors who established farm sites at the clan's legendary place of origin. Persons belonging to the same clan were expected to aid each other whenever the need arose. Clan chiefs had some influence over their clan. Clans provided a means to obtain more people for projects than were available in a single local group.

Before the 1930s ethnological studies of the Western Apache were amateurish and limited. Most whites believed the Western Apache was composed of tribes; that each tribe was composed of a number of bands; and that each band had a chief. This seemed to be apparent to them; the complexity of the Apache's social organization was not.

In the prereservation period the Cibecue group was composed of three bands, the Carrizo, Cibecue, and Cañon Creek, that lived in the river valleys for which they were named. The most prominent chief on the Carrizo during the 1860s was Miguel. A chief known as Captain Chiquito lived on the Cibecue, and another, Nock-ay-det-klinne, resided west of the Cibecue, probably on Cañon Creek. The White Mountain group occupied the land farther east and south and was composed of two bands, the Eastern White Mountain and the Western White Mountain. Esketeshelaw was the most prominent Eastern White Mountain chief.

There was one major anomaly in the Cibecue and White Mountain groups. Like Miguel, Pedro was a chief of a band living on Carrizo Creek. During a bitter clan dispute in the early 1850s, Miguel drove Pedro off the Carrizo. Pedro wandered with his people for nearly two years. Finally, Esketeshelaw permitted him and his people to settle in White Mountain territory, near present-day Forestdale. The location was close to Carrizo territory. After that Pedro's people began to be more closely associated with the White Mountain Apache, often intermarrying with them. Nevertheless, for many years Pedro's band and clan loyalties still leaned toward the Carrizo band.

In July 1869 Miguel and about forty members of his band guided three white men, Corydon Eliphalet Cooley and two companions, on an exploring and prospecting expedition through Cibecue country. The three men found Miguel and his people very friendly. That same month Maj. John Green led the first military expedition into White Mountain country; he and his men were also impressed by the friendliness of the Cibecue Apaches and Pedro.

In November 1869 Green returned to find a site for a military post. Five years earlier Esketeshelaw had visited the military at Camp Goodwin on the Gila River and offered them land for that purpose at the confluence of the East and North forks of the White River. During this return visit Green's men again found Miguel and Pedro and their people very friendly. Although Esketeshelaw and his people were also friendly, Esketeshelaw was somewhat evasive, perhaps because Cochise was visiting his camp at the time.

Green was convinced that the Cibecue Apache and the northern bands of the White Mountain Apache needed a reservation encompassing their own territory. They had repeatedly told him and his men that they wanted to stay in their homelands. In January 1870 a formal description of the new reservation was drawn up, and by the end of March it was approved by the commissioner of Indian affairs and the secretary of war. In May 1870 a post (which would soon be named Camp Apache, and then in 1879, Fort Apache) was officially established on the reservation on the land that Esketeshelaw had offered. The next month the Apaches began receiving beef rations from the military at the post.

At the same time Camp Apache was established, troops from Camp McDowell mistook some of Captain Chiquito's Cibecue Apache band for Tontos and attacked their camp, destroying their corn crop and taking several horses, saddles, bridles, and blankets. Rather than retaliate, Captain Chiquito's people reported the incident to the commanding officer of the new post. The Cibecue Apaches were trying hard to remain at peace with the whites.

Although Esketeshelaw tried to keep his White Mountain band on friendly terms with the military, some of his young warriors made it difficult. In March 1871 an Indian from his band lanced to death a clerk at the post trader's store. Two months later his people raided the quartermaster's beef herd and killed the herder. That summer Pedro's two daughters married Cooley, who had decided to stay in the area. Over the years Cooley often interceded on behalf of Pedro's band and did much to help them maintain peace with their white neighbors. The marriages to Cooley also brought Pedro's band into a close relationship with the military at Camp Apache.[2]

In August 1871 the first scouts at Camp Apache were enlisted. Seventy-five immediately volunteered, but only forty-four were chosen. All were from the Cibecue bands and Pedro's band. Their first duty was to arrest hostile members of Esketeshelaw's band. Six White Mountains were killed and fourteen were taken prisoner.

In September 1871 Vincent Colyer, the peace commissioner, visited Camp Apache. He selected the same land for the reservation that had been selected earlier. On November 9, 1871, President Ulysses Simpson Grant approved the establishment of the White Mountain Indian Reservation.[3] James E. Roberts, its first civilian agent, erected the agency buildings across the river from Camp Apache.

During the winter of 1872–73 Lt. Col. George Crook launched a campaign against the Northern and Southern Tonto Apaches and certain bands of Yavapai.[4] A scout company, composed of Cibecue Apaches and men from Pedro's band, under Cooley, served in the campaign. Four of the scouts were awarded the Medal of Honor. The subdued Tontos and Yavapai were settled on a reservation at Camp Verde.

During this period the troops at Camp Apache made frequent visits to Miguel's camp. They always found them peaceably disposed. Meanwhile Esketeshelaw's band had developed ill feelings toward the Cibecue Apaches and Pedro's band because of their friendship with the whites. In the spring of 1873 Esketeshelaw's people were accused of making attempts on the lives of several people at Camp Apache. The post brewer was shot through his right arm and side. Diablo, Miguel's younger brother, tracked down and killed the Indian who shot the brewer. Several travelers through White Mountain country disappeared and were later found dead. Depredations in the area steadily increased.

About this time Polone assumed the chieftainship of Esketeshelaw's band and Petone became the chief of Pedro's people.[5] Polone, aware of the trouble between his people and the military, told the military that he wanted to "get bad Indians."[6] He, however, could not control his young warriors any more than Esketeshelaw could. In the fall of 1873 there were reports of stock stealing, and soldiers traced the stock to White Mountain camps on Bonito Creek.

Crook issued an order in the spring of 1874 that all the Apaches must remain near Camp Apache and plant their crops only at such places as the military directed. The Cibecue Apaches and Pedro's band, who had not been involved in the troubles and had maintained peaceful relations with the whites, were most adversely affected by this order since they lived farther from the post than the White Mountain Apaches. The troublemakers, Esketeshelaw's band, were affected little, since they already lived nearby.

Of course, the Cibecue people did not want to leave their homelands and move into White Mountain territory, but they nevertheless complied with the order. The move was fatal for Miguel. Close contact with the White Mountain people led to frequent brawls. During one of them, Miguel and eight other Cibecue men and two White Mountain Apaches were killed.

Shortly after that Diablo became chief of Miguel's band. Diablo avenged the death of his brother and then enlisted as a scout. In the fall of 1874 the Apache leaders met at Camp Apache with Indian Inspector Daniels. Diablo said he wished only to be allowed to return to his home on the Carrizo. Petone also spoke on behalf of the Cibecue people, asking that they be permitted to return to their homes. On December 2, 1874, Diablo reenlisted in the scout company and was promoted to sergeant. Throughout this period, in spite of being moved from their homelands, Diablo, Nock-ay-det-klinne, Captain Chiquito, Petone, and Pedro maintained their friendship with the whites and were inclined toward peace.

The Cibecue Apaches' situation would soon worsen. The Indian Bureau had initiated a concentration policy whereby several agencies were to be closed and the Indians on those reservations moved to the San Carlos Agency on the Gila River. This consolidation would save the Department of Interior money: it would eliminate the expense of maintaining separate agencies. In February and March 1875 about 1,400 Tonto Apaches and Yavapais were brought to San Carlos from Camp Verde.

On June 16, 1875, the commissioner of Indian affairs ordered John Philip Clum, then the White Mountain Reservation agent, to close the Camp Apache Agency and move its property and the Apaches who were there to the San Carlos Agency. In compliance with these instructions the property and many of the Indians were transferred to San Carlos in late July. The military authorities were against the move but were powerless to prevent it. Many of the Apaches wanted to be near their homelands and argued against leaving Camp Apache. But only the Indian scouts and their families and relatives (Pedro and Diablo and their bands) were allowed to stay, until the scouts were discharged from the military.

Two months before Diablo's enlistment expired, however, he was discharged from the scouts and ordered to take his people to San Carlos. Dejected and bitter, on January 9, 1876, he led an attack on Camp Apache. It ended in failure, with three of his men arrested and confined to the guardhouse. Diablo then moved his band to San Carlos. He developed deep resentment and jealousy toward Pedro and his band for being permitted to remain at Camp Apache. About five years later Joseph Capron Tiffany, then the agent at San Carlos, remarked, "When Diablo came in with his band, it made a feud [with Pedro's band] which has never died down to this day, but has been a source of ceaseless trouble."[7]

Shortly after moving the Cibecue and White Mountain Apaches to San Carlos Clum established a subagency sixteen and a half miles up the Gila to alleviate overcrowding at the agency. The White Mountain Apaches moved to the subagency and camped near old Camp Goodwin. The Cibecue Apaches stayed at the agency, establishing their camps on the San Carlos River, to the north.[8]

Several years later, on August 30, 1880, a year before the Cibecue fight, Diablo's band attacked Pedro's band near Fort Apache. By the time cavalry from the fort arrived Diablo was dead, killed by Petone, Alchesay, and Uclenny of Pedro's band. A White Mountain chief, possibly Polone, was also killed.

In February 1881 Diablo's band, "supported by 35 other San Carlos Indians,"[9] left the agency and moved to the northern region of the reservation to avenge Diablo's death. They met Pedro's band near present-day Forestdale. In the ensuing fight Petone was killed, Alchesay was seriously wounded in the chest, and Pedro was shot through both knees. Tiffany reported, "Had not my scouts under A. [Albert] D. Sterling [chief of the San Carlos Indian Police] been there to try and arrest the murderers [of Diablo], and thrown themselves between them and Pedro's band to which these men belonged, the latter would, no doubt, have been annihilated."[10] When Diablo's band returned to San Carlos Sanchez assumed the chieftainship.

In March 1881 Eskiole, another popular Cibecue chief, was killed in a duel with one of his own band members. Many of the older Cibecue and White Mountain chiefs were now dead. Their old ways were gone. They had been through tremendous changes. Their removal to Fort Apache and then to San Carlos had forced them from their traditional homes and farm sites. It had disrupted family, band, and clan structures and caused serious social problems. The foundation was now laid for a cult movement that would lead to the battle of Cibecue Creek. The Cibecue Apaches were ready to listen to a medicine man who promised them that their old lifeway would return and their dead chiefs would come back to them. It was a concept totally foreign and abhorrent to traditional Apache beliefs.[11]

The concentration policy had continued after the Cibecue and White Mountain Apaches were moved to San Carlos. In June 1876 about 325 Chiricahuas were moved from the Chiricahua Reservation in southeastern Arizona to the San Carlos Subagency. In May 1877, 343 Warm Springs Apaches and 110 Chiricahuas were moved from the Warm Springs Agency, in southwestern New Mexico, to San Carlos. The total number of Indians at San Carlos was now more than five thousand.

The consolidation was terrible for the Apaches. Many of the groups had never been associated with one another, and their close proximity gave rise to mistrust and suspicion. There was bitterness and jealousy among them, and no friendly feelings between those Apaches already there and the new arrivals.

Although the Cibecue Apaches lived at the agency and the White Mountain Apaches lived at the subagency at the time of the Cibecue affair, contemporary whites were not at all consistent in their use of names for the two groups. Some referred to both groups as White Mountain Apaches, and others called them all Coyotero Apaches;[12] some called Pedro's band and the Cibecue Apaches White Mountain Apaches and the White Mountain Apaches Coyotero Apaches. This inconsistency will be apparent in the following chapters.

For approximately two years prior to the Cibecue affair and throughout its unfolding, the top commanders in the Military Department of Arizona remained the same. Bvt. Maj. Gen. Orlando Bolivar Willcox commanded the department. His headquarters was at Whipple Barracks, near Prescott, Arizona. Two regiments were then permanently stationed in Arizona and were, of course, under his command—the 12th Infantry (Willcox belonged to it and was its senior officer) and the 6th Cavalry, commanded by Col. Eugene Asa Carr. Carr's headquarters was at Fort Lowell, near Tucson. Altogether, the 12th Infantry and the 6th Cavalry had 1,324 soldiers (101 officers and 1,223 enlisted men) stationed at eleven posts scattered across Arizona.

Although Fort Lowell was about 225 miles south of Whipple Barracks, the relationship between Willcox and Carr had gradually deteriorated to the point that they detested each other.[13] On May 30, 1881, Willcox temporarily relieved Carr from duty at Fort Lowell and ordered him to command Fort Apache. Since Fort Apache was very remote, Carr presumed, probably correctly, that Willcox was banishing him. Carr arrived at Fort Apache as the Cibecue troubles were beginning.

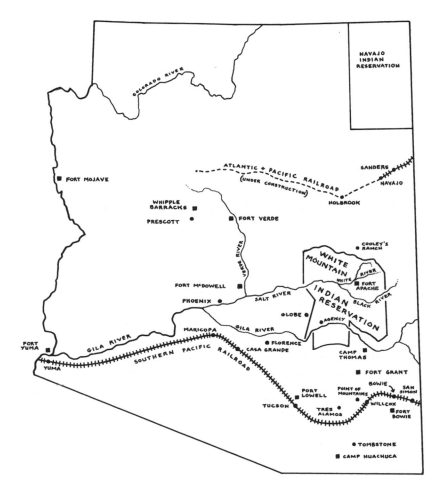

Arizona, September 1881

Chapter 1

TROUBLE ON THE RESERVATION

Several years after the transfer of the Cibecue and White Mountain Apaches to San Carlos the reservation agent granted the chiefs passes to move with their bands to the northern part of the reservation. A pass was for a specified period and for the chief and a specified number of men, women, and children. Some chiefs moved their bands north only for the summer; others stayed there. In the latter cases, the chiefs would come in to the agency and renew the passes just before they expired. Most who made this northward trip set up their villages along creeks and rivers. There they herded, hunted, planted corn, barley, and vegetables, and held dances.

In mid-May 1881 Nock-ay-det-klinne,[1] who was both a chief and a medicine man, obtained a pass from Joseph Capron Tiffany,[2] then the White Mountain Reservation agent, to move north with his small Cibecue Apache band. They left the agency and moved to Cibecue Creek, a remote area about 45 miles northwest of Fort Apache, and set up their summer camp. About a month later the whites at the agency and Fort Apache received disturbing reports about Nock-ay-det-klinne from Indians who had come from his village. The Indians said he was holding meetings to raise from the dead two chiefs who had recently been killed. They said the corpses of the chiefs were partly out of their graves and were resurrected to

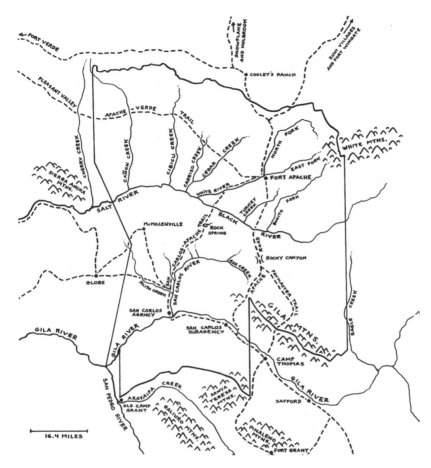

White Mountain Indian Reservation, 1881. When not away on passes, the White Mountain Apaches and three of the four Chiricahua Apache bands (the Chokonens, Nednhis, and Bedonkohe) lived near and were rationed from the subagency; and the Cibecue, Mojave, San Carlos, Tonto, Warm Springs, and Yuma Indians resided near and were rationed from the agency. (The Warm Springs Apaches were the fourth Chiricahua Apache band. They were known as the Chihenne to the Apaches.) The camps of the agency Indians extended about five miles down the Gila and seven to eight miles up the San Carlos River. The August 18, 1881, count indicated there were 4,994 Indians under the reservation agent's control: 2,726 at the agency, 573 at the subagency, 165 enlisted as scouts with the military, and 1,530 absent, mostly on passes in the northern region of the reservation. Pedro's band was not included in the counts, since they were not under agent's domain.

the knees and "visible to all Indians." Later the whites learned that during these gatherings the Indians were drinking *tizwin*, an intoxicant made from the mescal plant or corn, and dancing a peculiar dance. It was stepped to the monotonous thumping of tomtoms and continued until the dancers dropped from exhaustion.[3]

Colonel Carr arrived at Fort Apache on June 18, 1881, about when the whites first learned of Nock-ay-det-klinne's doings. The next day an Indian runner who had left Nock-ay-det-klinne's village that day came into the agency. Albert D. Sterling,[4] chief of the San Carlos Indian Police, learned from him that Nock-ay-det-klinne had announced he would give up his life if he could not raise the dead chiefs within seven days. Sterling immediately notified Tiffany.

At the time both Tiffany and Sterling thought more than one medicine man was involved. Tiffany quickly told Sterling, "Go to Cibicu[5] in time to protect the foolish medicine men but don't interfere until they have failed resuscitating the corpses in specified time. If it is then necessary for their protection bring them to the Agency and tell those chiefs that they shall not kill them, and that I shall not have any more such foolishness. Impress on their minds that all such actions are nothing more than the most utter foolishness and superstitions."[6]

Sterling took some scouts and went to Nock-ay-det-klinne's village. They counted the Indians and identified the bands of Nock-ay-det-klinne, Na-ti-o-tish, Es-ke-al-te, and Indaschin and part of Sanchez's band. Nock-ay-det-klinne fled into the nearby mountains that evening. Two weeks later Tiffany notified the commissioner of Indian affairs,

> Considerable excitement had been caused by a medicine man who had given out word that he was going to bring two chiefs who had been killed during the year (Di-ab-a-lo and Es-ki-o-le) to life and when he did he was going to be the ruler of the Indians as he would be a greater man than the Great and he would take care of the Indians and kill the white people in the Agency and etc. I sent scouts up to find out the truth of the report, as he had sent words to the Indians he had them alive up to the knees and I felt sure there was something wrong. They went and the followers tried to make them believe the man was talking to him but they could not hear what he said. They told him he hid and would come and tell me so. The

Col. Eugene Asa Carr. Courtesy National Archives.

Indians up at Cibicu said if he fooled them they would kill him. I have sent the scouts up to bring him in if they can find him. I shall make an example of him in order to deter any such foolishness, as it excited a great many foolish young warriors and bucks to the detriment of good order and the peace of the reserve.[7]

When the scouts returned to the Cibecue they found Nock-ay-det-klinne had again gone into the mountains. After they left Nock-ay-det-klinne returned to his camp. He called for more dances and asked the Indians for presents of horses, saddles, blankets, cattle, and food to complete the resurrections. The Indians gave him large numbers of these items, and the popularity of his dances increased. About July 14 he held dances near Fort Apache which attracted more Indians. After a while, however, some of the Indians suspected fraud and demanded the return of their sacrifices. Some threatened to kill Nock-ay-det-klinne if he did not keep his word or return their property.

Sometime between July 18 and 26, 1881, Nock-ay-det-klinne and Chiefs Na-ti-o-tish, Es-ke-al-te, and Ne-big-ja-gy (Nock-ay-det-klinne's brother),[8] came in to the agency and met with Tiffany. Tiffany did not then feel justified in arresting Nock-ay-det-klinne as he had only said he was going to raise two dead chiefs and asked for, and received, presents for the occurrence. Tiffany did, however, warn him to stop inciting the Indians. He also told the three chiefs that the scheming must stop, that they were being cheated and trouble would come. The chiefs agreed that Nock-ay-det-klinne should restore their presents. Shortly thereafter Nock-ay-det-klinne and the chiefs left the agency.

Nock-ay-det-klinne knew his followers would soon be so riled that they would recover their donations with force, if necessary, and might even kill him. He had to come up with a new scheme. In late July, he announced it: he could raise the dead of both friendly and hostile Indians, but "the spirits had notified him that the dead warriors could not return to the country until the whites had left it."[9] He fixed the date of the whites' departure at the time of the corn harvest (late August or early September).

Perhaps Nock-ay-det-klinne was not seriously advocating the departure of the whites but was simply trying to save face and his own life by tying the resurrections to an unlikely event. Tiffany

Joseph C. Tiffany. Courtesy Arizona Historical Foundation, University
Libraries, ASU.

believed Nock-ay-det-klinne was saying he would raise the dead of both friend and foe "to secure hostile favor, if he failed to excite friendly Indians."[10]

In any event, sometime during early August Es-ke-al-te and Sanchez joined Nock-ay-det-klinne's scheme. They claimed to be medicine men and began aiding him in pretending to be able to restore life to dead Indians. On August 4 Colonel Carr reported the situation to General Willcox:

> The Chief and Medicine Man of the band of Indians living on Cibicu Creek, "Nock-ay-det-klinne" by name, has been for two months holding dances with the object of raising from the dead Indians who have been killed. He called on me on the fifteenth after having held dances in this neighborhood, and informed me as above. He stated that he had not succeeded, but he had communication with the spirits of some of the dead Indians.
>
> It is now reported to me by Interpreter [Charles] Hurrle that Nockaydetklinne [sic] is telling the Indians that the dead say they will not return because of the presence of the white people; that when the white people leave the dead will return, and that the whites will be out of the country when the corn gets ripe. Hurrle thinks his next move may be to try to induce the Indians to hasten the departure of the whites, and that he may be working them up to a frame of mind suitable for the purpose. Pedro has moved his personal camp in, close to the post; says he is afraid of his enemies.
>
> I do not know whether all this is of any consequence, but feel it my duty to report it to the Department Commander.[11]

Carr was receiving other alarming rumors during this period. An Indian told the post's cattle herder that he "would fight soon and get even with him."[12] The post's sawmill engineer reported that an Indian told him "they liked him and when they broke out they would save him, if he would give them a horse." Another Indian told a soldier they "could take the post in 15 minutes after they commenced."[13]

On the nights of August 4 and 5 Nock-ay-det-klinne held large dances near Fort Apache. This gave the military and civilian personnel at the fort a chance to see how popular the dances had become. About eight or nine o'clock on one of the evenings Carr went to a dance in Pedro's village with Mrs. Carr; Clark M. Carr,

Bvt. Maj. Gen. Orlando Bolivar Willcox. Courtesy Massachusetts Commandery Military Order of the Loyal Legion and the U.S. Army Military
History Institute.

their fifteen-year-old son who was on vacation from school; Capt. Edmund Clarence Hentig; and George McCreery, the assistant surgeon.

Shortly thereafter Carr called his officers and important civilian employees together to discuss the situation. He often met with his key subordinates to discuss important matters and to ask for their ideas, opinions, and recommendations. Later, 1st Lt. William Harding Carter, who was in attendance, said that "nearly every officer at the post and the interpreters, [Sam] Bowman[14] and others, gave it as their opinion that they thought the Indians were very uneasy, showed a very different disposition from what they had done for years, and that they were only waiting to gather their corn to go on the war path. The feeling was almost unanimous that a general uprising of the White Mountain Apaches and possibly the Chiricahuas was about to take place."[15]

On August 10 Carr received a telegram from Tiffany, who was at the agency, seventy-five road miles south of Fort Apache. It said an Indian named "Coon Can" had come to the subagency and said the Indians would meet near Fort Apache on August 15 and "if the dead did not come up it was because of the whites and they must go."[16] Of course, Tiffany's message confirmed the rumors Carr was receiving. That same day Carr wired Tiffany:

> Sam Bowman thinks the White Mountains will break out when they have their corn gathered and cached. Hurrle thinks same, says they are making sacrifices. Indian doctor puts food in medicine lodge and pretends that the dead come and eat it, says that Indians think this doctor will be the head of all Indians; that he says the ground will turn over, the dead will rise and the Indians [will] be above the whites; that they will have possession of this post, that the soldiers will have to give up their horses to them, etc.
>
> Hurrle says they intend to have another dance here in Pedro's camp a week from next Saturday night which will be the 20th. It might be well to arrest the Indian Doctor and send him to Alcatraz,[17] but I would not like to take the responsibility as it might precipitate a war. Sam Bowman thinks our company of scouts will break when the others do. He says there is another medicine man at work also.[18]

Ezra Hoag, issue clerk at the San Carlos Subagency,[19] also heard similar reports. An Indian told him that Nock-ay-det-klinne had interviewed the bones of a dead chief and the bones said the "white man must go under and the Indians be on top."[20] He also told Hoag that he and one other white man would be permitted to remain at the agency.

On August 13 Carr received a telegram, dated the seventh, from Willcox directing him to arrest Nock-ay-det-klinne "if you deem it necessary, to prevent trouble, after consultation with the Agent at San Carlos."[21] Carr notified Tiffany of Willcox's telegram. He closed his message thus:

> I do not know whether it would prevent or cause trouble to arrest him. I think if it would be decided to arrest him that such measures should be taken as to make it certain that he be caught and secured and that it would be well to wait till there are more troops on the reservation. [Carr had nine officers, including himself, and 168 enlisted men at Fort Apache; 25 of the enlisted men were Indian scouts.] I might try to arrest him when he comes for the dance next Saturday [August 20] which will perhaps be soon enough. The Indians here say they expect all the Chiricahuas and Coyoteros here for the dance which will be four or five hundred bucks and I may not be able to arrest the chief in the midst of that number. It might bring on instead of prevent trouble.[22]

Tiffany forwarded Carr's telegram to Maj. James Biddle, asking, "You have more experience than me what would you advise?"[23] Biddle was the commander of scouting operations for southeastern Arizona and stationed southeast of the agency at Fort Grant. Biddle replied, "Suggested to General Willcox to arrest that medicine man near Apache and send him in irons to Alcatraz."[24]

Tiffany and the Indian Bureau inspector, Robert S. Gardiner, at San Carlos on a routine inspection,[25] were alarmed. They thought the White Mountain, Tonto, and San Carlos Apaches were being influenced by Nock-ay-det-klinne and reported rumors that White Mountain and San Carlos Indians were congregating near Fort Apache and hostile Indians in New Mexico under Nana were heading toward the reservation and were expected to join them.[26] Gardiner said the Indians were holding big medicine dances in various camps. Tiffany reported the White Mountain Apaches at the agency were making suspicious movements. He requested rifles and ammunition from the military and enlisted thirty additional scouts to help protect the agency. Tiffany's reply to Carr's communications about the situation reflected his fears: "I believe the medicine man is working for his own personal benefit and to keep property given by Indians under false representations and trying to excite them against the whites. I want him arrested or killed or both and think it had better be before dance next Saturday night."[27]

On August 15, the same day Carr received Tiffany's reply, he received another telegram from Whipple Barracks, dated August 13: "The two companies of cavalry at Thomas have been ordered to report without delay to you at Apache for temporary duty. The Commanding General desires that you arrest the Indian doctor, who you report as stirring up hostilities, as soon as practicable."[28]

Also on August 15, Carr wired General Willcox asking, at Maj. Melville Augustus Cochran's request, that two field pieces and a Gatling gun, with ammunition, be sent to Fort Apache for use in case the post was left with a small guard. Cochran was the commander of the infantry at the fort and would be left there with them if Carr and the cavalry went in the field.

Arizona was receiving torrential rains. The rivers were high and treacherous, and many overflowed their banks. Biddle was ordered to bring the two cavalry troops at Grant to Camp Thomas to temporarily establish his headquarters there and to send the two cavalry troops stationed at Camp Thomas to Fort Apache. Thomas was the military post closest to Apache, seventy-five road miles away. Biddle moved to Camp Thomas with the troops from Grant. However, he did not send the Thomas troops to Apache. He was reluctant to order them to cross the swollen Gila River, which was "higher than ever known."[29]

Carr's tough situation became tougher. A single telegraph line ran from Willcox, Arizona, through Grant to Camp Thomas and ended at Fort Apache.[30] There were no other telegraph lines into the fort. The weather downed the line between Thomas and Apache on August 15, leaving Carr with no quick means of communicating with the outside world. The military authorities at Whipple Barracks and in the Gila River valley were concerned. Four days earlier Tiffany had telegraphed Departmental Headquarters that Carr had informed him that there were six hundred Indians near Apache. The line went down before Departmental Headquarters or Biddle could telegraph Carr that the cavalry could not cross the Gila.[31] Although Willcox had directed Biddle to send a twelve-pound field gun and ammunition and a .45-caliber Gatling gun to Apache, the flooded river prevented Biddle from doing so.

On the morning of August 15, just before the line went down, Carr received a telegram from Tiffany:

> Have just heard from an Indian from Cibicu that the medicine men are there holding dances. That Pedro and Alchesay were there. Some San Carlos Indians and the friends of the deceased told them their medicine was no good. That they had given them their horses, burros and things and wanted to know when the men would come. The medicine men said they did not know when. That they would have a dance about it at Apache. They will leave Cibicu Tuesday [the 16th]. The names of the medicine men are Ka-klen-ney [Ka-clenny], Sanchez and Es-ke-el-tay [Es-ke-al-te].[32]

Obviously, Nock-ay-det-klinne and his partners in his schemes were still contending with doubters.

During the first several days after the telegraph line went down, Biddle, then at Camp Thomas, sent parties out several times to repair it. Sgt. Albert E. Grant, considered the best telegraph repairman in the department, went out with some of the parties. They were not able to string a new line across the Gila River (the first place from Camp Thomas where the line was down).[33] Biddle then sent out a detachment under 1st Lt. Gilbert Edmond Overton. They "worked all day with tools and animals" but without success; Overton nearly lost two of his men by drowning.

Two days after the line went down Biddle wired Departmental Headquarters: "If no orders are received to the contrary, I will proceed with the two Grant companies to Apache as soon as I can cross the river. See no necessity for remaining here."[34] At about the same time Departmental Headquarters notified Biddle of a rumor about troubles over outlaw cowboys operating along the boundary between Mexico and southeastern Arizona. The next day it wired Biddle: "Stay where you are unless you deem it necessary to go on. Nothing new from Apache."[35] On the following day Biddle replied: "Won't move to Apache with companies without urgent necessity for it. Troops may be required on the border [due to the cowboy problem]."[36]

On August 20 Welford Chapman Bridwell[37] came to Camp Thomas from San Carlos and reported "all was quiet at Apache and that the Indians were getting incensed against the medicine man and were likely to disband from disaffection among themselves."[38] Later that day Biddle telegraphed Bridwell's report to Departmental Headquarters with additional assurance: "If anything is wrong a courier from Apache would have come here. Carr was notified what time men would be on this side of river to see if anybody came."[39]

Also on that day, Biddle received a telegram from Tiffany providing more assurance that everything was calm at Fort Apache:

> Crit [lieutenant in the San Carlos Indian Police] . . . returned last night from White River, Apache, and reports several chiefs went with him and came back satisfied seeing or hearing nothing except that Crit says the woman who is living with Hunly [Hurrle] the interpreter at Apache circulated or caused to be circulated the reports about the killing and driving off [of the] white men. He says there is no such talk and has not been and that [Tiffany lists ten White Mountain Apache bands] have had nothing to do with it and that the chiefs will be here in a few days and tell me all about it. Crit, I believe, is a true scout, and I send this for what you may think it worth. There is no trouble on my reservation and I anticipate none there.[40]

On August 21, Biddle, then concerned over rumors that Nana was recruiting warriors from the White Mountain Reservation, wired Departmental Headquarters: "It is stated to me by Buford [Clay Beauford] that a very large number of Indians are now off the reservation and few men are drawing rations for a great many and the whereabouts of them must be unknown to the Agent even though he says to the contrary. . . . [Crit] just returned from Apache says all is quiet and nothing likely to happen."[41]

The following day, August 22, Willcox's assistant adjutant general (AAG) notified Biddle that he had received his dispatches of the previous two days and "as the Fort Apache scare seems to be over, the first thing now is to arrange for detecting and preventing Indians from leaving reservation."[42]

Biddle went to the subagency the next day to meet with Tiffany, Gardiner, and Sterling about the matter. After returning to Camp Thomas he reported, "There are Indians off the reservation but they are now being called in and the bands off have been visited by the Chief of Scouts, and from all information I can gather can't hear of any being in New Mexico. Saw an Indian at reservation who had been to Apache four days ago; all quiet there."[43] On August 25 Willcox ordered Biddle and the troops that had been moved to return to their home stations. Biddle was to keep the troops ready to help the military in New Mexico. Biddle immediately returned to Grant with the battalion he had taken from there.

The feeling that all was quiet at Fort Apache continued until the last day in August. Because of this and the continued high water in the Gila River, Biddle did not send out any more parties to try to repair the telegraph line. He thought if Carr needed to communicate with him, Carr would send couriers to the north bank of the Gila River, from which they could be seen by those at Camp Thomas.

Meanwhile, up at Fort Apache, Carr was also receiving information indicating that the chances of trouble were diminishing. On August 17 Not-chi-clish and Santo, both White Mountain chiefs who were temporarily living on the White River, a few miles below Fort Apache, came in to the fort with some followers to speak with Carr.[44] They wanted to discuss alarming reports they had heard. While discussing that matter, Not-chi-clish also told Carr that Nock-ay-det-klinne had been given more than one hundred head of stock to raise the dead. He added, "It will be years yet before the medicine man accomplishes what he undertakes and that by that time the medicine man will have all they own."[45] Not-chi-clish then said he and Santo were friends of the whites.

During their talk Carr concluded that some soldiers were frightening the Indians. Later that day he issued Order No. 125:

It has come to the knowledge of the Post Commander that some silly or evil disposed soldiers have been telling the Indians that we have sent for reinforcements and cannon and intend to remove the Indians off this reservation or to attack them or to do them some harm and have been bragging what we will do to them.

The Post Commander could hardly believe it possible that any soldier could be so foolish or wicked.

If it be simply folly it is unworthy of a man who is intrusted with the safety of the inhabitants and the credit of the Army. If any soldier can be so wicked as to deliberately try to create difficulties and misunderstandings with the Indians, the Post Commander hopes that the honorable men will put a stop to such conduct which can easily be done by frowning it down or if necessary reporting the offender.

Whatever may be the wish of a military man for war, it is his duty as a citizen as well as a servant of the nation to do nothing to bring it on but on the contrary to do everything in his power to avert it.[46]

Five days later Pedro and some of his men arrived at Fort Apache to talk to Carr. Pedro said he was concerned because the Mormons near Cooley's Ranch had met at Cooley's four days earlier, after learning that the Indians near Fort Apache were bad. The Mormons had said they were afraid. After Carr told Pedro that Nock-ay-det-klinne caused the scare, Pedro emphasized his friendship with Carr, Cochran, and the whites. Carr concluded the talk by telling Pedro "to tell all Indians they must be very careful not to scare the settlers" and that he "cannot make the settlers believe there is no danger when there is so much talk about, and the Indians go about with guns and threaten people."[47]

On about August 24 Carr called his officers together a second time. Carter said they were "questioned by Colonel Carr as to the result of any information they had been able to obtain as to the matter discussed before. Nearly all of the officers stated that they did not believe the Indians would break out as they had discovered that their plans were suspected and they had the rumor amongst them that troops and cannon were en route to the post."[48]

Nevertheless, Carr was still concerned about Nock-ay-det-klinne's influence. His orders to arrest him "as soon as practicable" still stood. Carr had hoped to apprehend him at the dance he planned to hold near Fort Apache on August 20. Nock-ay-det-klinne, however, became suspicious and canceled his plans. Carr learned Nock-ay-det-klinne was on a hunt but planned to return to his village on August 24 and then visit the camps next to Fort Apache for a dance three days later, on Saturday.

Carr wanted to apprehend Nock-ay-det-klinne before the dance. On August 23 he sent two Indian scouts, 1st Sergeant Mose[49] and Sergeant Chapeau, to his village to ask him to come to Fort Apache to talk on Thursday afternoon or Friday morning. When the scouts arrived at Nock-ay-det-klinne's village, they found he had not returned from his hunt but had sent word that he would arrive on

Friday. The villagers said he had arranged for a big dance at his village Friday night and might start for Fort Apache Saturday morning at ten o'clock. Mose returned to Apache and informed Carr. Chapeau remained at the village to deliver Carr's message to Nock-ay-det-klinne and to return to the post with him.

On Friday night an Indian came in to the village from the Salt River. He said the San Carlos Indian Police were en route to the village with a message for Nock-ay-det-klinne but were unable to cross the swollen river. The Indian said he had swum it. Chapeau waited until noon on Saturday for Nock-ay-det-klinne and then went to get him. Nock-ay-det-klinne told Chapeau that he would not come to Fort Apache until he found out what the police wanted of him. On Sunday, August 28, Chapeau arrived back at Fort Apache and informed Carr.

Carr thought the "San Carlos police story" was merely a subterfuge[50] and that Nock-ay-det-klinne was fast becoming defiant and avoiding the trip to Fort Apache. He realized he must travel to Nock-ay-det-klinne's camp to arrest him. He thought if there would be trouble, it would happen soon. The Indians were harvesting and caching their corn. The settlers were alarmed. Although he was expecting the arrival of the troops from Camp Thomas at any moment, he felt he could wait no longer.

That summer another situation also worried the military and Tiffany. On June 20, about when Nock-ay-det-klinne first announced he would raise Indians from the dead, Sterling informed Tiffany that he had received reliable information that a Navajo named Frank "was in the Tonto camps telling them [the] Navajoes were breaking out and desired them to join them."[51] The Navajo reservation was about one hundred miles north of the White Mountain Reservation. Sterling's intelligence was sent through the military hierarchy to the secretary of war. Tiffany also informed the commissioner of Indian affairs, saying it and a rumor that the government was about to remove the Indians from the reservation to a place unknown to them had created "considerable excitement"[52] among the Indians near the agency.

Several weeks later, on August 7, about thirty Navajos arrived at the agency with a large quantity of blankets to sell and trade to the reservation Indians.[53] They said part of their band was coming by

way of the Cibecue and would be at the agency the next day. Two
days later Tiffany learned they were saying they preferred to barter
their blankets for cartridges. Tiffany immediately stopped the
trading, whereupon the Navajos decided to leave. Tiffany put them
under guard until he could learn more of the situation. That night,
while Sterling was getting the information for Tiffany and Tiffany
was trying to decide what to do about the matter, a Tonto chief went
to the Navajo camp and visited for a long while. Finally Sterling
sent the Tonto back to his camp. The next day Tiffany sent the
Navajos away. During their visit Tiffany had reported that the
Tontos were uneasy. Later he said, "They [the Navajos] no doubt
came to see if there was any feeling of dissatisfaction among these
Indians and no doubt sent their men by the Cibicu to see what the
medicine man meant."[54]

After lunch on August 27 Clark Carr drove Carter and 1st Lt.
John Gregory Bourke,[55] Brig. Gen. George Crook's aide, to Pedro's
camp, a mile from Fort Apache, in a wagon. Colonel Carr had
asked Bourke to visit the camp. Bourke wrote about the request in
his diary: "[Brevet] General Carr had been very urgent in his
request to me to make this visit and . . . had made no secret of his
fears concerning the behavior of the Apaches. According to him,
'things wore an ugly look'—and there was 'more in it' than he
cared to talk about before the ladies of the garrison. . . . He asked
me very impressively to be sure and let the Indians see me and
know who I was: 'give them a good dose of Crook, they haven't
forgotten him and the licking he gave them. He is the only bulge we
have on them now.'"[56]

When Bourke's party reached Pedro's camp they found Pedro's
Apaches on a big tizwin drunk. All were armed, had their belts full
of ammunition, and were running and galloping on horseback
through their camp. Gar, Alchesay, and others talked to Bourke
about Crook and then asked him where he had come from. When he
replied that he had come from Navajo country, an Indian leaned
down from his saddle and asked, "When Navajo come?" The
Indians then explained that nine moons ago the Navajos had sent
word to the Apaches that they would come in August with many
goods and supplies "for all the Apaches and that they and the
Apaches were to be brothers." Carter later said, "We both regarded

the question with suspicion, because in the event of an uprising of the White Mountain Apaches it was believed by all in that part of the country that all disaffected young bucks of the Navajo nation would join them on the war path. The Apaches were acting in a more bold and saucy manner than I have ever known them to do and I have been among them eight years."[57]

Bourke wrote in his diary, "I didn't like the tone of this talk at all; if it meant anything at all, it meant that the Navajoes who had been surely for some months through dissatisfaction with their worthless Agent, [Galen] Eastman, had some idea of commencing hostilities in company with the White Mountain Apaches."[58] Carter later said, "Lieutenant Bourke's opinion was that these Indians were in for war, that he thought all of them would go."[59]

Chapter 2

AN AMBUSH FAILS

When Carr was ordered to arrest Nock-ay-det-klinne, the only soldiers stationed at Fort Apache were Troops D and E, 6th Cavalry; Company D, 12th Infantry; and Company A, Indian scouts. Second Lt. Thomas Cruse commanded Company A. Of his 25 scouts, 12 were from Pedro's band and 13 were Cibecue Apaches; thus Nock-ay-det-klinne was one of their own chiefs and medicine men.

With the permission of the military, the scouts attended Nock-ay-det-klinne's dances near Fort Apache. Cruse later said,

> After the medicine dances began around the post I noticed a change. Generally they [the scouts] are very ready to communicate anything they know or may have seen, but after these dances they became very uncommunicative and would not tell anything that was going on among the other Indians or among themselves. One morning the rumor was brought to me that they had told the Engineer at the saw mill that they were going to clean out the post and have it for themselves. I could not find out who made the remark from the scouts on inquiry. Formerly they had hung about the men's kitchens and quarters and would talk about themselves and their chiefs and all matters but after these dances they became changed to such an extent that all noticed it. On asking them, however, I could obtain no information.[1]

On about August 10 Carr asked Cruse for his opinion of the scouts' loyalty. Cruse replied that "he entirely distrusted his scouts in event of the rising of the White Mountains and believed all or nearly all would go with the enemy and recommended their discharge."[2] He based his recommendation on the scouts' change in conduct. He also told Carr that the main participants in any uprising would be friends and relatives of the scouts, and even if the scouts did not turn against the military, they would be of no use. Most officers at the post and Sam Bowman had the same opinion. On August 13 Carr telegraphed Departmental Headquarters: "It is the general impression here that the men of the Indian scout company will go with their friends if they break out. Please give me authority to discharge them or such of them as I may believe unreliable and enlist reliable ones in their places."[3]

Permission was granted, but the telegraph line went down before Carr could be notified. Carr did not receive the message granting approval until two and a half weeks after his request—after he returned from the Cibecue.

Routinely, every Sunday morning the scout company was inspected. Carr directed Cruse to take the scouts' guns after the August 14 inspection. He told Cruse to inform the scouts that he would keep their arms in his office to protect them from the rain. The guns were kept in the orderly room and only issued to those on herd duty, to those sent out on detached service, and to all of them on Saturday evenings for Sunday morning inspections. The scouts considered this a sign of distrust, but after Cruse had the interpreter smooth the matter over as best he could, they appeared satisfied.

Carr decided to take his cavalry and Cruse's scouts to the Cibecue and leave the infantry at Fort Apache. He did not feel comfortable bringing the scouts but had little choice. Later, he said, "I had to take the chances. They were enlisted men of my command, for duty; and I could not have found the medicine man without them. I deemed it better also if they should prove unfaithful it should not occur at the post [where there were officer's families, white civilians and government property]."[4]

On Sunday morning, August 28, shortly after Indian scout Chapeau returned to Fort Apache without Nock-ay-det-klinne, Carr told Cruse to let the scouts keep their guns after their inspection. About 10:00 A.M. the next day Carr left Fort Apache with 5 officers, 79 enlisted soldiers (Troops D and E, 6th Cavalry) and 23 scouts

Company A, Apache Scouts. This photograph was taken in 1880 at Fort Apache. Second Lt. Charles Baehr Gatewood is sitting in the center of the scouts, wearing a wide-brimmed, light-colored hat. Sam Bowman, Chief of Scouts, is standing directly behind Gatewood. Alchesay is to Gatewood's right. The left side of Alchesay's head is partially blocked by Gatewood's right hand. Courtesy National Archives.

(Company A, Indian scouts) to make the arrest.[5] He also took John Byrnes, guide; Charles Hurrle, interpreter; Charles (Nat) Nobles, chief packer; one cargador (principal assistant to the chief packer); four packers; and Clark Carr. Sixty soldiers, mostly of Company D, 12th Infantry, and several civilians remained at Fort Apache, with Major Cochran in command of the post.

Just before they left, Carr scribbled a message for General Willcox: "I sent word to Nock-ay-det-klinne that I wanted to see him. He does not seem likely to come and I am searching for his place on Cibicu to try to catch him."[6] Because the telegraph line

Infantry and Cavalry School at Fort Leavenworth, Kansas, class of 1891. First Lt. Thomas Cruse is the officer with the mustache on the far right in the second row. He is sitting off of the ground and his left shoulder is partially blocked from view by the soldier who is standing between the first and second rows (the soldier farthest to the right). Courtesy William H. Hay Collection, U.S. Army Military History Institute.

was down, Willcox did not receive the message until three days later.

It was not generally known that an expedition to Nock-ay-det-klinne's camp was planned. Carr had been secretive about the purpose and destination of the march. The scouts were not told which way to go until the force was moving out. Nevertheless, after they were notified they were going out on a march, they suspected their destination was the Cibecue.[7]

After the column crossed the White River, just outside Fort Apache, and reached the mesa on the other side, some Indians living along the river rode up and spoke to the scouts. Carr called these Indians and the scouts together and told them where the command was going and what he was going to do. He said he was not going to hurt Nock-ay-det-klinne but wanted him to come in with him. He told the curious Indians to go and tell their friends not to be alarmed as he was not going to bother them and there would be no trouble.

Carr took the Verde Trail to the Cibecue. Although this was the shortest route, the trail was rough, passing through mountainous country covered mostly with timber. The trail may have been boggy at places, but the region was then in the third day of a nine-day period without rain.

On the first day Carr and his battalion traveled about twenty-nine miles.[8] They were then winding through deep gorges with rocky sides. They camped for the night in a gorge where the trail crossed Carrizo Creek (Carrizo Crossing).[9] That evening, after supper, Carr issued each scout twenty rounds of ammunition.

> I called them around my tent and had a long talk with them. Told them I had sent for the medicine man to talk to him about the reports that he had said the whites would leave the country when the corn was ripe and etc.
>
> Mose [1st Sergeant of Company A] manfully defended his friend, but finally gave in to the idea that when there is a misunderstanding between friends they should talk it over.
>
> He then volunteered to go in advance and tell Nock-ay-det-klinne what was the object of the expedition. I told him he could do as he pleased; that I had sent once for the medicine man and he did not come, and now I was going to bring him; that I was not going to hurt him, but to show him that he must come when sent for. That if he had not said these things, he would be released at once; but that if he had, he and the Indians must be made to understand that they were not true—the whites were going to stay and etc. I then showed them the comet through my glass. Nock-ay-det-klinne had told me July 15th in reply to a question on the previous comet, that he had raised that comet. Perhaps these Indians thought that this was my comet.
>
> . . . I had also told him [Mose] and all the scouts to tell all the Indians they should meet, that my only mission was to get Nock-ay-det-klinne and that he would not be hurt and no others would be interfered with.[10]

About six o'clock the next morning Mose and a scout named Charlie left the campsite to talk to Nock-ay-det-klinne. On their departure Sergeant Dead Shot became acting 1st sergeant of Company A (the Indian leader of the Indian scouts). Carr now depended on Chapeau to point out Nock-ay-det-klinne's wickiup.

At seven o'clock the command left their campsite. During the morning they slowly climbed to the top of a canyon and onto the divide that ran between Cibecue and Carrizo creeks. In this area the trail was narrow. While passing over the "very high mountain ridge" that formed the divide, the command saw the four peaks of the Mazatzal mountain range, about sixty miles away. While they were on top of the ridge, a courier, John L. Colvig, caught up with Captain Hentig's troop, which formed the rear of Carr's column. Colvig's horse "had failed," probably from exhaustion. Cochran had sent him after Carr with two dispatches. Cochran was obviously worried.

To: [Brevet] General Carr
Sir:

After consultation with Captain [Alexander Bartholomew] MacGowan and [1st] Lieut. [Charles Garnett] Gordon I have decided to send a courier to Thomas with a dispatch, copy of which is enclosed, for your information. The dispatch referred to gives a full statement of the situation at this time (7 o'clock P.M.)

Major Cochran

To: Commanding Officer, Camp Thomas
Sir:

General Carr left this post this morning about 10 o'clock with the two cavalry companies and Company "A" Indian scouts, for the vicinity of the Cibicu for the purpose of arresting Nock-ay-det-klinne the medicine man.

Since he left the Indians about here have nearly all disappeared including the squaws of the Indian scouts and one scout left sick. Fifteen bucks in one party were seen by Lieut. Gordon going in the direction of General Carr's command all armed with rifles and with plenty of ammunition. Other parties saw nine bucks each armed with Henry rifles, going in same direction.

The circumstances look suspicious but of course we do not know what they intend to do. It is presumed however that they will at least hang on his trail and watch movements.

In case General Carr should get into a fight they might cut off his retreat on this post, or they may go at once and join the party with the medicine man, who is reported to have four or five hundred warriors in attendance upon his dance.

The total strength of the garrison is sixty men, sixteen of whom are in the sick report. The situation in my opinion is serious. It seems to me that there should be at least two cavalry companies here for an emergency.

Until this afternoon we did not consider the situation serious. Captain MacGowan and Lieut. Gordon with whom I have just consulted, concur in the foregoing statement, and both think it best to notify General Carr of what has transpired since he left the post. A courier will go to him tonight.

Under the circumstances, if General Carr should need assistance we could not possibly send out more than Captain MacGowan's company and this would leave the post with a very small guard, not strong enough to protect post.

Major Cochran[11]

Hentig immediately ordered one of his men to bring the messages forward to Carr. The soldier reached Carr as he was beginning his descent into the valley of the Cibecue. Carr read the messages and then continued onward. Their trek down the divide required caution to prevent falls. The mountain slope was so steep the trail zigzagged. At one place there were irregular stairs of stone that were difficult for the horses and mules to traverse.

About one and a half miles from the Cibecue and three miles from Nock-ay-det-klinne's village, a trail branched from the Verde Trail. This secondary trail ran diagonally up the valley, across high, open ground, through a beautiful grassy slope that stretched from the hills to the timber along the Cibecue. It was the shorter route to Nock-ay-det-klinne's village.

From this fork the Verde Trail crossed rocky and rolling country directly to Cibecue Creek. The place where it crossed the creek was known as the Verde Crossing. On the other side of the creek another secondary trail ran up the creek, just outside the bushes and undergrowth of the creek bottom, to Nock-ay-det-klinne's lodge. In this area cornfields were scattered about in the creek bottom. Where the Indians had not cleared the bottom for cultivation, there was brush. In many places it was thick. The banks of the creek, which were sometimes steep, extended ten to twelve feet above the creek bottom, on top of which was an open plain with a scattering of junipers but no heavy timber or thick bushes. Carr later described the creek as "a small mountain stream, across which you can jump in many places, and step in some; and the brushy bottom does not average one hundred yards in width."[12]

About one or two o'clock in the afternoon Cruse, Byrnes, and the scouts reached the fork. The scouts suggested they continue on the Verde Trail. Cruse, however, would not decide which to take and waited until Carr's approach. Cruse and his command then started off on the Verde Trail. When Carr reached the fork he realized Cruse was taking the longer route. He knew that because the previous night he had managed to get Mose to tell him that Nock-ay-det-klinne lived two or three miles above the Verde Crossing. Carr thought the scouts wanted to stay on the Verde Trail to get to water more quickly. He did not know they had stopped to drink when they passed water about two miles back.

Rather than take the longer route, Carr sent Hurrle to tell Cruse and his men to take the trail to the right. They had gone about a third of a mile past the fork when Hurrle reached them and gave Cruse the message. The group then switched to the other trail. Later Cruse said, "When we started off to go on the other trail they [the scouts] exhibited a good deal of symptoms of anger and one or two of my company said they were very angry because we did not go the other trail."[13] Cruse, however, did not report their dissatisfaction to Carr.

Several officers studied the situation later. Almost all concluded that the scouts had tried to lead the force into an ambush that the Indians had set up along the creek bottom. From all indications, that was probably the case. Of course, Carr and his men were not aware of it at the time. In fact, Carr was looking for a place to make camp later in the afternoon—after he made his arrest. He thought the open area just ahead, next to the creek and just north of the Verde Crossing, would make a good campsite.

Before the command changed its direction there were no Indians, other than the scouts, in sight. Once it did, Indians started to come out of the creek bottom in groups of two and three. Most headed toward Nock-ay-det-klinne's village. When the command was about two miles from the village, Sanchez, whose band lived on Carrizo Creek, twelve miles north of Carrizo Crossing, came up from the creek bottom. He was unarmed and riding a white pony. His face was painted red, but that was an ordinary occurrence. Indians frequently came into Fort Apache with painted faces.

Sanchez shook hands with Carr and told Hurrle that he was going home. He rode to the rear of the column and then back to the creek bottom. Later, when Carr's officers and key civilians thought back on the events, they believed Sanchez was counting the soldiers when he rode down their column. As Sanchez rode back to the creek bottom, Hurrle told Carr that he was not heading in the right direction to go to his home. Carr then looked back and saw him riding toward the bottom. Carr, however, thought he might be returning to the creek bottom to get some of his family or friends. In any event, Carr did not want to show the Indians any signs of distrust.

Before the command reached the Cibecue, they stopped on a little knoll to rest. They were then about a mile from Nock-ay-det-klinne's camp. During the rest Carr questioned Colvig about the state of affairs at Fort Apache. Colvig said he did not think they were as bad as reported in the dispatch as he had not seen any Indians during his journey to reach the column.

Carr concluded that the Indians whom Cochran had reported were following him had not gone far in his direction and had gone elsewhere. He turned to Assistant Surgeon George McCreery, sitting next to him, and said he "thought they were getting a little alarmed up at Apache."[14] Carr knew that in the direction the Indians were reportedly heading there were several trails leading to Indian camps and villages down the White River. In fact, the trail to the San Carlos Agency forked from the Verde Trail a few miles from the post.

As the command approached the point where the trail crossed the Cibecue, the scouts asked Carr to stop and camp before crossing the creek. They said the grass was better on this side, and there were cornfields across the creek. (The scouts did not want the command's horses and mules to eat the Indians' corn.) Carr responded that he had come a long distance to get Nock-ay-det-klinne before setting up camp. The command continued onward, directed by Chapeau.

Cibecue Creek. This photograph was taken near Cibecue, Arizona, in the general area where the Cibecue battle is believed to have been fought. Photo by Eric Collins.

After crossing the stream, which was not quite belly deep, the force moved the short distance to Nock-ay-det-klinne's village. From their approach the village sat on a low mesa, about twenty feet above the creek bottom and eight to ten feet higher than the plain on that side of the creek. This mesa extended up the creek as far as the men could see. The trail to Nock-ay-det-klinne's lodge ran between the bluff on which the Indian village was situated and the bushes of the creek bottom. Here the path was narrow because the bushes came up against the foot of the bluff.

Cruse, Byrnes, and the scouts reached Nock-ay-det-klinne's wickiup first. When they arrived Mose came out with Nock-ay-det-klinne and introduced them. After they shook hands Cruse told Nock-ay-det-klinne that Carr wanted to see him. The medicine man then asked where Carr was. Cruse said he was on his way. Carr soon arrived with his troops. The time was 3:00 P.M.

Carr moved forward to meet Nock-ay-det-klinne, who was standing in front of his lodge with Mose and Charlie. The two shook hands. Carr recollected the meeting:

> I told him through the interpreter what I had come for, as I had told the scouts the night before. This was told him in the presence of the other Indians, in their own language, so all should understand. [There were only about three male Indians around, besides the scouts.][15] . . . I then told him I would treat him as a friend till those charges had been investigated and if not true he would be released. He had already denied them. He showed me a pass from the Agent for himself and others to plant corn on Cibicu for 60 days, dated May 13th, and extended July 13th for another 60 days.
>
> I told him the Agent wanted me to bring him in to talk & etc.
>
> He made [an] excuse for not coming before, that he had a patient to attend, and the Indians would have blamed him if he had left the sick man; but said he had cured him, and he had gone home this morning and he, Nock-ay-det-klinne, was now ready to go with me. I told him that was all right and if it was all explained he would be released in a few days. I then ordered a guard detailed [one noncommissioned officer and eight men]; told him who was in charge of that, Sergeant [John F.] McDonald, Troop E, 6th Cavalry; that if he tried to escape he would be killed. He smiled and said he did not want to escape, he was perfectly willing to go.
>
> I then told him that if there were an attempt at rescue he would be killed. He smiled at that also, and said no one would attempt to rescue him. I also told him he could take part of his family along with him.
>
> This talk was all in the presence of other Indians, purposely to reassure them and make a good case to their minds. Mose at times repeated and explained, when he did not seem to catch the meaning of Interpreter Hurrle.
>
> I thought that the possession of his person, as a hostage, would make them particularly careful not to bring on a collision.[16]

Chapter 3

THE BATTLE ON THE CIBECUE

As Carr prepared to leave Nock-ay-det-klinne's camp he told his officers the command was going to proceed down the creek to find a camping place. He knew "almost exactly"[1] where they were going to camp since he had noted the ground at the Verde Crossing earlier that day. He directed Troop D to follow behind him, then the pack train, followed by Nock-ay-det-klinne and his guard, then Troop E. He ordered Cruse, with his Indian scouts, to travel beside Nock-ay-det-klinne. The officers' suspicions of the scouts had diminished somewhat because they appeared "altogether indifferent"[2] about the taking of the medicine man. Carr then turned his command around, by file, to leave the area. "Quite a good many squaws"[3] were about, but only a few Indian men (besides the scouts). Only one Indian showed some signs of hostility. He was about one hundred yards from Nock-ay-det-klinne's lodge. He was totally naked, obviously drunk on tizwin.

As Carr left he had the bugler sound the call to forward. His headquarters staff, Troop D, and the pack train followed directly behind him. At that point a break in his column occurred. Nock-ay-det-klinne delayed the rest of the column while he got his personal belongings and a horse and then entered his lodge and began to eat.

When 1st Lt. William Stanton realized what was happening, he urged Sergeant McDonald to move out with his prisoner at once.

Apache wickiups. Typical Apache homes, similar to those at Nock-ay-det-klinne's village. This photograph was taken at the San Carlos Indian Agency. The date is unknown. Courtesy National Archives.

McDonald immediately got Nock-ay-det-klinne to mount his horse and move forward. During this delay of about ten minutes, Carr and the front half of his command followed the trail through its narrow part, then disappeared around a sharp turn and entered the heavy growth of cottonwood trees, high willows, and underbrush in the creek bottom. The sharp turn, which was on the trail they had come in on, was about a quarter of a mile from Nock-ay-det-klinne's camp.

About when Carr turned toward the creek, Sergeant Dead Shot came up to him and complained that the guard would not let Nock-ay-det-klinne's friends travel with Nock-ay-det-klinne. Carr responded by saying that some of his friends could come in and see him after camp was made. Dead Shot then returned to his scout company.

Carr and the group traveling with him followed the trail through the creek bottom, winding in and out of the trees. It was about two hundred yards from the sharp turn to the point where the trail crossed the creek. At the creek Carr had the bugler sound water call.

The trail there was rather steep, and the soldiers had to crowd into the river to water their stock and then go up the bank single file.

After passing through the creek bottom Carr left the trail he had been following and turned south on an old trail that went around the growth, past an old ranch, and down the east side of the creek to the campsite he observed earlier. The campground was about two miles south of Nock-ay-det-klinne's lodge.

Meanwhile, as the latter half of Carr's command waited for Nock-ay-det-klinne to get ready, about fifteen armed Indians approached. As the column departed Cruse and Byrnes were in front, followed by the guard and Nock-ay-det-klinne with the scouts in front and behind them, then Troop E. Before this group reached the narrow portion of the trail, more Indians came up from down the creek and also moved along with them. All the Indians were armed; most were mounted. As a precaution, while Cruse, the scouts, and Nock-ay-det-klinne and his guard stayed on the trail (which was on the flat below the mesa), Stanton and his men turned to the right and went up on the mesa and passed through the Indian village. There Stanton saw many women and children but few men. He moved about three hundred yards on the plateau of the mesa before descending back to the flat.

At the start of the sharp turn in the trail, an old trail departed from it and ran down the west side of the creek. While Stanton was on top of the mesa, Cruse inadvertently missed the turn and took the old trail. Shortly thereafter Stanton and his troop came down to the flat and united with Cruse's party. Stanton and Cruse then discussed missing the turn. When it was mentioned to the scouts, they said there was a better crossing a short distance downstream. The two men then decided to continue to the better crossing.

After the two officers conversed Stanton and his troop marched on Cruse's flank. As they moved down the creek several more parties of armed Indians from downstream came up and traveled with their column. Others came out from the adjacent bluffs and ravines. They crowded around Nock-ay-det-klinne's guard and Troop E. As each new party arrived there was hurried conversation and excited talking. Generally, when Apaches fought, they stripped off all their clothes except their breechclouts. Most of these followers wore only a breechclout and a belt of cartridges.

Stanton and Cruse viewed the situation differently. Stanton noticed the excitement among the Indians but did not think they had hostile intentions. He was never apprehensive of an attack. He later said, "Their intentions appeared to be friendly. Many of them whom I knew addressed me, and also to other men in each company whom they knew."[4] Cruse was worried. He said, "In marching along I thought once or twice that there was danger of our being attacked. I thought that they acted in some what of a threatening manner."[5] Although he was concerned about the Indian followers, he did not notice anything peculiar about the scouts.

Meanwhile, as Carr exited the brush in the creek bottom, he went through a sunflower patch. After clearing the patch he sent for Captain Hentig, who was behind him with his troop. When Hentig arrived the two men engaged in idle talk that was typical on a march. Carr remarked that he was glad everything passed off so quietly; that he had thought there might be a little trouble but now believed all was well. Hentig agreed. The two men congratulated themselves. Carr later recollected, "I said to Capt. Hentig that I was rather ashamed to come out with all this force to arrest one poor little Indian. Capt. Hentig put on his saturnine expression and said but little; but evidently considered it a case of great cry and little wool."[6] During their conversation Hentig laughed and said he was surprised they got Nock-ay-det-klinne.[7]

About when Carr sent for Hentig, three hundred to four hundred yards after crossing the stream, Carr received a report that the latter part of his command had separated. Carr then turned to his right, looked over the brush and trees, and saw the separated force moving down the other side of the creek with Nock-ay-det-klinne. He remarked, "Well, it is all right now, everything seems quiet and they are coming on."[8]

As the two columns moved down the creek Carr and other members of his column occasionally saw the rear column over and through the trees. Though Carr saw some Indians around the rear column, he was not too concerned since they were naturally curious and had an interest in Nock-ay-det-klinne. He expected to be notified if there were any indications of trouble. No uneasiness was reported to him, though he could have easily been told. In fact, he received no word from the rear column.

About three hundred yards before Carr reached the area where he planned to camp, he halted his column. He rode forward with Hentig, McCreery, and his bugler to decide where to place each element of his command. After looking over the area he decided they would camp on top of a mesa, just up the bank from the creek bottom. After he, with Hentig's assistance, decided where to place each element he had the bugler sound advance for the remainder of the front column.

Carr's headquarters staff and Troop D reached the campsite about 3:15 P.M. As they rode up Carr showed Carter where to place Troop D, the pack train, and Troop E. He also showed him where to put his tent and headquarters staff. Carter then asked where to camp the scouts. Carr told him to put them at the foot of the mesa (in the creek bottom) opposite the pack train—between the two troops and close to Carr's tent.

After Carter had the guard details made (for their horse and mule herd, the pack train, and the camp)[9] and showed the men where to camp, he started toward Carr. The colonel was then sitting with Hentig and Clark Carr next to where his tent was being pitched. McCreery was also with them, lying on the ground.

At that time some men at the campsite saw Cruse and Stanton and their men coming down the other side of the creek, about two hundred fifty yards away. The rear column was nearly opposite their campsite, perhaps a little north of it. As Carter walked toward Carr Acting Sgt. Maj. Frank H. Mandeville stopped him and reported that a large party of armed and mounted Indians were moving with the rear column. Carter looked across the creek, saw them, then told Mandeville that he thought there was no cause for alarm. Carter continued onward to see Carr.

When the rear column was one hundred fifty to two hundred yards above the campsite it came to an old trail that crossed the creek and then a cornfield. Both Nock-ay-det-klinne and the scouts said they did not want to cross there. Nock-ay-det-klinne said he did not want the corn trampled; the scouts said they did not want to get their feet wet. They mentioned that there was a dam ahead on which they could step across and stay dry. Cruse and Stanton decided to continue down the creek and cross at the dam. Stanton later said that as they were about opposite the campsite, he could see Carr's tent and the men of Troop D.

The dam was at the point where the Verde Trail crossed the Cibecue, no more than two hundred yards below Carr's camp. Near that point there was a small, narrow hill, dotted with cedars and covered with brush, that stood twenty to twenty-five feet higher than the creek bottom. The Verde Trail and the trail that the rear column was following met near this hill.

As the rear column drew near the dam they saw another large party of twenty or thirty armed Indians, most of whom were mounted, on the hill. Stanton later testified, "There was considerable shouting and excitement as we crossed the creek near the place where [Brevet] General Carr was in camp. . . . I know now that there was a large village below where we crossed the river."[10]

As the column had moved downstream, Stanton at one time counted forty male Indians. He said others joined the command after he made his quick count, and he had seen others coming in from below. He thought there were about two hundred warriors nearby. All, except for three or four who had bows, were armed with guns. Cruse said he saw about seventy-five Indians.

When the rear column turned to cross the creek, almost all the Indian followers joined the Indians on the hill close to the crossing. Approximately twenty-five of them, however, continued with the column and crossed the creek with Nock-ay-det-klinne and his guard. As they moved back upstream toward camp, Cruse was in front, followed by Sergeants Dead Shot and Dandy Bill and the other scouts, then Nock-ay-det-klinne and his guard with Troop E.

About fifty yards before the group reached Carr's tent, Cruse rode ahead and around to the rear of the tent to where Carr and his officers were sitting. The front column had been at the campsite ten or fifteen minutes. Carter had just reached Carr. Cruse reported to Carr for duty as officer of the day and asked where he should put Nock-ay-det-klinne and his guard. Carter then informed Carr that armed Indians were coming toward camp with the guard and Troop E. Cruse later said, "[I then] stated [to Carr] that things looked very squally as we came along. I think that was my language. He asked me what it was and I remarked that a great many armed Indians were coming out from the ravines. I said a lot. He asked me 'What do you mean by a lot, forty-fifty-one hundred or two hundred?' And I said, 'I don't know how many there were, sir.'"[11]

While they were talking Nock-ay-det-klinne and his guard arrived with the Indian followers. Carr directed Cruse to place Nock-ay-det-klinne and his guard near the pack train, which was then being unloaded; Carter to take the scouts to the place where they were to camp; and Hentig to get the followers out of camp. Hentig got up and walked with Carter toward the Indians. They then separated.

Hentig stepped toward the followers, waved his hand, and said "Ucashee," which means "go away." Carter went to Dead Shot, the ranking sergeant of the scouts, since Mose was with Nock-ay-det-klinne. Carter told him to bring the scouts to the edge of the mesa on which the command was making camp, away from the other Indians. Dead Shot did so. Carter then showed them where they were to camp (at the foot of the mesa). Dead Shot responded by pointing to the place and saying, "Too hot."[12] Carter then told him to camp on top of the mesa near the rest of the command.

At this time Carter noticed the scouts had arranged themselves in a line about two or three yards apart along the crest of the mesa. Dead Shot was near the center of the line. The scouts were standing there, with the butts of their .45-70 Springfield rifles on the ground, facing toward the camp. Their backs were to the nearby brush and shrubs of the creek bottom. From where they were standing the ground sloped down eight to ten feet to the bottom. The bushes that formed the undergrowth in the bottom were quite dense and extended outward from the creek for thirty to forty yards. It continued on the other side of the stream.

Regarding Carter's latest location, Dead Shot pointed to an anthill and said, "too many ants." Carter then told him to move out in front of the ants and camp in the grass. Dead Shot replied in Apache, "It is all right."[13]

Carter then noticed that the scouts appeared to be listening to the conversation between Hentig and the Indians whom he was ordering out of camp. However, he thought everything was all right and started toward Carr's tent, fifteen to twenty yards to the left of the scout's line (up the creek from them). About then, the scouts dropped their guns into position of load and loaded them. Also, an Indian on horseback in the midst of the followers started delivering "quite a harangue"[14] in a loud voice to all the Indians, both followers and scouts.[15] Carter had walked only about fifteen feet from the end of the scouts' line when he heard the Indian making such a loud noise that he turned around. He later said the Indian was calling out "as if giving orders to them."[16] Carter saw that the scouts were listening intently to what this Indian was saying. The Indian then called out something in a loud tone, jerked his gun out of the holster on his saddle, and gave a war cry. Carter quickly turned toward Hentig and yelled for him to look out.

Cruse had turned away from Carr and walked about ten feet to carry out his orders regarding the placement of Nock-ay-det-klinne and his guard when he heard the Indian on horseback "call out something in a loud tone."[17] He then heard the war whoop, then a soldier call out, "Watch out, they are going to fire."[18] Immediately thereafter one or two shots were fired from among the Indian followers. The war whoop, the caution, and the volley were almost simultaneous. The time was about 3:30 P.M.[19]

The Indian on horseback was in the middle of Troop D's camp. The men of the troop had taken their saddles and bridles off their horses. Their horses had been turned loose and driven together and placed in charge of the herd guard, then composed of one sergeant and three privates.[20] Most men of the troop were scattered about among their saddles attending to the usual tasks required to prepare camp. Some were sitting, and others were standing. Some were placing their blankets, others were making fires, and some had gone for water. Their arms lay on their saddles on the ground where they had taken them off. A detail was out getting wood. The cooks had started preparing dinner. The Indian on horseback was only twenty-five or thirty feet from the cook boxes where the cooks were working.

After the first shot, a scattering of fire took place from among the Indian followers. Carter quickly looked at the scout company to see what they were going to do. He heard Dead Shot say something to them in Apache and then saw them immediately raise their guns and fire in the direction of Hentig and Troop D. Some scouts knelt; others stood up when they fired. They fired at approximately the same time.

Carter quickly drew his revolver and fired at Dandy Bill. He was the scout nearest to him—only twelve to fifteen feet away. He then realized he was alone and decided to try to get behind the corner of Carr's tent, still five or six yards from him. Before he could reach it the sergeant major, lying in the grass near him, yelled for him to drop. Carter turned around and faced the scouts just as a number of them raised their guns to fire a second volley. Carter instantly dropped in the grass. The bullets passed over him.

After the followers and scouts initially fired their guns, they dropped down the slope at their rear, taking cover around the brow of the mesa. Carr immediately yelled for every man to stand fast. The men of Troop D dropped to the ground or rushed to get behind their saddles or whatever other protection they could find. The soldiers of the headquarters guard had just finished pitching Carr's tent and were busy putting up another. Some of them also rushed to their arms. Most packers and some other civilian employees were already at or near their arms. By the time the scouts had fired their second volley, several of Carr's men had retrieved their guns and begun to reply to the fire. Soon more men reached their guns, and there was firing from all around the campsite.

As soon as the command began to return the fire the scouts and Indian followers began to break and run down the mesa toward the thick brush and weeds in the creek bottom. Their retreat was not orderly: some ran pell-mell into the brush without stopping; others fired their guns as they dropped down the slope. Once the Indians reached the creek bottom they took cover in the timber and underbrush and fired into the campsite. By then more of Carr's men had reached their guns and were returning fire.

Immediately after the scouts' second volley, Carr came around the corner of his tent and passed over Carter. Carter told him the scouts had just fired and retreated into the brush. Carr went up toward the mesa that the scouts had just left, then down toward the place where Hentig had told the Indians to leave the area.

Just before the first fire Stanton had ridden through the camp to its north side with Troop E. When he had turned his troop in line to dismount, Carr came out and told him to move them a little farther upstream. Stanton wheeled them into columns of fours and proceeded. They were advancing toward their new location when the first shots were fired. Stanton quickly turned his troop into line and looked around to see where the firing came from.

When Carter had notified Carr that the scouts had gone into the brush, Carr yelled to Stanton to dismount his troop and drive the Indians from there. In the confusion and noise Stanton did not understand the order. Carr told Carter to take the order to him. Carter then ran over to Stanton and repeated the command. Stanton immediately dismounted his men and led them down to the edge of the brush and trees in the creek bottom. They charged through the bushes, attacking the Indians' left flank. His movement quickly cleared the bottom. Some hostiles went out the other side of the brush and ran across an open flat, directly across the creek from the campsite, toward a red bluff about five hundred or six hundred yards west of the campsite. Others ran through a grove of large cottonwood trees across the creek and below the campsite, while many retreated to the little hill on the other side of the creek close to the crossing, about 350 yards from Carr's camp. Later, Carr said Stanton's movement with his troop "saved the day."[21]

After clearing the creek bottom Stanton and about five men formed a skirmish line on the other side of the creek, near the west edge of the brush. The line extended the length of the camp. Shortly thereafter the command's horses and mules were taken down to the bottom and tied to the brush under its bank. McCreery also moved to the safety of the bottom, where he attended to the wounded. There was a moment of respite during the retreat of the Indians. The command improved its defenses by setting up breastworks of packages, rocks, and whatever else was available.

When the Indians reached cover at their new positions they resumed fire. For a few minutes it was so intense that Carter told the men with him to lie down. About then Carr came over to Carter and ordered him to command Troop D, in addition to performing his duties as regimental adjutant.

Typical of an Apache fight, all the men could see of the Indians were the puffs of smoke from their rifles. Carr's tent was struck a number of times. One box of canned goods in a breastwork was riddled and the cans set leaking. Most of the fire came from down the river in the direction of the cornfields and from the hill on the opposite side of the creek near the crossing. Some came from the red bluff, from among the cottonwood trees, and from the high ground near them. The hill at the crossing was closer to the camp

than the other bluffs and the cedars and brush on it provided con-
cealment. Carter later said, "It was the most dangerous spot that we
had to contend with."[22]

During the battle Cruse acted as a rover, going to all parts of the
field, until Carr assigned him command of several men to protect
the south and east sides of their camp. The hostiles fired at the
troops until dark. At about that time Carr placed Cruse in command
of Troop D.

Cruse later wrote,

> During the first fifteen minutes of the action, while [Brevet]
> General Carr was engaged in disposing his troops for defense, he
> had forgotten his fifteen-year-old son Clarke [Clark], who had come
> on the march with us. Suddenly he remembered that he had not seen
> Clarke since the first shot, when the boy was seated on the ground
> not more than fifty feet from the Scouts. The General's emotion was
> apparent when he called the boy's name, then turned to the
> bystanders and asked if they knew where he was. There was an
> ominous silence for a second, then Clarke answered calmly:
> "Here I am! What do you want?"
> I think that Clarke was the only person in the whole command
> who got the slightest degree of enjoyment out of the whole fight. He
> had a small Winchester .44 and had got to shoot it to his heart's
> content with none to say "Don't!"[23]

Just before the firing started Nock-ay-det-klinne and his guard
had taken their station beyond the packs and begun unsaddling.
When it began Nock-ay-det-klinne dropped and started crawling
toward the brush. Sergeant McDonald, though shot in the right leg,
saw him moving and shot him through both thighs. Trumpeter
William O. Benites, seeing he was still alive, drew his revolver and
shot him in the neck.[24]

First Sergeant Mose was the only scout who remained loyal. He
stayed with Nock-ay-det-klinne when he came into camp and went
to the packs with him. He was with him and his guard when the
firing started.[25] Cruse said,

> Mose at first dropped down but some of the scouts were firing on
> the pack train and the men, and some of the men called out, "shoot
> him, quick, he's getting a gun," and both Lieut. Carter and myself
> then called out, "Don't shoot him, he is all right." And called to him

to come over there to where we were. I guess about five feet, or five or six perhaps, and he come and laid down by us and staid there until we turned him over to a soldier. Lieut. Carter told him to take charge of him and watch him. I had an enlisted man take his gun away from him.[26]

Hentig was shot in the back when the Indians began their attack. The bullet entered about an inch to the right of his spinal column and passed through his heart, instantly killing him.[27] He was only four or five yards from the line of scouts. According to Eugene Condon, the farrier for D Troop, when Hentig went to the Indian followers and told them to go away, the Indian riding the horse did not seem willing to go. He wanted to go down into the brush. But Hentig wanted them to go out the same way they came in. Sergeant Dandy Jim then walked between Hentig and the mounted Indian. Hentig caught him by the shoulder and said, "Ucashee." Dandy Jim replied, "I am a soldier." Hentig then said, "Well, if you are, go to camp" and pushed him around to the left with his hand.[28] Dandy Jim walked behind Hentig looking sideways at him as he went along. When he was about four yards behind him, he kneeled on his right knee and fired at Hentig's back. Hentig threw up his hands and said "Oh, my God" and fell on the ground.[29]

Pvt. Edward D. Livingston, Hentig's personal orderly, was also killed at the beginning of the fight. When the scouts initially fired their guns, he was immediately in front of their line with his back to them—only about five yards away. He was hit two or three times. One witness said he was spreading Hentig's blankets on the grass when shot. Another said he was sitting on a rock.

About "half a minute to a minute" after the first fire, a bullet struck Pvt. John Sullivan in the head, killing him.[30] He was one of the few men of Troop D who had not yet dismounted. Apparently he was not killed instantly. A witness said as he fell off his horse he "saved himself as much as he could but finally fell on the ground."[31]

Pvt. William Miller had gone down into the undergrowth of the creek bottom to wash; he was killed in the bushes.[32] Another soldier, who accompanied him, made it back to camp safely.

After the soldiers of Troop D had arrived in camp their horses were turned loose and driven down to the water. When the firing started the packs were off the pack mules, but most still had their aparejos on and were standing about their place of unpacking. The saddle mules, however, were stripped, and most had joined the horse herd, which was then south of Carr's campsite, about forty yards from Hentig's troop. The sergeant of the herd guard was reporting to the officer of the day for orders.

The herd, which had come up from the creek bottom several minutes before, stampeded when the firing started. A few Indians, including Sanchez, immediately went for the animals and drove them south, down the creek. Three soldiers were with the herd. Two were in the thicket near the creek (some horses and mules were probably still in the brush), and the third was in the open. Pvt. John Sonderegger, the herder closest to the stream, and Pvt. Ludwig Baege, who was herding in the open about twenty yards from camp, were shot by the Indians as they rushed to capture the herd. Sonderegger died four hours later at the campsite.

About half an hour after the firing began some men thought they saw Hentig move, though McCreery had pronounced him dead earlier. He was laying one hundred feet in front of Carter's line. Pvts. Richard Heartery and Henry C. Bird, both of D Troop, volunteered to go forward with Carter to get him. When they dashed forward the Indians "loosed a terrific fire."[33] A bullet struck Bird. After Carter got Hentig's body back behind cover, he helped Heartery, who was assisting Bird back to their breastwork. Their effort was fruitless; Hentig had died earlier. Bird died about five hours later at the campsite.[34]

Just before the fight Colvig went to the creek bottom. He was in the creek getting water, about forty yards from Carr's tent, when he heard two or three shots and then as many as thirty more. He immediately ran up to the top of the bank. He peered over its crest and saw the Indians firing on the troops from their skirmish line. Colvig stayed there and watched the fight until Stanton's troop charged them. His viewpoint was about sixty yards from the Apache skirmish line.

William McGuire, a civilian packer and blacksmith with the pack train, was shoeing a mule when the fight commenced. His gun was laying on his saddle about twenty-five yards away. When the firing started he ran to it, laid down, placed it across his saddle, and fired at the hostiles. He was about thirty yards from their skirmish line.

Pvt. John Burton, Troop D, said,

> Directly after arriving in camp Lieut. Carter ordered a detail to go
> out for wood. I was detailed with a packer and one enlisted man and
> three mules for the purpose. We went about half a mile above the
> camp where some wood was lying near an old Indian tepee. While
> on the way up we met Dead Shot on a horse—about half the way to
> the wood. He passed me and went on into camp. About then I saw
> another Indian sitting in the path—an Indian called Ka-clenny—who
> asked me where I was going. I pointed to the wood and told him I
> was going after wood. He motioned his hand and told me to hurry
> up and go ahead and became very much excited at the same time. He
> was at this same time undressing, had his moccasins off and was
> pulling off his drawers. As I rode away, another Indian rode up. Ka-
> clenny jumped up behind him and rode on towards the camp. I went
> on to the wood, tied the animals and was just gathering the wood
> when there was a volley fired in the camp.[35]

As night fell Carr queried his officers, the guide, the chief
packer, and others for their opinion about what to do next. He found
they were "pretty unanimous in the wish to get out of there." Carr
also saw no object in remaining. He decided it was best to get back
to Fort Apache as soon as practicable. From the dispatch he had
received from Cochran that morning he knew there was "great
alarm" at the fort. He also knew that even a few hostiles could set
up an effective ambush along the trail back to the post and any wait
would give them more time to do so.[36]

After dark the soldiers gathered the bodies of the dead. Hampered
by the darkness and the high brush, they could not find Private
Miller, who was killed in the creek bottom. Carr directed that a broad
grave be dug under his tent to bury the corpses. Later, Carter said,
"I wrote in my own book the position and age of the body as well as
I could see by the moonlight to write and placed it on the breast of
each one, showing what his name was and when he was killed and
that he was buried on the 30th day of August by our command."[37]

The grave was widened twice, for Privates Sonderegger and
Bird, who died while it was being dug. Carr said, "When all was
ready, I said over them as much of the service as I could remember
and had taps sounded. This served for 'good night' to them, and
also to indicate to Indians that we were going to sleep. To fire

volleys over the graves would have been to notify Indians that we were burying these at night with the intention of moving at once."[38]

Shortly after the fight at Cibecue Creek, Sergeant Mandeville wrote the following poem.

"On the Cibicu"

Brave General Carr commanded—
Well and true.
The troops who fought in blue,
On August thirtieth, eighty one,
    T'was on the Cibicu.

Traitorous scouts, they did their work,
Then ran away,
When brave boys opened fire on them;
Then E Troop charged most gallantly
Across the bottom low and deep;
Those murderers ran—they fairly flew—
To "foot hills," far beyond
    The roaring Cibicu.

Gallant Hentig to fall was number one,
And Livingston was two,
Poor Miller fell as number three,
Then Sunderriger pierced through;
Then Bird the gallant, brave, and true,
His captain's corpse went to;
He fell performing duty well,
    This on the Cibicu.

Sullivan was number six to fall.
A soldier brave and true;
Then Mickey Foran met his fate;
A thorough soldier—an honor to blue.
Bagge—wounded in the shoulder deep—
McDonald in the leg;
Brave boys they suffered terribly,
Would not complain or beg.
This numbers all our comrades true,
Murdered, wounded—died
    On Cibicu.

Gallant Carter and Cruse—brave men—
And McCreery, God bless him,
Did surgeon's duty, yes more too;
Handled his carbine steadily,
Assisting soldiers true.
To wounded quickly he did go,
Though lead missiles thickly flew;
Cared nought, his duty would perform,
    T'was on the Cibicu.

Young Clark M. Carr, a boy in teens,
Not accustomed to such scenes,
Did bravely, nobly, for one so young,
Handled well a soldier's gun.
Assisted much the boys in blue,
    Fighting hard at Cibicu.

The grave was dug; no shroud, no coffin;
Rolled in a soldier's blanket;
One by one we laid the corpse in;
"Earth to earth," "ashes to ashes";
"Taps" true. "'tis still as death."
Comrades murdered in the blue,
    By traitorous scouts at Cibicu.

Comrades! "revenge is sweet";
To us it is and more;
With gallant Carr to lead us
We'd make the valleys roar.
With love for the murdered in our hearts
We'll hunt the Apache from his lair:
Nor cease to fight with all our might,
And God protect us in the right,
Till all the murderers bite the earth,
Shall we be content.
Never falter; revenge 'tis true;
    Our battle cry, "The Cibicu."[39]

It required some time after the burial for the men to get some
supper, arrange the packs, and pack the mules. Since there were not
enough mules remaining to carry all their supplies and march

rapidly, some items had to be left behind. They left flour, bacon, canned goods, saddles, aparejos, and other equipment of the pack train. Preference was given to leaving the goods belonging to Cruse's scout company.

Before leaving they cut the flour bags and spread the flour on the ground. They destroyed all other goods and equipment that were to remain. All serviceable arms and ammunition that could be found were taken. Years later Carter wrote,

> Before leaving the field [Brevet] General Carr sent Lieutenant Carter to examine the body of the Medicine Man and determine if life was extinct. Strange to say, notwithstanding his wounds, he was still alive. The recovery of this Indian, if left in the hands of his friends, would have given him a commanding influence over these superstitious people, which would have resulted in endless war. General Carr then repeated the order for his death, specifying that no more shots should be fired. Guide Burns [Byrnes] was directed to carry out the order with the understanding that a knife was to be used. Burns, fearing failure, took an ax and crushed the forehead of the deluded fanatic, and from this time forward every person murdered by these Apaches was treated in a similar manner.[40]

The force left the battle site about 11:00 P.M. Years later Cruse recalled, "Everyone had been strictly warned against noise and straggling. We felt that the canyons were alive with Apaches and, after the fight, they would be as alert as ourselves."[41] Since the Indians had stolen about half their horses, most of the men of Troop D had to walk.

Carr placed Cruse in charge of the advance guard, which consisted of Mose, as guide, and some dismounted men of Troop D. Carr, Carter, and the headquarters staff, along with the remainder of Troop D, came next. Then came the pack train with the ammunition and other supplies and Troop E with the three wounded men under McCreery's care. Stanton was with the rear guard, which was composed of six or eight men.

The wounded men were Private Baege, shot in the shoulder, Pvt. Thomas J. F. Foran, shot through the intestines and bowels, and Sergeant McDonald, shot in the leg.[47] They rode on horses with men behind them to hold and steady them in their saddles. These attendants were relieved every few minutes.

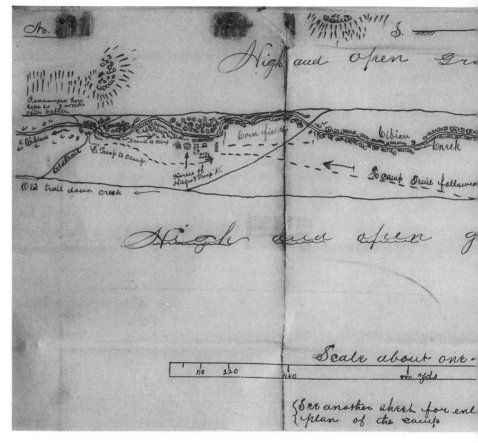

Three participants in the Cibecue battle drew maps of the fight. Sgt. Frank H. Mandeville drew a map for some friends while at Camp Thomas, probably in early September 1881 (see Wharfield, *Cibicu Creek Fight in Arizona: 1881*, 41). Second Lt. Thomas Cruse presented his sketch of the Cibecue fight during the trials of the mutinous Indian scouts in November 1881. Both Cruse's and Mandeville's maps were critiqued during Carr's

The command's first accident occurred in some brush while climbing up the divide. Carter described the incident:

He [Carr] directed me that in case anything happened to any body or the packs during the march that the word should be passed to the head of the column, and that the command would halt until the

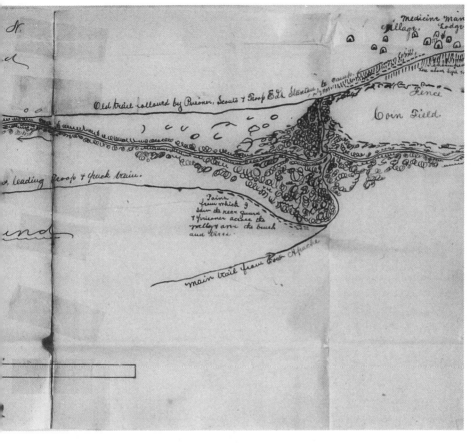

inquiry. They were considered generally correct but with some errors. Mandeville's map was judged less accurate that Cruse's.

The sketch above was drawn by Col. Eugene A. Carr, from memory, after his court of inquiry in August 1882. It was included in a letter to the adjutant general of the army on January 6, 1883. It was never critiqued.

words "all right" were passed to the front. We had gone about I should judge a mile and a half when the first word came to halt. I rode out of the column and started back to see what was the matter and it was very dark and I met Lieut. Stanton who told me that one of the pack mules had fallen over the bank I should judge twenty-

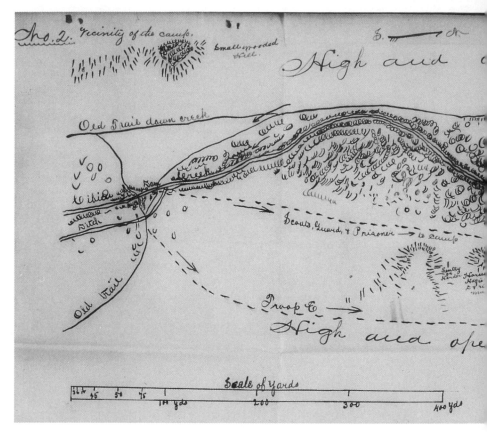

This sketch of the Cibicue battleground, with an enlarged plan of the camp, was also drawn by Colonel Carr.

five feet deep. Almost immediately the pack mule ran by me in the dark with apparently nothing on. The packer came up and said the cinch was broken and the mule had dropped his aparejo and the load. No one knew what we had lost until the next day and then we found that the mule was loaded with ammunition and one sack of flour.[43]

When the command reached the top of the divide, about nine or ten miles from the battleground, a mule missed his footing and

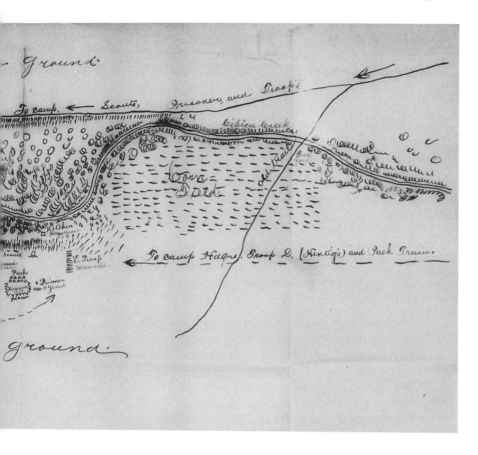

rolled down the mountainside. This incident was not reported to Carr until daylight.

From these two accidents three thousand rounds of ammunition, packed in four small boxes and one large box, were lost. A few weeks later Lt. Col. William Redwood Price, while searching for the hostiles on a trail south of the Cibecue, found a spot where a large supply of ammunition had been distributed. The ammunition was believed to be Carr's.

The mule that rolled down from the mountaintop also carried a satchel containing Carr's papers, clothing, and other personal belongings. About three weeks later, when Carr returned to the Cibecue, he found some of the papers and the empty bag strewn along the trail.

During the middle of the night, when the second accident occurred, the command took a wrong turn and almost lost another mule. Carr recollected the event about two months later: "One mule was missed about 2 o'clock A.M. 31st after we turned back from taking a wrong trail; this was, I think reported to me at the time, if so, I had already waited a long time to get the command and trains on the right track, and thought it useless to wait any longer; still, hoping the mule would follow the bell or the command which it did."[44]

Because of the turn back Cruse was now in the rear of the column with McCreery and three privates who were helping McCreery with the wounded. They were having serious problems. John F. Finerty, a *Chicago Times* war correspondent who interviewed Carr's troops several weeks later, described the situation.

> Foran, a young Irish recruit, refused to lie down under fire, and was shot through the bowels. The brave young Dr. McCreery placed him on a horse and brought him more than half way in, helping him to mount and dismount, which he did frequently, owing to the intolerable agony of the wound. He had to be tied on his horse finally, but broke the ropes and hung head downward, writhing in torture. He was straightened in the saddle, but on reaching the top of the great hill [the divide] he said: "It's no use, doctor, I'll never live to get to the bottom of this." He begged to be untied, and when his request was granted he suddenly sprang a yard into the air and fell at full length, perfectly dead.[45]

While McCreery, Cruse, and the three attendants struggled with Foran, they dropped behind the column. Part of the way they carried Foran in their arms. He died shortly after sunrise. They lashed his body across the saddle of an Indian pony and led it forward, trying to catch up with the command.

In the meantime the command had stopped at a little spring over the top of the mountain. They stayed there about an hour. During that time Cruse and McCreery's party arrived. They had been behind the command (without Carr's knowledge) for several hours. They reached the spring as Carr was starting to give precautionary orders covering the passage of Carrizo Canyon. Carr felt that if the Indians were still going to attack the command, it would be while they were in that defile.

Shortly thereafter the column moved out. Their descent into the canyon was made alertly and with all expectation of volleys from the far rim. Before the advance guard reached the creek a detail moved to its banks to protect the guard while it forded the stream. The guard then crossed the creek and moved to the mesa on the other side. Not a shot was fired.

When Carr realized the trail was safe the main column splashed across the creek and climbed the steep trail out to the mesa. Carter described the remainder of the journey: "We then marched on to Cedar Creek, and as some of the men were very tired and had begun to straggle a little we halted again. It was about five miles from Carrizo Creek to Cedar Creek. We halted and took off the packs and the men all got what they could to eat. When everything was ready and all the men were in line, we took the dead man off of the horse and put him on the mule so that we would have no more trouble and marched into the post."[46]

Before the command reached Fort Apache, probably when it was near Cedar Creek, it met two prospectors on the trail. They told Carr that only one Indian (Severiano)[47] had preceded them toward the fort. The column arrived back at Fort Apache at about 3:00 P.M. On the military side, seven soldiers were killed and two wounded,[48] and forty-two horses and seven pack mules were killed, wounded, or missing. All the men who had been struck belonged to Troop D, except McDonald, who was detailed from Troop E. Nock-ay-det-klinne was the only known Indian casualty.

Carr estimated that less than sixty Indians, including the scouts, attacked his command at the onset of the battle and fewer than two hundred fought his force at any time during the fight. Almost all damage done to his command occurred in the first volleys, while the Indians were close to their camp. The bullets passed through the bodies of all the killed and wounded.

Until the moment before the attack all the officers with the command thought the Indians' conduct was docile. Later Carter said, "I felt perfectly secure, and I thought everybody else did. . . . If I had had any feeling of insecurity, I don't think I would have

Monument to the soldiers killed at Cibecue Creek. The noncommissioned officers of Troops D and E, 6th Cavalry, raised funds for this monument. Photo by Dr. Joe Nickolas.

walked down amongst them myself."[49] And about fifteen years later he wrote,

> That the loss was no more was due in a great measure to the coolness and courage of [Brevet] General Carr.
>
> A situation better calculated to try the mettle of a command could scarcely be imagined. Having effected the object of the march,—the arrest of a notorious and mischief-making medicine man,—without difficulty, and with no resistance on the part of his people, the troops had set about making camp for the night, when suddenly they were fired upon, not alone by the friends of the medicine man, but by their own allies, the Indian scouts, who had hitherto been loyalty itself.[50] The confusion and dismay which such an attack at such a time necessarily caused, might well have resulted in the annihilation of the entire force, and constituted a situation from which nothing but the most consummate skill and bravery could pluck safety.[51]

Finerty reported,

Talking of Carr, his conduct at Cibicu has won for him the lasting respect of his soldiers. He never took to cover, and when a sergeant called out: "For God's sake, General, get under cover or you'll be killed sure," the gallant old chief replied coolly: "Oh, God d———n these whelps, they can't hit me, God d———n 'em." And they couldn't.

I asked a soldier who was in the fight, how the General happened to escape.

"D———d if I know," said he. "The General waltzed around there in the open, and the bullets seemed to shun him. I expected him to fall every moment, but devil a fall did he. He issued his orders just the same as if he was on the parade square, only a d———d sight cooler."[52]

Chapter 4

THE HOSTILITIES CONTINUE

The day after Major Cochran sent Colvig to Carr with his worrisome message he prepared Fort Apache against attack: "We put everything in the best shape for defense. Surplus arms and ammunition were removed to the commissary storehouse; water barrels, tools, etc., etc., were placed in this building ready for use, if needed. There we intended to collect the women and children, and if compelled to do so, make the final stand."[1]

Late that night, while Carr was on his way back to Fort Apache, Severiano came in to the post. He said he had been out hunting his cattle all day, and while returning about sunset, nine Indians fired at him. The Indians told him, "We have been fighting the soldiers and have killed some of them and we will get you and Cooley too."[2] Severiano said he then jumped on his horse and rode to the post as fast as he could.

Cochran suspected Severiano of treachery but did not feel justified in arresting him. Before daylight, in anticipation of an attack, Cochran had reveille sounded. At daylight he sent Pvt. John Welch down the Apache Road to Camp Thomas,[3] seventy-three miles away, with the following message.

To: Commanding Officer, Camp Thomas
   Savianna, a Mexican captive, arrived here at 12:15 A.M. and
reports that the Indians have been fighting the troops all day and

some soldiers are killed. Courier sent to [Brevet] General Carr on the 29th instant has not returned, should have been here early yesterday morning.

No word from General Carr, hurry troops forward.

Please telegraph my dispatch of the 29th to Dept. Hdqrs. and to Col. [of Volunteers] Biddle if you have not done so. Also telegraph substance of this letter at once. Settlers have been warned. It is important that you repair at once your section of the Apache telegraph line.

Party of four mounted men are at Ash Creek guarding property and should be reinforced from Thomas. The two men at Black River ferry have been ordered in.[4]

During the morning the post trader came to see Cochran. He said he had just heard a rumor from Indian sources that five of Carr's officers and most of his soldiers had been killed. "I investigated the rumor as far as possible and became satisfied there was something in it, but could not tell how much," Cochran said later.[5] He immediately wrote another dispatch for delivery to Camp Thomas.

To: Commanding Officer, Camp Thomas
General Carr's command reported all massacred at the Cibicu. Hurry up reinforcements, no time to lose, post threatened. If General Carr had not expected reinforcements within two days he would not have gone out. Please telegraph this to Dept. Headquarters and to Colonel [of Volunteers] Biddle.[6]

Thomas Owens, a civilian mail carrier between Camp Thomas and Fort Apache, volunteered to take the dispatch. He left the post at noon. Shortly thereafter, while traveling through Seven-Mile Canyon, about four miles from Fort Apache, Indians attacked and killed him. Others had the same fate. Cochran sent Pvt. John Dorman, Troop D, 6th Cavalry, to bring in Pvts. Peter J. Bladt and Edward Winkler, Company D, 12th Infantry. They were tending the ferry at the point where the Apache Road crossed the Black River. Dorman reached the ferrymen and helped them hide their property. They then set out for the fort. As they approached the plateau of Seven-Mile Hill (about 12 miles from the ferry and 8 from Fort Apache) hostiles ambushed them. All three were slain. A short while later three Mormon men traveling north in a wagon (Henderson, Chesley, and Daniels) passed by the spot where the soldiers were killed. At the top of Seven-Mile Hill Indians ambushed and

Fort Apache, Arizona, ca. 1883. An Apache camp is in the foreground. Photo by Ben Wittick, courtesy Museum of New Mexico, negative no. 15677.

From the ridge in the background Pvt. Will C. Barnes signaled to the worried soldiers at Fort Apache that he saw cavalrymen approaching the fort on the trail that Carr took to the Cibecue. He received the Medal of Honor for this dangerous deed. Photo by author.

killed them. Soldiers had warned them of the danger before they crossed the Black River, but they had decided to continue their trip.

Meanwhile, the soldiers at Fort Apache continued to prepare to defend their post. Many civilians came in for protection. Cochran ordered that arms and rations be given to those who needed them. At about 1:00 P.M. Cochran sent the telegraph operator, Pvt. Will Croft Barnes, out on a horse with a flag and field glasses. Cochran told him to climb the high mesa just north of the post and signal with the flag if he saw Indians or soldiers. At about two o'clock Barnes signaled that he saw two cavalrymen slowly approaching from the direction taken by Carr.[7] Cochran anxiously waited for them on the parade ground. In a short time the two riders came into sight. They were Sgt. Frank H. Mandeville and a private—both from Carr's command. On their arrival they gave Cochran and the other anxious listeners who had gathered around a full account of the affair at the Cibecue. At about 3:00 P.M. Carr arrived back at Fort Apache and assumed command of the post.

That evening Indians raided John Phipps's ranch, about a mile southeast of where the soldiers and the Mormons had been murdered. They drove off Phipps's stock and killed Johnny Cowden, an old man employed at the ranch. Cowden was shot in the head while eating dinner. Phipps heard the shots, guessed they were fired by Indians, and hid in the underbrush until night.

The next morning, September 1, Carr furnished mounts to friendly Indians and sent them out to spy. From them he learned of the killings along the Apache Road. While men were digging Foran's grave at the cemetery, about six hundred yards east of the post's buildings, the Indians "commenced to demonstrate."[8] The grave diggers, as well as the men at the nearby sawmill, rushed to the post. At about 2:00 P.M. the Indians began firing into the post from the bluffs on every side. The soldiers formed a skirmish line around the fort. They loopholed the walls of buildings and made breastworks of rocks, logs, wagons, and whatever else was available. During the first hour of the shooting the Indians' fire was heavy, particularly from the northeast side. They continued their fire on two sides of the post for several hours. The post quartermaster, Captain Gordon, was wounded severely in the leg while on the firing line; a ball hit him squarely in his shin and entered about an inch.[9] Carr's horse was struck while he was riding it.

During the engagement the Indians slowly circled toward the south. Some set fire to buildings up the creek (the gardener's house and others), northeast and east of the post, and stampeded a large herd of cattle. They then charged toward the post, dismounted, and opened fire. As they approached the sawmill, about four hundred yards from the quarters, Carr became worried they might burn it. He ordered Captain MacGowan—commanding the defenses on the east side of the post with Company D, 12th Infantry, and the civilians—to take part of his company and take possession of the mill. MacGowan did so.[10] He and some civilians then held it.[11]

After the thwarted charge the Indians fired at the post for a while with no effect, then withdrew to the nearby mountains. About dark they gave up their attack, and "some were seen going on the road to the north."[12] The next morning only a few Indians were in sight.

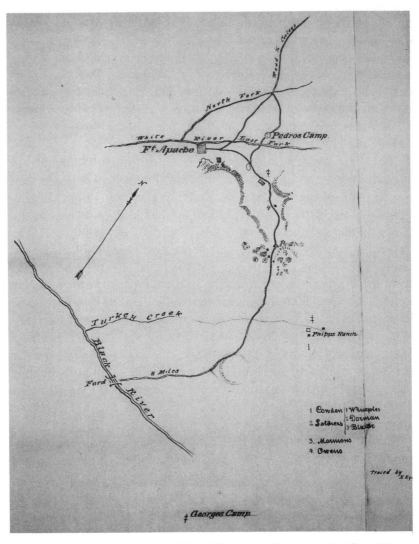

Locations of the August 31, 1881, killings near Fort Apache. Capt. Harry C. Egbert included this sketch in his December 10, 1881, report on the Cibecue troubles.

While preparing for the attack Carr had armed four prisoners, two of whom belonged to the 9th Cavalry. After the fight he reported that they fought bravely and recommended that their offenses be pardoned.

During the fight Carr again demonstrated his bravery to his troops. Finerty, the *Chicago Times* reporter, wrote, "He rode all around under fire on horseback. Bullets rained around him. His horse was hit in the hoof, but nothing touched him. Hang me, if I can explain it at all. Lieut. Gordon no sooner showed himself than he was hit in the leg."[13]

During the attack or shortly before it started the hostiles pulled down the telegraph line into the fort in several places and beat it with stones until it broke. They then took the pieces away. (The line was already dead: it had been down more than two weeks.)

Five days after the attack Carr sent Troop F, 6th Cavalry (commanded by 1st Lieutenant Overton), and 2d Lt. Wallis Olwin Clark's Indian scout company out to bury the people killed near the fort.[14] Owens's remains were discovered when a dog was seen nearby. His body was stripped of clothing. He had been shot through the head, and his skull was crushed, "almost to a jelly."[15] The faithful dog, who had been without food for six days, was shot through the shoulder and so lean he could scarcely walk. He was sent back to the fort and was adopted by Carr.

Next, in the middle of the road, the burial party came upon the burned-out remains of the Mormons' wagon. It was held together by its iron framework. Henderson's charred remains were among the ashes. He had been tied to the axle tree of the wagon before it was set on fire. The sickening odor of the burning flesh was so terrible the Indian scouts passed on, refusing to bury the body. That night there was a rainstorm. The next day Clark went back and buried Henderson. The corpses of the other two men were strung along the road at intervals of a few hundred yards. Evidently, when the attack occurred, they jumped from the wagon and ran but got no farther than where their bodies were found.

All three men had been shot twice and their brains beaten out. Later an *Arizona Citizen* correspondent interviewed some privates in Troop F. They said, "In a box on the road were a number of empty, reloadable cartridge shells, which the Indians had evidently thrown from the wagon before destroying it. The supposition that the shells were the result of a desperate defense is not tenable, inasmuch as a part of them were still in the box, the balance having fallen on the road when the box was thrown from the wagon."[16]

Along the road and close to where Henderson perished the burial party found breastworks sufficiently high to cover the body of a man. The fortifications were covered with grass, obviously to prevent being seen. Finally, the burial party came across the corpses of the three soldiers. Their skulls were broken. They had also been shot through the head[17] and their bodies horribly mutilated.

Eleven days later John Finerty traveled the road while moving from Camp Thomas to Fort Apache with Capt. [Bvt. Maj.] Tullius Cicero Tupper and Troop G, 6th Cavalry. Finerty wrote,

> Just as we approached the plateau [of Seven-Mile Hill] we observed two oblong heaps of stones on our right hand and one upon our left.
>
> "They are graves," said the Major. "No doubt there are buried the two soldiers who were employed at the ferry and the man who went to warn them."
>
> This subsequently proved to be the fact.
>
> A hundred yards further on we came upon another grave on the right-hand side of the road. A red pocket-handkerchief, held by a stone, waved from its summit, and produced a ghastly effect. Another grave appeared on the other side of the road. . . . In the trees, fifty yards off, we saw the debris of his [Henderson's] wagon, in which the Apaches burned the poor fellow. . . . He had some kerosene oil on his vehicle, and with this the bloody wretches consummated their infernal work. A few charred bones, no fragment being over an inch square, are all that remain of gallant Henderson.
>
> Both the soldier and citizen victims traveled carelessly enough by daylight, and ran into the Indians where they least expected. . . . Their graves will long be a terrible reminder to travelers along that lonely road.[18]

On September 1, the day of the attack on Fort Apache, George L. Turner, Jr., left Globe, Arizona, for the Middleton Ranch to notify them of the troubles.[19] The ranch was about sixty miles from Globe and eight miles from Pleasant Valley, near Cherry Creek, about thirty miles west of the Cibecue battle site.

On the way Turner stopped at the Moody Ranch and gave them the news. He stayed there overnight and then continued his journey the next morning with Henry Moody. The two men arrived at the Middletons at about 10:00 A.M. and informed them of the danger. The Middletons immediately decided to leave the ranch the following morning with Turner and Moody for a place of safety.

About three o'clock that afternoon, however, seven Indians came up to the ranch house and asked permission to camp at a nearby spring. All had carbine needle guns and belts full of cartridges, except one who had only a pistol. When asked if they knew of the Cibecue fight, they said they did not—that they had been out hunting. They then borrowed a kettle. A short while later they borrowed bread. The Middletons' suspicions quickly diminished as they appeared to be friendly. Previously many other Indian parties had stopped by. The parties had always been treated kindly and returned everything borrowed.

Later that afternoon Mr. Middleton was making boxes at a workbench at the side of the house. His twelve-year-old son was sitting on the end of the bench, and Mrs. Middleton was at the milkhouse with her three youngest children (the youngest was four years old), about twenty steps from the house. Turner was standing near the milkhouse talking to Mrs. Middleton. Moody and the Middletons' seventeen-year-old daughter, Hattie, were sitting in the doorway of the house, where she was sewing, and the Middletons' oldest son, Henry, was in the house. Three Indians were standing near Mr. Middleton, another was in front of the house outside the yard fence, and the other three were at the milkhouse, one of whom was only four feet from Turner.

Suddenly one Indian yelled "Now," and they all fired their guns and ran for cover. One ball passed through Mr. Middleton's hat; another passed through his shirt without injuring him. Both Moody and Turner were killed instantly. Turner was shot three times, once over the left eye, once in the left arm, breaking it, and once through the breast. Moody was also shot three times, once in the right ear and twice in the breast. He fell "near and across the doorway, his head and shoulders hitting a box which stood near."[20] The ball that struck him in the temple first grazed Hattie Middleton's forehead, cutting off a lock of her hair.

The Middleton Ranch, ca. 1880. The Middleton Ranch was about ten miles southeast of present-day Young, Arizona, at a mesa now named Middleton Mesa. Photo courtesy Dan Thrapp, who obtained it from Leroy Middleton.

Henry, on hearing the gunfire, grabbed his rifle and ran to the front door. He saw the Indian who had been standing in front of the house running toward the corral. He raised his rifle and shot him through the hips. He then shot again, killing one Indian as they were seeking cover under a bank. Henry then ran to the back door to get another shot at them. Just as he located them an Indian hiding behind a large rock on a nearby hill shot him through the left shoulder.

Meanwhile, the other Middletons scampered to the house. As Mrs. Middleton and her three little children ran to it, the Indians fired a volley at them but missed. When all were inside they closed and fastened the doors. They then barricaded the doors with tables, beds, and chairs. The Indians continued their attack for about three hours, during which they drove off all twenty-two of the Middletons' horses.

As night fell the Middletons' became afraid that the Indians would come back in the darkness and set fire to their house. They stayed inside until midnight, when the moon went down, then moved about two miles to a point up on a mountainside. There Mr. Middleton hid his family in brush and left for Pleasant Valley to get help. When Middleton reached the valley he enlisted the aid of George Church. While he and Church were returning to the hiding place on the mountainside, they met the Indians. The hostiles fired at them and ran them back toward Pleasant Valley.

The two men took a roundabout route to the hiding place. They reached it long after sunrise. Church then had one cartridge left. Since the area seemed to be full of Indians Middleton decided to take his family to Globe. While en route, at eight o'clock that evening, they met a party of six men who had come out from the town to rescue them. The group reached Globe during the afternoon of the next day, September 4.

The military later determined that there had been twenty-one hostiles in the area around Pleasant Valley. Besides attacking the Middleton Ranch, they burned Church's house, skirmished with Edward Rose, killed a valuable stallion and stole ten horses belonging to George Turner, Sr., and drove off all the Tewksburys' horses, except sixteen head, mostly Morgan brood mares, which they killed. No one knew how many cattle were slain; some were found dead on open rangeland.

Chapter 5

RUMORS ABOUND

The telegraph line to Fort Apache remained down for almost a month, until the night of September 9. Lacking facts, the rumors received in the Gila River valley and consequently up the military hierarchy about the Cibecue battle, the attack on Fort Apache, and the hostiles' activities, were many and usually exaggerated.

On September 1 General Willcox telegraphed his first report of the battle to his superior, Maj. Gen. Irvin McDowell, the commander of the Military Division of the Pacific, headquartered at the Presidio of San Francisco:

> Have rumors, more or less authentic, that Carr had fight on 30th at Cibicu Creek crossing, Verde trail; and no information has been received from him since. Courier due at Apache on 30th has not reported. Indians from reservation report at Thomas that troops have been whipped. They say a lieutenant and several soldiers killed, and report Fort Apache taken, but which is not credited; but the situation is serious.
>
> . . . I hope the outbreak is not universal. . . . The rumors are conflicting. I do not believe Fort Apache was taken.[1]

McDowell quickly retransmitted the message to the adjutant general (AG) of the army in Washington, D.C., to inform Gen. William Tecumseh Sherman, general of the army, of the situation. Sherman's AG immediately notified the secretary of war, Robert Todd Lincoln.[2]

Maj. Gen. Irvin McDowell. Courtesy Massachusetts Commandery Military Order of the Loyal Legion and the U.S. Army Military History Institute.

The next day Major Biddle sent a severer message to Willcox.

Stirling [Albert Sterling], chief of scouts at Agency, saw Mickey Free[3] who was there at the fight, but come right in. He says medicine man was arrested by a lieutenant, supposed to be Cruse. Medicine man's brother said "Shant arrest my brother" and killed Cruse. Troops killed medicine man. Scouts close to troops poured their fire into them, killing most of the officers and a great many men. Then the massacre took place. A few got away holding together and trying to fight their way back to Apache, but supposed they must have been killed from the number stated by the Indians. Pedro's band attacked Apache, but must have been repulsed. He now holds the cañon through which the road to Apache runs.[4]

The essence of Biddle's message was forwarded to McDowell, then to Sherman and to Lincoln. Willcox also notified McDowell, "Tiffany telegraphs report from Subagency, an Indian named Nickey [probably Mickey Free] brought word that [a] number of chiefs are coming in with their bands, but that Pedro with all his band and others are on warpath. That Carr's command including himself, six officers and sixty-four enlisted men were killed day before yesterday: also that Pedro's men had killed seven or eight men, including an expressman between Apache and Thomas."[5]

First Lt. Harry Leland Haskell, Willcox's reliable and trusted aide, then at Grant, reported to Willcox: "Runners arriving at Agency confirm killing of Carr's whole party, 60 to 110 men. . . . [I]t seems beyond doubt that Carr and command were killed."[6] Haskell then informed him,

The most reliable information we can get through the Indians and in all their stories they fully sustain each other in that the outbreak is confined to the White Mountains bands principally these of Pedros, Santos, and Uilpitas numbering in all about four hundred warriors. The Indians say the arrest of the medicine man who led in the inciting of this people to bloodshed was a signal for a massacre for to begin and that Lieut. Cruse was shot dead by this man's brother who in turn was killed by a shot from one of the Sergt's of Cruse detachment who fell pierced by five bullets. The scouts then shot the men of the cavalry detachment down before they could raise their carbines and many of the White Mountain warriors armed themselves with their weapons and the fight continued all day. A party kept together fought their way out of Cibicu Creek but Mickey Free thinks that Pedro's band has killed them all and says it was this band which killed the expressman who is probably the mail rider for this place together with eight others about seven miles from Apache. Mickey states he saw this killing himself being hidden in the rocks. Sterling, chief of Maney's scouts, was here yesterday and says that from all the information he can gain that Peltay, Indian Sergeant, was the man who shot Lieut. Cruse; that the scouts shot Genl. Carr and the officers almost immediately and finished the cavalry detachment at the same time.[7]

Newspapers across the country printed these rumors as though they were fact. The headline for the story on the front page of the Sunday, September 4, edition of the *New York Times* said,

SHOT DOWN BY INDIANS

Gen. Carr and His Command Murdered.

A massacre by the White Mountain Apaches—seven officers and from sixty to one hundred and ten privates killed—fired upon by their own scouts in trying to arrest a "medicine man."[8]

An Associated Press report read,

San Francisco, September 3rd.

A Tucson despatch to the STAR has advices from Fort Grant to the following effect:

Three couriers have now come into Camp Thomas, all bringing the same news, that [Brevet] General Carr and command have all been massacred by White Mountain Indians, thirty-five miles from Camp Apache; one hundred and ten men and seven officers were killed. The officers must be General Carr, Captain Hentig, Lieutenants Carter, Gordon, Stanton, Overton and Dr. McCreery. The White Mountain Indian Reservation is located about one hundred and sixty miles north of Wilcox [Willcox] near the line of New Mexico. The tribe numbers about fifteen hundred in all. They can muster about four hundred warriors.[9]

The military in the Gila River valley first learned of the fight shortly before 9:00 P.M. on August 31, when Private Welch, who had left Apache that morning with Cochran's dispatch containing Severiano's news of the fight, arrived at Camp Thomas.[10] Immediately the commander of Camp Thomas, Capt. John Ludlow Viven, wired the message to Major Biddle at Fort Grant. At the time Biddle had only four cavalry troops nearby: Troops A and F, 6th Cavalry, at Grant; and Troops B and C, 6th Cavalry, at Camp Thomas. He quickly ordered the troops at Thomas to move to Fort Apache. He also mustered Troops A and F. At 11:45 P.M. he left for Camp Thomas with them.

Troops B and C and Lieutenant Clark's scout company, all under the command of 1st Lt. Henry Pratt Perrine, left Camp Thomas the next morning. They had to ferry across the swollen Gila River in small numbers on a raft, using a rope and pulley system anchored on each side of the river. They did not leave the north side of the Gila until three o'clock that afternoon. Biddle arrived at Camp Thomas a few hours before their departure from the river, at 11:30 A.M. Shortly thereafter he sent telegrams to Captain Tupper at Camp Huachuca with Troop G, 6th Cavalry, and Captain William Augustus Rafferty at Fort Bowie with Troop M, 6th Cavalry, ordering them to move to Thomas with all their available men. He also ordered Lieutenant Overton to march to Fort Apache with Troops A and F. The next day Biddle notified Capt. Curwen Boyd McLellan to bring his Troop L, 6th Cavalry, from Fort Lowell to Thomas via old Camp Grant.

Overton also experienced difficulties crossing the Gila. His command did not complete the crossing until the following morning, September 2. While they were crossing Biddle received a telegram from General Willcox ordering him to divert a cavalry troop to the San Carlos Agency. Indian Bureau inspector Gardiner had telegraphed the general that the agency was endangered by hostiles and a military force was needed there. Biddle reluctantly diverted Troop A. Overton did not leave the far side of the Gila with Troop F until 10:00 A.M.

Before Overton left Biddle ordered him to make a forced march to overtake Perrine and assume command of the three-troop force. Biddle also told him "to send no couriers or small parties back except to save the command."[11] He was very concerned about the strength of Overton's command, since it was not much larger than Carr's two-troop force, which reportedly had been massacred. The hostiles were thought to be holding Seven-Mile Canyon.[12] Biddle believed there were "straggling Indians on the trail that would

Cavalry troop crossing the Gila River in the 1890s. Courtesy U.S. Army Military History Institute.

likely kill any small parties travelling over it."[13] He had also received a rumor that Navajos were on Ash Creek, between Apache and Thomas, with hostile intentions.

Overton overtook Perrine at the Black River. The next night, at Turkey Creek, they left the Apache Road and moved cross-country to avoid the dangerous Seven-Mile Hill area. They arrived at Fort Apache about 3:00 A.M. without seeing any sign of the hostiles.

After Willcox received the initial reports of the Apache troubles he realized the situation was serious, though the reports were conflicting. During the morning of September 3 he left Whipple Barracks with Maj. Abraham Kerns Arnold, his acting assistant adjutant general (AAAG), and a clerk to move to Thomas to establish a headquarters in the field. He wanted to be at the front to personally command the effort to subdue the hostiles. While the "doom and gloom" rumors were being published and Overton and his men were moving toward Fort Apache, Carr was trying to contact the outside world. On the night of September 2 he sent two civilian couriers, John Colvig and Nat Nobles, the chief packer, to Camp Thomas with his report of the Cibecue battle and the attack on the fort. They came back to the post later that night saying they saw Indians and could not get by them.

The next night Carr sent Colvig and the regular mail carrier with two soldiers to Fort Wingate. Cooley and two other civilians accompanied them part of the way. Carr also dispatched Lieutenant Stanton's Troop E to carry his report to Camp Thomas. Stanton covered the part of the road that was in the mountains that night. While on Turkey Creek Hill his advance patrol reported back that they saw fires near the road. On examination Stanton found a recently abandoned camp and evidence that a box of ammunition had been opened. Most likely the camp was Overton's, who had probably just left the campsite to move cross-country to Fort Apache.

Stanton's force arrived at Camp Thomas at about 7:00 P.M. the next day, September 4, some twenty-four hours after leaving Fort Apache. The soldiers at Thomas were relieved and elated to see them. Stanton yelled the military casualties across the Gila as he and his men began the time-consuming task of crossing the river. His verbal information was quickly telegraphed up the military chain of command to Sherman.[14]

Meanwhile Willcox was worried about a general uprising among the Indians. On September 2 a sergeant who had been guarding abandoned property at Ash Creek came in to Thomas and reported having seen Indians in that area. He said they had held war dances, tried to take his stock, and pointed their guns at him. He deduced they were Navajos from the silver on their horses.

The fear of a large-scale uprising spread to the highest levels in the War Department on September 5, when General McDowell telegraphed General Sherman:

> The outbreak in Arizona appears very general. The hostiles are reported along the Southern Pacific road from Wilna [New Mexico][15] to Bowie, a distance of 100 miles. They pursued the west bound train of the third near Wilna for six miles and attacked Fort Bowie the same night.

. . . Nothing yet heard from Apache. I trust Gen. Sheridan [Lt. Gen. Philip Henry Sheridan, commander of the Military Division of the Missouri] will be able to send troops by the Atlantic and Pacific [rail]road[16] to try and open communication with Apache from the north. It is surmised by the commanding officer of Camp Thomas that the attack on that point has been repulsed, but it is not known.

. . . A large party of hostiles crossed the railroad between Stein Pass[17] and San Simon going north. This presents a very serious outbreak, and gives rise to fears that the hostiles have been successful in the attack on Apache, or expect to be.[18]

McDowell was reporting false rumors. The hostiles did not chase a train, nor did they attack Fort Bowie. The reports of large bands of Apaches near the railroad tracks were never authenticated. These rumors were reported direct to McDowell's headquarters by the general superintendent of the Southern Pacific Railroad, A. N. Towne, who had received the information from the conductor of a westbound train. False reports of Indian sightings and hostilities were common during Indian troubles.

Towne also notified General Willcox of the conductor's report. His report to Willcox, however, was more embellished than the one he sent to McDowell. Unlike McDowell, Willcox immediately knew it was false. However, Willcox was receiving numerous other reports of Indian sightings and depredations. The rumors were from locations across central and eastern Arizona and western New Mexico. Willcox thought most were false but was not certain. Settlers often reported false Indian incidents hoping troops would be sent to their settlement to provide protection.

Realizing there were not enough troops in Arizona to handle widespread hostilities, Willcox recommended that the citizens at exposed places take their own rifles and organize themselves as minutemen for their mutual protection. The secretary of war authorized the sale of 250 arms and 50,000 cartridges to the settlers for their self-protection[19] and two hundred .50-caliber Sharps carbines, with ammunition, to the Southern Pacific Railroad Company to arm its employees.

Willcox and his staff doubted the loyalty of Clark's scouts. They also thought 2d Lt. Albert Sidney Bailey's scouts were unreliable and might prove treacherous. As the agency and military authorities determined which reservation bands were faithful, the military filled its scout companies with Indians from them.[20]

The military's response to the Cibecue troubles was tremendous. During the first two days of September Willcox and Biddle ordered the entire regiment of the Sixth Cavalry, all the cavalry under Willcox's command, into the field near the reservation. In addition, they ordered three infantry companies stationed within the Department of Arizona to the troubled region.[21] Willcox also telegraphed the AAG of the Division of the Pacific, at San Francisco: "Please hurry forward all the troops you can spare to report by telegraph en route, as they come."[22]

The Division of the Pacific was composed of the Departments of Arizona, California, and the Columbia. In response to Willcox's request McDowell immediately ordered two 1st Cavalry troops under Major George Bliss Sanford and five 8th Infantry companies under Lt. Col. John Darragh Wilkins, all from the Department of California, to Arizona.[23] On September 6 McDowell ordered Company A, 8th Infantry, stationed at San Diego Barracks, California, under Capt. George Mitchell Brayton, to Fort Lowell.[24] These soldiers were rushed to Arizona via the Southern Pacific Railroad line, which had opened across southeastern Arizona the previous year.

In response to the potentially explosive situation north of Fort Apache, Willcox wired Sheridan: "It is reported that the White Mountain and other Apaches, to the number of 400, have commenced hostilities near Apache. It looks serious. Navajoes reported saucy. Will you look out for them and the A&P [Atlantic & Pacific] railroad? Can you render any other assistance?"[25]

Also during early September the *New York Herald*, the *Chicago Times*, the *Arizona Citizen*, and the *Arizona Star* rushed correspondents to the area.

Meanwhile, Biddle and Willcox were having communication problems. The problems began on September 1, when Biddle wired Willcox that he would leave for Fort Apache with the troops from Fort Grant. Willcox responded by ordering him to stay at Camp Thomas until more definite news was received from Fort Apache and of further movements of the Indians. The next day Biddle notified Willcox, "[I] will remain here as you direct but would have

Origin of military units sent toward the Cibecue troubles. These units came from seven states or territories.

preferred going [with Overton] as the command is not much larger than Carr's, which if information is correct, was easily used up."[26] Willcox then ordered Biddle, "Wait no longer, but join command and push for Apache. Answer at once."[27] Biddle replied that all the troops had been sent forward; there weren't enough men left to escort him; and he did not think he could overtake them if he did start. Later that night Maj. Samuel Nicoll Benjamin, Willcox's AAG, responded: "Dept. Commander is anxious to strike them [the hostiles] before their numbers are increased, and put as speedy an end to the outbreak as possible. . . . The General does not wish to detain you at Thomas longer than to get a survey of the situation and form definite plans of operation [against the hostiles]."[28]

Biddle then notified Willcox that his plan of operations was to wait for the arrival of Captains Tupper, McLellan, and Rafferty with their cavalry troops, move north with them to Fort Apache, and then proceed against the hostiles. "With the force I will then have . . . [I] will be able, I think, to clean things up," he added.[29]

At 9:30 that night Benjamin sent Biddle another telegram: "Make sure you have force enough before attacking. Bring up all you need from the rear and make best disposition you can for San Carlos. Suggest that [Capt. May H.] Stacey take care of Grant and Bowie. Telegraph you today that the General leaves for Willcox in the morning and wishes you to command the column in person."[30] By then Biddle was hesitant to act without General Willcox's express orders. He feared his actions might interfere with some of Willcox's plans.

At 3:00 P.M. the next day, September 3, Biddle received another telegram from Benjamin, dated the previous day: "Comd'g General insists upon your going out to the cavalry en route to Apache and halting them till you bring up enough to make a sure fight."[31] Lieutenant Haskell, who had just arrived at Camp Thomas, was shown this telegram. He quickly telegraphed Benjamin: "It is impossible to carry out this order, only 6 mounted men can be had for that duty until Rafferty comes [from Fort Bowie]. Biddle is preparing to go, but it is not safe, [I am] . . . sure [the] General [doesn't] . . . understand situation fully. It would be murder to send out men in this way."[32]

At 10:30 P.M. Biddle received another telegram from Benjamin: "Dispatch from Haskell just received. If road is not safe, you are to wait for Rafferty's company and go on with him. Report fully."[33]

At midnight Rafferty and his Troop M arrived. At noon of the following day Biddle left with them for Fort Apache. Shortly thereafter another telegram arrived at Camp Thomas for Biddle:

The General approves your remaining at Thomas and considers it fortunate under the circumstances to gather up a force sufficient to meet any emergency. His dispatches were sent from Prescott under the impression that Overton was within easy reach. Your views coincide with his own and he does not wish the command flithered away in small numbers. The first object should be to open effectual communication with Fort Apache and be ready to wipe out the hostiles wherever they may be.[34]

On September 4, after Willcox received word that Biddle had left for Fort Apache, he had Arnold send Biddle another telegram. It ordered Biddle to return to Thomas with Rafferty's troop "for the purpose of perfecting your organization as planned in your late dispatches, with the view of assuming offensive operations."[35]

The commander of Camp Thomas immediately sent a courier to Biddle with the two messages. The next day the commander wired General Willcox: "Courier sent out yesterday, returned, went as far as Rock[y] Canyon, did not overtake Biddle, saw Indian ponies and smokes in canyon. Hazardous to send less than 75 or 100 men."[36]

Several days later Biddle wrote about his journey:

I left the ferry at Thomas at 3 P.M. Sept 4th.[37] Marched over the trail and into Rocky canyon, arrived there about 3 A.M. on the morning of Sept 5th. Unsaddled and remained in camp until about 6:30 A.M. Marched two miles where I had to go into camp on account of torrent rushing through the canyon from the almost incessant rains from the time of starting.[38] Remained at that point four hours for water to go down; moved out reached Black River at 7 P.M. of the 5th having marched 14 miles, making 50 miles in all. Next morning tried to cross Black River, but it was impossible, boat on the other side and the rope broken. Next day worked all day, got the rope over and the boat from off the shore; tried to cross evening of the 8th but found we could not get over without losing some of the animals and it would take us all night. Waited until next morning and when about half the command was across Lieut. Overton with the battalion [Troop F and Clark's scout company] arrived acting under instructions from Col. Carr. I would here state that I have known this road for six years but it never was in such a condition as at present and is perfectly impassable for wagons or ambulances with the lightest loads generally conveyed.[39]

Biddle's and Overton's forces camped together that night— September 9—three miles north of the river. The next morning the couriers arrived with the two messages from Willcox. The two forces then broke camp. Overton and Troop F went back to Fort Apache; Biddle returned to Thomas with Rafferty and his troop.

Apache Indians at the Apache Road. Date unknown. Courtesy Special
Collections, University of Arizona Library.

Since Overton had found Clark's scouts ineffective and they were
of doubtful loyalty, Biddle took them back with his force. After
Biddle's party arrived back at Camp Thomas General Willcox
ordered Clark to San Carlos to discharge his scouts and immediately enlist a new company.

Chapter 6

CONFUSION AND MYSTERY REIGN

Shortly after being notified of the Cibecue fight General Willcox wired the agency asking about the reservation Indians. Tiffany replied, "Hostile, White Mountains; Yumas, Mojaves, Warm Springs and Chiricahuas appear to be friendly; Tontos, Coyoteros and most of San Carlos profess friendship, but are neutral. Don't think there are over four hundred hostiles, four hundred friendly and balance can't say."[1] Two days later, on September 3, Tiffany reported that fourteen Apache bands, of 220 men, were involved in the hostilities. He listed the number of warriors in each band and the chief of each. All were Cibecue and White Mountain Apaches. He based this revised estimate on the bands camped in the Cibecue region and near Fort Apache when the hostilities occurred. Throughout the events that followed the attack Tiffany frequently updated his estimate. Willcox used these estimates and Tiffany's counts of the Indians that had not come in to the agency and subagency to estimate his active foe.

On hearing of the hostilities most friendly Indians out on passes immediately headed for the agency or subagency. On September 2, while they were arriving, Tiffany notified Willcox.

One of Santos Band came in from Cibicu, says the White Mountain Indians tried to get some San Carlos and Chiricahuas to join them. They refused and are coming into the Agency. The Cibicu or White

San Carlos Indian Agency, 1895. An Indian camp is in the foreground. Courtesy National Archives.

> Mountain Indians who fought Col. Carr are up near junction of White and Black Rivers and the junction of these rivers from the Salt River. They sent word by this Santos Indian that they were not going out, but going to stay where they are and if the soldiers wanted them to try and get them. I take this only for what I think it worth. It is reported to me, some of Pedro's band White Mountains are down Ash Creek, if so, they are probably watching the movements of troops toward Apache, either to convey the news to Indians there or to ambush or attack in the rear. . . . We had an alarm this evening which proved a false one, but while out with Indian Scouts I found San Carlos Indians coming in to defend Agency and a whole band of Yumas and one of Mojaves came up for same purpose.[2]

The Tontos also hurried in to the agency. They volunteered to help fight the hostiles if they could have arms. They did not want pay— if they could have the plunder. A couple of days later Nodeski, a friendly Apache chief who had been living on Cherry Creek, came in to San Carlos. He said hostiles had threatened him and he then immediately left for the Agency, leaving his crops, cattle, and possessions behind.

Willcox, nevertheless, was worried about the friendly Indians. He asked Tiffany to keep them near the agency and subagency until the "excitement" was over. Willcox believed the hostiles had spies at San Carlos who would report troop movements to them. He was also concerned that agency and subagency Indians "may steal away and commit depredations on the sly."[3]

As early as September 2 Major Biddle suspected many hostiles were having second thoughts about remaining out. He notified General Willcox: "I think a good many of the Indians that was in the fight have got frightened at what they did and have started for the Agency and to avoid the consequences."[4]

Some hostiles were indeed coming in to the agency. On September 5 Lieutenant Haskell reported that Tiffany's Indian police arrested an Indian at San Carlos who was in the Cibecue fight. Three days later two of Cruse's scouts came in to San Carlos and surrendered.[5] They brought in their guns and ammunition (twenty rounds). They said that when the scouts started firing at Carr's soldiers, they left for the agency. Two days later Tiffany informed Willcox that he had arrested two men of Sanchez's band. The men said they had nothing to do with the battle—that they heard the firing and ran away.

On September 7 Willcox wired McDowell's headquarters: "There are all sorts of rumors but my present belief is that hostiles are all north of the Gila and mostly in the White Mountains and Mogollon Country."[6] Willcox also telegraphed Brig. Gen. John Pope, the commander of the Department of the Missouri:

> Agent Tiffany reports but two hundred sixty bucks out on warpath mostly [in the] White Mountains. No signs of their leaving. [Col. Ranald Slidell] Mackenzie[7] may not seem to be needed but if we can crush the hostiles a desultory war will be prevented. The treacherous scouts must be killed quickly or they will be likely to join Nana in New Mexico. Please instruct your officers to hang on the spot all old scouts that may be caught. Will telegraph Fort Bayard[8] on first report of hostiles moving south.[9]

In addition, Willcox wired Pope asking him to look out for the Navajos, to protect the working parties on the Atlantic and Pacific Railroad, to send ammunition to Fort Apache at once, and to keep the route open between the railroad and Fort Apache for ammunition and supplies. Pope quickly replied. He said Col. Luther Prentice Bradley would leave Wingate for Fort Apache on the eighth with the extra ammunition from there,[10] Mackenzie was coming, and the Navajos were quiet. Pope immediately ordered infantry to guard the railroad personnel.

Willcox also notified Carr that he should determine exactly where the hostiles were and move offensively as soon as possible. Carr replied that he had no knowledge of their whereabouts. Willcox was concerned. He sent a message up his chain of command asking for money to pay large rewards to agency Indians to serve as informants. However, he soon found they would not go out except in large bodies, so he did not pursue his request.

Meanwhile, Carr began to send troops out on assignments near Fort Apache. On September 6 he sent Overton and Troop F out to bury the people killed near Seven-Mile Hill and to scout near the head of Turkey Creek. Overton did not see any sign of Indians; he thought the recent rains might have obliterated any that may have existed.

Two days later Overton and his troop left Fort Apache to repair the telegraph line. They arrived back at the post on September 10 after repairing it down to the Black River. That night Carr sent a party through Seven-Mile Canyon. He believed, perhaps from a report by friendly Indians, that hostiles were still in the canyon. The soldiers found none but destroyed caches containing corn, hides, and camp equipage. During the next few nights Carr sent a scouting party up the East Fork and another down the White River. Both were unsuccessful in locating the hostiles.

During this period Carr asked Willcox for horses, pack mules, and scouts. He was also short of ammunition. He planned to resume the offensive if he learned the whereabouts of the hostiles. But he did not.

Throughout the Cibecue aftermath Tiffany believed Pedro's men were deeply involved in the hostilities around Seven-Mile Hill and the attack on Fort Apache and included them in his estimates of the number of hostiles. His belief was based on information he received from Indians at the agency and subagency, many of whom had come in from the northern part of the reservation and were strongly

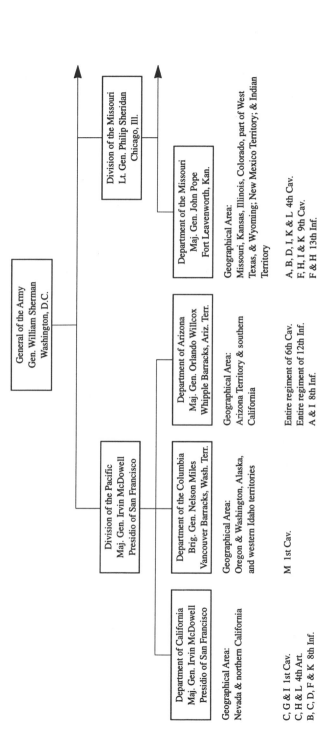

General of the Army
Gen. William Sherman
Washington, D.C.

Division of the Pacific
Maj. Gen. Irvin McDowell
Presidio of San Francisco

Division of the Missouri
Lt. Gen. Philip Sheridan
Chicago, Ill.

Department of California
Maj. Gen. Irvin McDowell
Presidio of San Francisco

Geographical Area:
Nevada & northern California

C, G & I 1st Cav.
C, H & L 4th Art.
B, C, D, F & K 8th Inf.

Department of the Columbia
Brig. Gen. Nelson Miles
Vancouver Barracks, Wash. Terr.

Geographical Area:
Oregon & Washington, Alaska,
and western Idaho territories

M 1st Cav.

Department of Arizona
Maj. Gen. Orlando Willcox
Whipple Barracks, Ariz. Terr.

Geographical Area:
Arizona Territory & southern
California

Entire regiment of 6th Cav.
Entire regiment of 12th Inf.
A & I 8th Inf.

Department of the Missouri
Maj. Gen. John Pope
Fort Leavenworth, Kan.

Geographical Area:
Missouri, Kansas, Illinois, Colorado, part of West
Texas, & Wyoming; New Mexico Territory; & Indian
Territory

A, B, D, I, K & L 4th Cav.
F, H, I & K 9th Cav.
F & H 13th Inf.
A & I 15th Inf.

Units in the Department of Arizona at the completion of the Cibecue troubles and their chain of command. In addition, a detachment of ten enlisted men and an officer of Battery A, 4th Artillery, from the Department of California, moved to Yuma to fill in for Company E, 12th Infantry, which was ordered to Camp Thomas; and a detachment of Company F, 15th Infantry, from the Department of Missouri, was stationed at the terminus of the Atlantic & Pacific Railroad to guard supplies for Fort Apache.

suspected to have been involved in the hostilities. On September 10, however, Carr reported that 32 men, 67 women, and 105 children of Pedro's band were at Cooley's Ranch. This was most of his band. Carr stated that the men (which included Alchesay, Uclenny, and Bottalish—the most prominent members of the band) were friendly.

A situation was developing which soon caused a terrible personality clash between two high-ranked military officers involved in the operations to engage the hostiles. This clash should not have happened. It developed because General Sherman, in his impetuosity, erroneously convinced himself that the Cibecue affair was the result of an organized attack on Carr's command by an established group of Indians. He thought this band was continuing to lurk about as though they were Sitting Bull's Sioux, and the army needed to chase them down, have a grand battle, and give them a good "clearing out." This was not quite the case, and Willcox and McDowell did not disabuse him.

Willcox kept both McDowell and Pope well informed. He telegraphed them his plans, his troop movements, the suspected hostile locations and their numbers, and everything else that he thought was important for them to know. Many of his reports, however, were detailed and difficult for someone at Sherman's level and not familiar with eastern Arizona to understand.

Pope passed the intelligence he received from his sources, including Willcox, to his superior, General Sheridan. Pope and Sheridan telegraphed summaries of the situation using statements that were easy for someone away from the action to understand. Sheridan, a good friend of Sherman's, knew how to tell Sherman exactly what he wanted to hear.

> Sept. 6. From my information today it is almost certain that no other Indians than the White Mountain were engaged [in] the recent attack on Carr. General Pope is accumulating a good strong force at Wingate to watch the Navajoes or operate to help McDowell. There has been great exaggeration on the reports concerning the White Mountain difficulty.[11]

> Sept. 6. The trouble in Arizona seems to be confined to [the] White Mountain Apaches. Colonel Bradley has moved out from Wingate to

relieve Apache if necessary. Pope will soon have sufficient troops concentrated at Wingate to give to Willcox all the assistance he will require.[12]

Sept. 10. Have been in free communication with General Pope on the subject of the troubles about Fort Apache. The trouble is confined to the White Mountain Utes,[13] and there is as yet no reason to believe that it will spread. Bradley has gone towards Apache with two companies of cavalry and three of infantry and will soon be joined by Mackenzie with six companies of the Fourth. Additional companies of infantry are being collected at Wingate and the nine companies of Infantry at Uncompahgre [Colorado] will be sent there if necessary. . . . If I get the slightest information that will lead one to believe that the trouble will spread, I will send the whole of the Third Cavalry and one regiment of infantry from the Department of [the] Platte, one from Texas and one from Dakota and one more can be pushed out from [the] Department of Missouri. We cannot prudently spare these forces, but will take the chances as the cold weather is coming on and the Indians will keep quiet in the north.[14]

Sept. 11. General Pope telegraphed me last night that advices from Willcox are to the effect that there was no connected attack of Indians on Fort Apache; that what occurred was a mere temporary outbreak occasioned by arrest of medicine man and unexpected firing of some of Carr's scouts which killed Hentig, and six men. There have been no depredations since the firing on burying party the day after officially reported. General Pope expresses some doubts as to whether the Indians will fire on the troops now advancing on them from every direction.[15]

Sept. 12. In every case where the wishes of the General of the Army have not been anticipated, they will be carried out. There has not yet been sufficient developments of the condition of affairs in Arizona to warrant specific action by the troops of this Division any further than the advance of Bradley towards Apache.[16]

Unfortunately, McDowell did not recognize the difficulty with Willcox's reports and forwarded most of them verbatim to Sherman. Sherman found them so confusing that he could not understand what Willcox was doing about the situation. The reports did not provide Sherman with the information he needed to determine what steps he should take. Nevertheless, Sherman gave McDowell his views.

Sept. 7. No further orders from me necessary. Will approve most severe measures as a punishment for the treachery of the Apaches.[17]

Sept. 10. The quicker the insult involved in General Carr's retreat is avenged, the sooner the fighting will be over.[18]

Sept. 11. I expect Willcox to destroy the renegade Apaches. . . . [I] don't care about details. . . . The best and only way is to give General Willcox absolute authority to act, and leave him free to accomplish the only end desired—the punishment of the Apaches who are known to be hostile. I only want to hear results not intentions.[19]

Sept. 12. I think that the troops must whip and punish the Apaches, or the effect will be bad. Every Indian who aided in the attack of General Carr's party must be killed or arrested and held for trial, the sooner the better. Then, if he has not troops enough, [Brevet] General Mackenzie will enter Arizona from the direction of Wingate or Craig,[20] when every Indian outside the San Carlos Reservation will be treated as hostile. There must be no half way measures.[21]

When McDowell received the third message, he notified Sherman's AG: "General Willcox is under no restrictions as to his operations against the Apaches save those imposed by the General of the Army. I had given him no orders and had not intended giving him any to hamper him in any way whatever."[22]

Of these four messages from Sherman, McDowell's headquarters transmitted only the third down to Willcox. When Willcox received it he provided Carr, Price, and Mackenzie with his interpretation of it: "He [Sherman] expects General Willcox's troops to destroy the renegade Apaches without giving him any of the details whatever."[23] As a result, for the next six days, until September 17, Willcox did not send any information about the Cibecue troubles, or about what he was doing to resolve them, up his chain of command.[24] Sherman did not like this. He wanted to know what Willcox was doing. This lack of information made him dissatisfied with Willcox's handling of the Cibecue affair.

Chapter 7

ANXIETY IN THE HIGH COMMAND

To reach the front General Willcox and Major Arnold took a stage from Prescott to Maricopa. From there they took a train to Willcox. They then moved to Grant. The general was busy during their journey: at towns with telegraph facilities he sent and received many telegrams concerning the Cibecue troubles.[1]

Biddle returned to Camp Thomas from the Black River on September 11. While he had been away Troop G, 6th Cavalry, Company H, 12th Infantry, and Company I, 8th Infantry, had arrived there. The next day he and Haskell traveled to Fort Grant and met with General Willcox. They briefed him on what they knew about the situation.

Willcox and Arnold arrived at Camp Thomas at 4:00 P.M. on September 15. Company E, 12th Infantry, had reached the post the previous day. On September 16 Bailey's Company D, Indian scouts, Troop A, 6th Cavalry, Troops G and I, 1st Cavalry, from California, and McLellan's Troop L, 6th Cavalry, arrived there. McLellan and his troop had been delayed because they could not cross the flooded Gila River farther downstream, north of old Camp Grant, and had to take a roundabout route via Tres Alamos and Point of Mountains.

Other cavalry and infantry units were also arriving at their initial destinations on the reservation. In addition, Carr was receiving more troops. Stanton's Troop E, which brought Carr's report to Camp

Fort Thomas, Arizona Territory, 1885. Courtesy U.S. Army Military History Institute.

Thomas, left Thomas to return to Fort Apache on September 11 and arrived there on the fourteenth. While en route it was caught in the heaviest storm of the season. The rain started during the afternoon of the eleventh and continued until five o'clock the next morning. Fort Apache recorded three inches of precipitation from the storm. The next evening the region received another rain; however, it was light. The rivers in the region again rose to high levels.

During the morning of September 15 Tupper and his troop left Camp Thomas for Fort Apache with 2d Lt. Charles Baehr Gatewood and his fifty newly recruited Yuma and Mojave scouts. John Finerty, the only newspaper correspondent who went into the field with the soldiers, traveled with them as he thought Carr would be involved in any fighting that might occur.[2]

Tupper's force had to be ferried across the Gila on a raft, a few at a time. While one group was crossing the river the ferryboat suddenly veered, throwing Pvt. Fred K. Seelhorst and another soldier into the "swift and treacherous" water.[3] The other soldier swam to shore, but Seelhorst drowned. Tupper and his men reached Fort Apache on September 17.

Meanwhile, McDowell's and Willcox's relationship with Sherman was worsening. On the day Willcox reached Camp Thomas, Sherman, who had not received an update from Willcox in five days, telegraphed McDowell: "Neither Willcox's or your dispatches are clear. What I expect is action, results, not speculation. All Apaches outside the reservation must be killed or captured, and if any of them take refuge on the reservation that must not save the guilty parties who fired on [Brevet] General Carr's command."[4]

Although McDowell did not pass this telegram down to Willcox, he did respond: "Willcox is for the moment out of telegraphic communication. . . . I do not know in what respect my despatches are not clear to you. Your directions as to Apache matters have all been communicated to Willcox and he is as you wish left absolutely free to carry them out and is not to trouble you further with speculative plans or details only results when he has achieved them."[5]

Sherman replied the next day:

> Your dispatch of last night is received, and on the theory that all of General Willcox's troops are in the field beyond the reach of the telegraph, converging on the hostiles, I will await results. [Brevet] General Mackenzie is concentrating at Fort Wingate prepared to enter Arizona via Apache, and [Brevet] General [Edward] Hatch is also at Fort Craig prepared to move toward San Carlos, and I await a call from you to give the orders to advance. I want this annual Apache stampede to end right now, and to effect that result will send every available man in the whole Army if necessary. But of course it will be far better if General Willcox can do this without extraneous help. I must go to Chattanooga next Monday [September 18], and would like to act before I go, as it is confusing to have telegrams follow me for answer away from the records. . . . [When] the troops from New Mexico are called on to help, . . . I may indicate a common commander for all the forces employed against the Apaches.[6]

Sherman had inferred from McDowell's telegram that Willcox was out of telegraphic communication because he and his troops were converging on the hostiles. At that time they were not. Willcox and his staff for his Headquarters in the Field were moving from Fort Grant to Camp Thomas.

McDowell immediately passed Sherman's latest telegram down to Willcox. He also sent Sherman a reply:

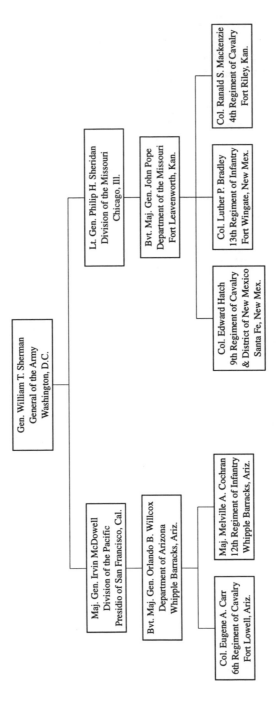

Chain of command of the principal officers involved in the Cibecue aftermath. This chart shows the commander, the organization he commanded, and the location of his headquarters. Willcox and Pope commanded in accordance with their brevet rank, major general. Pope's actual rank was major general; Willcox's was colonel.

Your telegram of today received. The last word from Willcox about the troops from New Mexico was of the tenth. He then telegraphed he thought Mackenzie had better halt at Wingate for further developments. I do not venture to advise against his wishes. He telegraphed on the seventh however that he had requested Pope to reopen route for supplying Apache from nearest station on A & P Railroad and send some ammunition to Apache.

[Lt. Col. Rufus] Saxton[7] just informs me that the washed out road from Thomas to Apache is now so bad that supplies cannot be pushed through from this side and are blocked up at Thomas. I ask therefore that communication be opened and supplies be sent as requested by Willcox of Pope.

. . . Willcox is reported by the papers to have just arrived at Thomas and I hope to hear from him tomorrow.[8]

Meanwhile, Sherman and Sheridan were wiring each other expressing their frustrations:

[Sherman to Sheridan] Before going to Chattanooga where I expect to meet you the 21st, I want to make what orders are necessary to counteract the bad impression by Carr's affair near Fort Apache. Where is Mackenzie?[9]

[Sheridan to Sherman] Your dispatch of this date [Sept. 15] just received. The best reply I can make to you concerning your inquiry and the condition of affairs is to transmit the last dispatch received from General Pope. Of course your information is better than mine as you hear from California [McDowell's headquarters]; but I would advise that no orders be given until you see me at Chattanooga when we can talk over the condition.[10]

[September 13, Pope to Sheridan] Although I received dispatches from military sources in Arizona everyday, no one appears to know anything of the whereabouts of hostile Indians nor indeed anything whatever about them, although there are rumors that somebody has run off stock, no reports even of any attack by Indians or any hostilities of any kind since the first outbreak has been received. It appears to me that such of the Indians as were concerned in the late outbreak near Apache are hiding away, as much stampeded about what they have done as the people of Arizona are. Messengers have come through from Apache to Wingate without molestation and the telegraph line from Apache to Willcox on Southern Pacific Railroad open. I repeat my opinion telegraphed you some days since that the whole affair will die out and be saddled upon Carr's Indian scouts. Mackenzie leaves today with three (3) companies of Fourth Cavalry to take command in Navajo Country, his other three companies will push through to Wingate day after tomorrow. He will have eight cavalry and eight infantry companies as soon as his last three cavalry companies arrive there. He is ordered to move towards Apache forwarding all trains of supplies that may be there from Wingate to Apache and to keep open safe communication between these points and to use his whole force against any hostile Indians either Navajos or Apaches. I do not believe he will fire a shot.[11]

[Sherman to Sheridan] Dispatch received. My information from Generals Willcox and McDowell is so indefinite that it is not worth repeating. Willcox is beyond reach of the telegraph and I infer all his troops are converging on the hostiles east and south of Apache.[12]

[Sheridan to Sherman] During last night and today [September 16] I have received several despatches from General Pope and one from Mackenzie. All they contain is about this; no hostility need be apprehended from Navajoes and there are no hostile Apaches in New Mexico. Pope says Willcox has sufficient troops. The number of hostile White Mountain Apaches is supposed to be about one hundred and eighty (180) as only a portion of the tribe is supposed to be on the warpath. Pope thinks hostiles want to talk and come in of which I, myself, have no doubt as I have seen the same thing before. He suggests a settlement of the trouble by arrangement in that way. I myself have no suggestions to make. It is time some thing should be done. I must confess I am disgusted with the whole business. If you have no objections I will direct Mackenzie to unite with Bradley and if he feels strong enough to march on the enemy. This is what I supposed Pope intended to do from previous des-patches or at least to march as far as Fort Apache; if Mackenzie does not feel strong enough I will direct him to unite with sufficient of Willcox's troops to make himself strong enough and then attack. As to what is being done by the troops in Arizona, it is a mystery to me. There is nothing to be done in New Mexico as far as my judgement goes. I submit the information and the suggestion(s) herein for what you have to say on the subject.[13]

[Sherman to Sheridan] I have your despatch of yesterday [September 16]—also one from McDowell. The latter reports Willcox moving towards the theater of operations from the south, but owing to the state of the roads he asks that provisions and ammunition be sent to Fort Apache from the direction of Wingate. Please order this to be done. Also let Mackenzie move towards Apache keeping his men and horses as fresh as possible till Willcox calls on him for help, or until he is ordered to advance by me. Let General Hatch have similar instructions at Craig.

I will give Willcox a fair chance to punish the Apaches with his own men but if he is too dilatory, or if he calls for help, I will give orders to Mackenzie to pitch in with all the troops in that quarter, regardless of department lines.[14]

During the previous few days Willcox had taken some steps toward dealing with the situation. To segregate the hostile Indians from friendly Indians he had decided to establish a "peace line" around the agency and subagency. When Tiffany was informed of the idea, he requested it not take effect until the friendly Indians could be notified and given enough time to bring in their families. On September 16, the day after Willcox arrived at Camp Thomas, he issued Field Orders No. 11. The orders said he was establishing the peace line, effective September 21, and any Indians found outside its limits would be considered hostile, except scouts, runners, and others in the military service and the friendly Indians of Pedro's band near Fort Apache. Tiffany immediately informed the reservation Indians.

The same field orders divided the vast area of the reservation into three military districts and assigned the 6th Cavalry, 8th Infantry, and 12th Infantry units in the area for the Cibecue aftermath within the districts. Colonel Carr was ordered to command the District of Apache, which included the country north of the Salt and Black rivers and east of Cibecue Creek. Lieutenant Colonel Price was placed in command of the District of the Verde, which included the western area of the reservation and the country farther west, including Globe, Florence, and the Tonto Basin. Major Biddle was ordered to command the District of the Gila, the area south of the point where the Apache Road crossed the Black River, including Fort Grant, Camp Thomas, and Willcox Station.

Meanwhile, Indians were continually coming into San Carlos in groups of eight to ten families. Four members of George's band arrived at the subagency on September 11 and said their band would be in within five days. During the morning of September 14 two friendly Apaches (Nodeski and Torseli) came in to the agency from Nodeski's camp up the San Carlos River.[15] Nodeski said he had talked to the hostiles. After Tiffany learned the details he wired General Willcox:

> Nodeski . . . reports the hostiles are calling him out at midnight to talk. They would not go in to his camp or he go to them but talked across the arroyo some 2 or 300 yards. They wanted them to come and join hostiles and they got 1 box of ammunition at the Carr fight and since then 5000 rounds more, that the bands were on Cibicu and would die there. They wanted to know if I had sent the soldiers to arrest the medicine man, and how the people who came in were treated to all of which Nodeski told them that he did not know, if they wanted to talk to come and talk to me, that he was going to stay with the Agent. They told Torseli that when Jim Cook[16] came down with scouts from Apache to Thomas [earlier in September] they were concealed on both sides of the road but did not fire into them because they did not want to hurt the scouts. After this they went back into the hills. I will have that place watched by some of my scouts.[17]

The next day Tiffany sent Willcox another message: "A woman came into Subagency and reports that Chief George's band are hemmed in on Black River not far from San Carlos and Apache Trail by the Cibicu hostiles. She says there are 64 hostile men all armed with Government guns and had two boxes of cartridges besides those they had in their belts and threatened to kill George and his party if they attempted to leave. . . . I give it for what it is worth and think it important for you to know."[18]

On September 16 Tiffany informed Willcox that he had received more reports from incoming Indians which led him to believe the hostiles were indeed on the Black River. "Sanchez is no doubt the leading man of the hostiles from what I can learn," he added.[19]

Four days earlier, Carr, at Fort Apache, had notified Arnold and Tiffany: "People from Cooleys seem to think hostiles in force on or about Cibicu. Others think they are in mountains east of here or heads of Turkey creek and Bonito."[20] To determine the validity of these rumors Carr started sending his troops out on longer-range scouting missions. On the night of the fourteenth he sent 2d Lt.

John Y. Fillmore Blake with a detail of twenty-five men of Troop B, 6th Cavalry, to the head of Cedar Creek. They returned the next day, having traveled more than sixty miles in twenty hours. On their return Carr notified Willcox: "Indians generally have been moving towards Cibicu, packing corn and etc."[21] Willcox then wired Pope: "Result of Carr's scouting so far shows Indians still in Cibicu. Inform Mackenzie."[22]

Blake's scouting party was the sixth that Carr had sent out; the last four had left at night. During the night of September 15, several hours after Blake's return, Carr sent 1st Lt. Louis Aleck Craig with fifty men out to scout south and east of Fort Apache. They returned the following day without finding hostiles.

Meanwhile, important events were taking place at the subagency. During the evening of the fifteenth Bonito arrived. The next day George and his band arrived.[23] Both men blamed the hostilities around Fort Apache on Pedro's band. At that time, however, Carr was reporting that Pedro's band was friendly:

> Cooley came in [to Fort Apache] this morning [September 16] with about 150 men, women and children of Pedro's band and those who have been living with them for some time past. Probably 14 bucks came in, rest still at Cooley's. Will telegraph names as soon as can.
>
> Cooley has the most perfect confidence in the friendliness of these people and wants part of them to remain at his place for its defense.
>
> Cooley says he had an Indian with the hostiles who came in last night and reports that they were on Tuesday 13th, about three miles below the trail crossing of Black River near a round hill above mouth of White Mountain Creek [White River]. His story agrees to some extent with your information. Says he counted ninety-eight good guns, twenty-five pistols and three small boxes of ammunition. Cooley has idea that there were about 150 bucks, but I will get it more certain when I see Alchesay. They were ferrying their women and children across and sending them to San Carlos. Women crying and don't want to go; men saying they expected to die and wanted women and children away.
>
> . . . Cooley is confident that hostiles are on mesa between this and Black River. I cannot think so, but will have to look there when ready to start.

Bonito. Courtesy National Archives.

Sanchez. Photo by Henry Buehman. Smithsonian Institution Photo No. 45,889.

Cooley says that Moseby's [Mosby's] and George's Indians as
well others were in the attack on this post, Sept 1st. That they killed
the people on the road and then joined with the others S.W. of here.[24]
Says Sanchez killed several people to the west, say about Pleasant
Valley and brought in 50 or 60 head of stock.

Sanchez is no doubt the general leader.[25]

Based on these reports of the hostile's whereabouts and intentions
and the number of Indians Tiffany was reporting out and supposedly
hostile, Willcox believed there were two groups of hostiles, and
they were waiting for him. He believed one was near the junction of
the Black and White rivers and the other was still on the Cibecue.
He and his staff quickly planned a massive offensive operation to
find and punish them. It consisted of four separate commands,
composed of sixteen cavalry and infantry units and five Indian
scout companies.

The plan was to confine the hostiles in the basin formed by the
Salt, Cibecue, Carrizo, White, and Black rivers by sending the four
forces in simultaneously from different directions.[26] Price, northwest of the reservation near Fort Verde, was to push for the Cibecue
with his force. Carr, at Fort Apache (southeast of the Cibecue battleground), was to move to the Cibecue with his command. McLellan
and a 6th Cavalry battalion was to move north from Camp Thomas
to the Black River, then west along its north bank. Sanford and his
1st Cavalry battalion was to move north from the San Carlos Agency
to the Black River. Troop A, 6th Cavalry, was the only cavalry troop
in Arizona not participating in the advance.

On September 16 Price left Fort Verde for the Cibecue, starting
his movement for the operation. The next day, as Sanford and
McLellan left Camp Thomas, Tiffany traveled to Camp Thomas to
visit General Willcox. Shortly after arriving he learned Sanchez was
planning to come in to the agency. He quickly wired Sterling, back
at the agency: "[Brevet] Genl. Carr telegraphs Sanchez is coming
into San Carlos tomorrow, may be to have a talk and may be not.
Have your scouts ready and watchful. If to talk keep him until I
come, but disarm him if he has arms or any of his men with him.
Have scouts spot them; if saucy and you can't arrest him without
trouble, kill him, but if he sends word and wants to talk to me, guard
him until I come. Tell [Bvt. Lt.] Col. [May Humphreys] Stacey."[27]

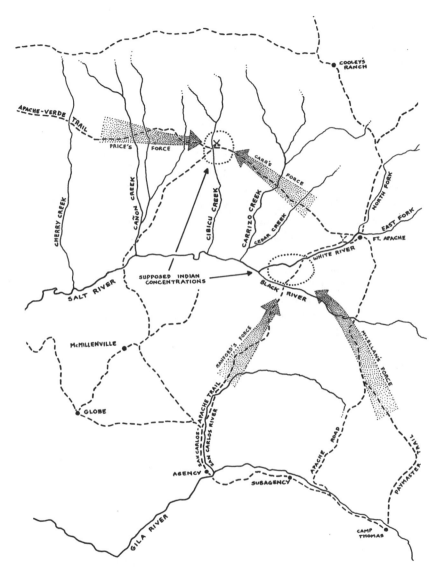

Willcox's strategy to engage the hostiles

Meanwhile, Sherman was growing more impatient. He expected action. Since he was not receiving any information from Willcox or McDowell, it appeared to him that little, if anything, was being done. Finally, McDowell wired him.

As bearing on your question of yesterday [September 16] saying you were waiting a call from me to give orders for Mackenzie and Hatch to move to Arizona, I send you the following just received from Willcox dated today at Fort Thomas as follows:

Dispatch received. Am very busy. Outbreak being fast reduced to treacherous scouts and a few others. Think I have received all your telegrams, but have not taken pains to keep you informed as events are constantly changing and the General of the Army said he wanted no details and nothing but results. . . . George's and Bonito's bands of White Mountains have come in and charge the mischief on the very people Cooley reports friendly. I have been in telegraphic communication with Carr for a week but he has accomplished nothing for want of scouts. These he will get today. I do not need Hatch or Mackenzie—may as well halt. Expect supplies through from the north side and starting a working party on Rocky Cañon road today for such transportation as pack trains and light wagons afterwards. Cannot supply Apache this route. . . . Have ordered Carr to strike at Cibicu. Price should be about up there too. Meantime I have fixed peace lines close around San Carlos and given till the 21st for Indians to draw in. This will not prevent operations against known hostiles or runaways from the reservation.[28]

A short while later Willcox sent McDowell another telegram. In it he said, "My troops seem to me sufficient; but I would like supplies sent down to Apache from Wingate, or such point as they may be delivered by railroad company under Pope's guards."[29] McDowell also forwarded this message up to Sherman. Willcox wired Pope the same day: "Other bands coming in besides those at Cooleys. Mackenzie may as well halt where he is till my troops strike the Cibicu and results are known"[30] and "Please send Bradley's surplus ammunition to Carr."[31]

Meanwhile, Sherman was sending McDowell another forceful message:

Your dispatch of yesterday [September 16] is received, and I will instruct General Sheridan to cause Mackenzie's force to advance near to Fort Apache, to supply it amply with provisions and ammunition, and to hold his force ready to assist General Willcox, who will be allowed to punish the hostiles in his own way, and by his own troops if he can. In like manner General Hatch will have an auxiliary force at Craig. Let Willcox know these facts, and that the Apaches must receive such chastisement now that a repetition of the Carr affair will be impossible. Our accounts from that quarter are very meager.[32]

When McDowell forwarded this telegram to Willcox, Willcox realized the situation with Sherman was fragile and he must keep him informed. He quickly wired McDowell: "Following is present situation of forces moving towards the enemy."[33] His message was very detailed. It thoroughly explained where his troops were, what they were doing, what they were going to do, and how they would operate to engage the hostiles. Unfortunately, McDowell did not forward it to Sherman.

Earlier that day Willcox's AAAG, Major Arnold, sent Carr orders for the movement:

You will have Gatewood's scouts, with Tupper today, and the General Commanding wants the hostiles struck effectually. You will move a sufficient force to the Cibicu, to make sharp and quick work of the hostiles that are left. You will not neglect to secure the Indians who have already come in and those who remain near Cooley's. All Indians who do not wish to fight must come or be brought within the peace line and the sooner the better. Bonito and George are in and charge most of the killing upon the people whom Cooley is now trying to screen. It is likely that all are implicated and none will be allowed to escape. The Gen'l relies upon your good judgement and prompt action.[34]

Carr sent a lengthy response. He said he would move as soon as Tupper arrived but complained that his force was small and that he had not been furnished the horses he had frequently requested. He said he could move with only 193 men from the six cavalry troops that were with him but did not think he should make any detachments until he found that the hostiles had scattered. Regarding the securing of Pedro and his band, he said,

I think the Indians who have already come in are sufficiently secure, as they are under the guns of the fort. They came in, 17 bucks, 45 women and 62 children, see my separate dispatch giving

names, upon my invitation, to gather their corn, and I will not arrest
them without positive orders, against which I most earnestly protest,
and request that if such orders be given, they may be executed by
some other person. Those at Cooley's are about 15 bucks with about
50 women and children, all under charge of fifty settlers, who with
their 150 women and children have confidence in them and expect
them to help protect their wives and children.

I do not believe that these Indians were engaged in the murders,
or in the attack on the post. Moseby properly belongs to George's
band, altho' of late living with Pedro's people, who comprise three
or more small bands or parts of bands. The murders were committed
in the country where George and Bonito had cattle. The mail carrier,
Owens, was killed near Bonito's camp. I have no doubt but that
some of our scouts were in those murders, and in the attack on the
post, but believe that some, or most of George's band were so also.
It is of course, difficult to say who were, or who were not, in it, but,
this is no time to drive into hostility any who may be wavering; and
I think that if all the Indians of Pedro's band, so called, were
arrested, and taken under guard to within the peace limits, some
would go hostile as soon as they could escape, and in fact, that some
would evade arrest and go hostile at once.

Cooley has, of course, his own interests to subserve, but, he
certainly does not want war on the northern border, and depends on
Pedro's band to help avert it, and if they should prove treacherous, I
think it better for us, whose trade is war, to risk the danger, than to
precipitate it upon the settlers.[35]

Willcox quickly responded: "There has not been time to purchase
and forward more horses; but one hundred and fifty are promised
for your regiment. As you feel your force is inadequate, the
movement on the hostiles will be delayed. Don't do anything rash
with the friendly Indians that you have around you—nothing precipitate or impracticable expected."[36]

Shortly thereafter Carr replied that his force was not inadequate
for the movement and that he should move to help Price. Willcox
then notified him to continue the operation as scheduled. In the
meantime, however, Willcox had sent General Pope a message that
he would soon regret: "How near to Apache is Bradley? Did not
mean to include him in the halt. There are still one hundred fifty
(150) hostiles, and from Carr's small force they may make trouble

enough yet. Please let Bradley push on, *followed by Mackenzie.*"[37] Willcox then informed McDowell of his message, stating, "Carr seems a little uneasy about the strength of his command for attack."[38] McDowell immediately forwarded Willcox's message to Sherman.

The next day Willcox sent McDowell another telegram bringing him up to date on what was happening. He added, "Inquire of [the] General of the Army whether it was not intended that Bradley and Mackenzie should at least communicate with me. I hear of them only through Pope. Pope said Bradley was to march on the eighth and would bring ammunition to Carr but Carr had not heard from him or his ammunition up to last night. He will need more ammunition if the hostiles fight hard."[39] McDowell forwarded only the portion of Willcox's message quoted above. However, before he sent it, he received a shocking message from Sherman:

> General Sheridan and I are committed to be at Chattanooga Wednesday. Therefore I want today to make absolutely clear my judgement at this distance for your information but not to be communicated to your subordinates. If Mackenzie crosses the Mogollons to Fort Apache, I will be forced to give him supreme command of all the troops operating against the Apaches, because of his rank and great ego. This will not necessarily interfere with Willcox's administrative control of his Department, but will reflect on him and especially on Colonel Carr who seems to have remained at Fort Apache, almost, if not entirely passive. I wanted both these officers to strike the Apaches a blow that would inspire at least respect, but if Mackenzie gets there he will surely carry things with a high hand.
>
> General Pope already has the necessary orders to help and I will not confuse him by any more.[40]

McDowell immediately responded:

> I feel called upon in justice to my subordinates to ask a suspension of your condemnation. They may have and I am disposed to believe they have done the best they could under the circumstances in which they have found themselves and are eager to take the offensive at the earliest moment practicable. At all events Mackenzie's rank as a matter of course will give him command at Apache and of operations from that point, and this in the ordinary course of service under the articles of war.[41]

The next day, September 20, Sherman replied:

> I have not condemned your subordinates, but the case calls for immediate and coherent action. Every day of delay increases the chances of the hostiles. Willcox himself said he has troops enough till within the past few days, and now he seems to be waiting for them and for ammunition. That you may understand the case as it appears to us at this distance, I will cause to be telegraphed to you the despatch of General Sheridan of Sept 16th and my answer to him of the seventeenth (17th)—Mackenzie's and Bradley's command still belong to General Pope's Dept. but the moment they come into Arizona they fall under the Dept. command of Gen. Willcox, only that when fighting is to be done one officer must command and he on the spot.[42]

Meanwhile, Sherman notified Sheridan of Willcox's request for Bradley and Mackenzie, adding, "I had been in hopes that Carr would long since have retrieved his loss of prestige by some positive action, and that if Mackenzie reaches Fort Apache, I will be forced to give him absolute command of all the troops operating against the Apaches, which will be a reflection on Carr and Willcox too."[43] Sherman then sent Sheridan another message:

> Gen. Willcox seems to be waiting for ammunition and for reinforcements at Apache. You may instruct General Pope to hurry forward these supplies and troops and that if Genl. Mackenzie reaches Fort Apache I want him to assume command of all troops in that Quarter and proceed to punish and subdue the hostiles. The Department Commander, Gen. Willcox, is at Fort Thomas and is assigned to that command by superior orders of the President and his authority as such commander must be respected, but if Gen. Mackenzie will make an end to Apache Wars he may be sure of his reward.[44]

Sherman sent a copy of this message to McDowell, who notified Willcox that the "Gen'l of the Army expresses great impatience at the state of affairs in the Dept. If Col. Mackenzie comes to Apache he will take command of all troops in the field."[45]

Chapter 8

THE HOSTILES SURRENDER

At noon on September 18 Carr left Fort Apache with Troops B, C, D, E, F, and G, 6th Cavalry, and Gatewood's scout company, thus beginning his part of General Willcox's operation to engage the hostiles.[1] That afternoon they marched twelve miles on the Verde Trail to Cedar Creek Crossing. They then camped for the night. From there Carr sent a message back to Fort Apache for transmittal to Willcox: "About two miles east of this place crossed trails of about forty a week old, going south, some shod. This would take them toward the place designated by Cooley three miles below the Apache and San Carlos Crossing of Black River where all the hostiles were on Tuesday 13th. I suppose however they have left there, and if not, Sanford can take care of them and I will execute your orders of yesterday to proceed to [the] Cibicu."[2]

The next day Carr marched his force to Sanchez's village on Carrizo Creek.[3] They found the village empty. After spending the night there they moved to the Cibecue battleground. John Finerty, who went with them, wrote,

GEN. CARR'S CAMP. Cibicu Creek, Arizona (Scene of Indian Attack), Sept. 20.—We made another twenty-mile march, or more, from Sanchez's farm to this place today. The trail was pretty bad all through, until we cleared the ravines and came out on this fine valley, which witnessed a few weeks ago one of the most exciting episodes of Indian history. As we passed the defile we came upon a dead government mule, with the afaragos [aparejos](panniers) still on. This animal had been shot in the fight, and, of course, stunk infamously.

We noticed the Indian scouts in a group down by the river bank, where the plain was broadest, and rode in that direction. As we approached, the air was filled with a horrible odor, which we had no trouble in distinguishing as the dreadful smell that exhales from decomposed humanity. We were not long in discovering the cause. The Indians, after Gen. Carr retired, had desecrated the graves of the slain, and there on the polluted ground were extended, in mutilated, unrecognizable hideousness, the bodies of the once stalwart and handsome Capt. Hentig, of the 6th Cavalry, and four soldiers. An attempt had been made to cut them into pieces. One of the captain's feet had been carried off, and the leg bones lay bare in the sickening sunlight. A hand had also been carried away, and he was otherwise cruelly dismembered. His face had been smashed in with a rock. His blue shirt still clung to his frame, which lay partially face downward, and his pantaloons, with the stripe of his rank on, were cast beside the repulsive remains. Maggots wiggled around his head and neck, and it was utterly impossible to identify in that terrible wreck the finest man, physically, and the most popular line officer, personally, of the 6th Cavalry. What poor, miserable worms we are, anyhow! I pity the vain creature who is proud of a physique that a few days of sun and wind can destroy almost as utterly as if it had never existed.

The four soldiers equaled, if they did not excel, the unfortunate captain in horribleness. All were more or less cut up, and the air for hundreds of yards all around stunk so desperately that some of the recruits vomited.

Down in the brush lay another body, that of a soldier named Miller, who had gone down to gather firewood, also badly decomposed, and the head entirely gone.

Gen. Carr detailed Lieut. Cruse with a party to rebury the remains. This was done effectually, the graves being marked carefully; but the odor still remained, because of the decomposing matter which had drained from the bodies while above the earth.

I have seen so many awful sights that I have grown somewhat case-hardened, but I think the remains of Hentig and his unfortunate companions capped the climax of my horrine experiences.

. . . We were soon in camp, out of range of the charnel-smell, and enjoyed our suppers as if we had seen nothing of an unusual nature.

GEN. CARR'S CAMP. Cibicu Creek, Sept. 21.—The Indian scouts found three superannuated old squaws—abandoned by their relatives because they could not walk far—in a corn field today, and brought them in. The poor old wretches were badly scared. One looked to be at least a hundred years old. . . . They belonged to the medicine man's village, and say they have seen only one man and one woman since the day after the massacre.[4]

Carr camped at the battlefield for three days.[5] While there he sent scouting parties up and down the Cibecue for twenty-four miles. They did not find any recent signs of the hostiles.

On the morning of September 23 Carr sent Captain Tupper with Troops C and G and Gatewood's scouts down the east side of the Cibecue to scout the country along the Black River near the mouths of Cibecue and Carrizo creeks.[6] Shortly thereafter Carr left the battleground with the rest of his force, heading back to Sanchez's village. While en route he met McLellan, who was moving to the Cibecue with his battalion in accordance with his latest orders from Camp Thomas. The next day, while at Sanchez's village, Carr sent another message back for Willcox:

I arrived at Cibicu 20th found the graves violated and the bodies horribly mutilated. Capt. Hentig's skull broken, brains gone, both feet and one hand cut off, and shot fired into his arms. Miller's head cut off and body dragged about, but ring left on his finger which will be sent to his sister. Livingstone and other's heads mashed and etc. Our war correspondent, Mr. Finerty could not stand the stench. Rearranged and reburied them—Medicine man's body had been removed. Great abundance of corn at his village, dry and green, also beans, melons and pumpkins. My command with over 300 animals fed on it for two days. McLellan's command would be fed last night and still some left.

There were three old squaws, one blind, abandoned by them.

. . . When ready to move I formed my command and fired volleys over the graves and then marched for this place.[7]

Carr then moved his command back to Cedar Creek Crossing and camped for the night. During the night 1st Lt. John Brown Kerr, the 6th Cavalry adjutant, arrived with more men.[8] The next day, the twenty-fifth, Tupper and his detachment rejoined Carr.

Captain McLellan and Troops L and M, 6th Cavalry, and Lieutenant Bailey and his scouts left Camp Thomas, starting their

Officers at the Pine Ridge Agency, South Dakota, winter 1890 to February 18, 1891. Standing, left to right: Reporter from the *New York World*, 2d Lt. Lunsford Daniel, 1st Lt. Elon F. Willcox, Capt. Folliot A. Whitney, Maj. Tullius C. Tupper, 2d Lt. Charles D. Rhodes, 2d Lt. Richard B. Paddock, 1st Lt. George L. Scott, Maj. David Perry, 1st Lt. George H. Sands, Maj. Emil Adam, 2d Lt. John J. Pershing, 1st Lt. Adelbert Cronkhite, 2d Lt. Hugh J. Gallagher, Capt. Frank West, 1st Lt. Augustus P. Blocksom, 1st Lt. John M. Stotsenburg, 1st Lt. Frederick G. Hodgson. Seated on camp

stools, left to right: Col. Eugene A. Carr, Lt. Col. Albert P. Morrow, Capt. John B. Kerr. Seated on the ground, left to right: 1st Lt. Edward E. Dravo, 2d Lt. George M. Williamson, Capt. William M. Wallace, 1st Lt. Benjamin H. Cheever, Jr., 2d Lt. Robert L. Howze, Capt. Adam Kramer, Capt. William H. Carter, Capt. William Stanton. Seven of these officers (Tupper, Blocksom, Carr, Kerr, Wallace, Carter, and Stanton) were involved in the Cibecue battle and/or the military operations after the fight. Courtesy U.S. Army Military History Institute.

portion of Willcox's campaign, during the afternoon of September 17. They moved up the Paymaster Trail and then the Apache Road until they reached Black River Crossing. At that point they crossed the river and scouted down its north side. Near the mouth of the White River, on the south side of the Black River, they found a strong fortification built by the hostiles. McLellan concluded that about forty-five Indians (Sanchez and his followers) had been there. Although he and his men figured the Indians had left the site several days before their arrival, they did find, in that area, "a few fresh tracks going down [the] Black River."[9]

McLellan then moved his force up to the Cibecue battle site. They probably arrived there during the afternoon of September 23. Since Carr had just left the place their stay there was not productive. On the morning of the twenty-fifth they left the site for Fort Apache.

On September 16 Lieutenant Colonel Price left Fort Verde via the Verde Trail. Much of his command was scattered over the western region of the reservation. The various forces joined him as he moved down the trail. His command was composed of Troops H, I, and K, 6th Cavalry; Company F, 12th Infantry; Companies C and F, 8th Infantry; 1st Lt. Frederick Von Schrader's company of twenty-five Hualpai scouts; and 2d Lt. Francis Joseph Andrew Darr's company of fifty San Carlos scouts. Veteran guide Dan O'Leary was the assistant superintendent of the pack train.

Price found the roads in terrible condition due to the recent rains. The poor road conditions caused some of his wagons to break down, and he had to send pack trains back to retrieve the rations. As he approached the Cibecue battle site he sent his two scout companies out from his main force "to discover, if possible, any signs of the enemy." Later, he wrote about their approach: "On the 25th broke camp [at Cañon Creek] shortly after dawn and marched towards Cibicu, at 2:30 P.M. received report from Lieut. Von Schrader that he had seen smoke early in the morning coming from Cibicu Valley, that he had cautiously approached and found the villages along the creek in flames."[10]

Price reached the battlefield at 3:15 P.M. He "found many traces of cavalry having recently passed over the ground and all traces of Indians obliterated by them."[11] The signs were made by Carr's force, who had left the site two days earlier, and by McLellan's battalion, who set the villages on fire that morning when they departed the area. Price camped on the Cibecue for three days. While there he sent his scouts out to the north, south, and east to search for signs of the hostiles. These searches convinced him "that the majority of the Indians had moved in a southerly direction or towards San Carlos."[12]

On September 17 Major Sanford and Troops G and I, 1st Cavalry, left Camp Thomas for the San Carlos Agency, starting their part of the campaign. That night 2d Lt. Stephen Crosby Mills arrived at Camp Thomas. Willcox immediately ordered him to meet Sanford at San Carlos, recruit a company of Indian scouts, and join Sanford's command. The next day Mills hurried to the agency and formed his company, composed of twenty Yuma Indians.[13] Sanford's battalion and Mills and his scouts left the agency on the morning of September 19. They headed up the San Carlos–Apache Trail to where it crossed the Black River.

The next day, while en route to the river, Sanford captured an Indian man and woman who were moving down the trail (toward the agency) with several horses. The two Indians told him that Sanchez and four other chiefs were on their way to the agency to surrender with their bands. Sanford allowed the man and woman to proceed. Three or four shots had been fired when Sanford's force met the two Indians. One of Tiffany's far pickets, a Yuma scout, learned of the shooting and hurried to the agency to notify Tiffany. When he arrived his horse was nearly dead from fatigue. He told Tiffany that Sanford struck some Indians and had a small fight. Tiffany notified General Willcox. Later that day Tiffany and Willcox learned what actually happened. By then, however, the news of a fight had spread widely.

On hearing of the fight Sterling, chief of the San Carlos Indian Police, headed up the trail toward the site of the supposed battle. He found Indian women and children coming down the trail toward the agency. They wanted to be certain of being inside the peace lines, which were to take effect the next day. They said that while coming down the trail they saw soldiers (Sanford's battalion) moving up it and turned off into side cuts to avoid them.

During the morning of September 21 Sanford reached the Black River. Later that day he notified Willcox: "Hostiles appear to have all left this vicinity, going toward San Carlos. Scouts found a large camp north, signs of plenty of stock a few miles west, this morning, lately abandoned."[14] Willcox posted Sanford's force at the Black River, where it remained for four days. During that period Sanford sent Mills and some of his scouts out to look for hostiles and to find McLellan. Mills did not find either.

On September 18, while all four forces were in the field, Cooley returned to his ranch from a trip to Fort Apache and found that Naduntes, who he had sent to the hostile's camp on the Black River, had returned. Naduntes brought back old Esketeshelaw, who had been the chief of George's band for many years, with ten men and twenty-six women and children.

Esketeshelaw told Cooley that Tiffany had sent three men to George to encourage him to come in to the agency. He also told him that before George left for the agency, George told Sanchez that he would arrange for the surrender of the rest of the hostiles at the camp, including Sanchez. Esketeshelaw said all hostiles at the camp had crossed the Black River on the fifteenth—the day he and Naduntes left the camp—with the intention of getting to the agency. "The Indians were all anxious to see the Agent as they said they were not to blame for what they did,"[15] he added. Naduntes confirmed Esketeshelaw's statements.

Cooley immediately wrote a letter with this information and sent it by courier to Fort Apache. Later that day he sent Naduntes to the fort with a second letter. In both letters he expressed his concern that all the hostiles would be "taken in" by Tiffany and escape punishment. In the second letter he said that there were then 120 hostiles (men, women, and children) at his ranch.

Major Cochran, commander of Fort Apache in Carr's absence, immediately telegraphed Cooley's information to General Willcox.[16] The general notified Tiffany and told him that if the hostiles who were at the Black River did come in, they must surrender themselves and their arms to U.S. troops. Tiffany replied that George, who had been at the agency for three days, had not mentioned anything to him about negotiating for Sanchez or the hostiles.

Shortly thereafter runners arrived at the agency from the hostiles' camp. They told Tiffany that some of their men wanted a safeguard to come in to talk to him about settling the situation without further trouble. Tiffany gave them the safeguard. A few minutes later Tiffany received intelligence from another Indian runner that the hostiles were quarreling among themselves: some wanted to make peace; others did not. Tiffany then informed Willcox that he had positive information that sixty or seventy hostiles were on the Black River near the crossing of the Apache and San Carlos Trail during the previous night and that morning.

The next morning Sanchez came in to the agency and met with Tiffany. He agreed to surrender himself and his band uncondition- ally. He then sent for his men and told Tiffany they would be in within two days. Shortly thereafter Tiffany notified Willcox of what transpired. Near the end of his message he stated, "I believe the backbone of the trouble is broken."[17]

The next day, September 21, Sanchez arrived at the agency with four other Cibecue chiefs—Indaschin, Na-ti-o-tish, Es-ke-al-te, and Ne-big-ja-gy.[18] They met with Tiffany and agreed to surrender with the men then with them. All agreed to surrender their arms. They said they would call in the balance of their bands, and they would arrive in three or four days. Tiffany designated a camp for them four miles from the agency and placed Nodeski in charge of them, subject to his orders.

Before their meeting ended Sanchez told Tiffany that he believed some of George's band was with the party that attacked Fort Apache. Sanchez also said that some members of his own band were connected with the murder of Turner and Moody at the Middleton Ranch. Tiffany quickly sent this intelligence to General Willcox.

After the meeting Tiffany notified Willcox that the chiefs agreed to surrender themselves and their bands to the military. Tiffany also informed him that they wanted a fair trial and good counsel to represent them if they were tried. Willcox's AAAG replied, "[The General] accepts the stipulation set forth in your dispatch, namely, their unconditional surrender of themselves and arms. He agrees to give all fair trail and counsel to represent them."[19]

During this period Willcox continued to keep McDowell fully informed of what was happening. He also kept Pope abreast of the events. On receipt of Sherman's message of September 20 (in which Sherman said he had not condemned Willcox and Carr but immediate and coherent action was needed), McDowell realized he had misread Sherman. He replied,

> I beg you will please bear in mind your instructions to me to allow Willcox absolute freedom to carry out his plans to effect the object in view; also your orders not to send you any details, or plans, or intentions, only results. For this reason, I did not report to you the movements of troops as ordered by Willcox, but may now state that Willcox reports this morning an engagement of Sanford's, and that Cochran at Fort Apache reports that one hundred and thirty hostiles, men, women, and children, have come in at Cooley's and that all hostiles had crossed the Black River to go to Agency and surrender to Agent Tiffany. Carr reports he reached one of the hostile villages, and found no hostiles.
>
> Willcox further states he has notified Agent Tiffany and the several commanders of the troops gathering around the hostiles that the hostiles must surrender to the troops unconditionally.
>
> Agent Tiffany tells Willcox he has communicated with Sanchez who offers to come in and surrender his band, that he told him he must do so unconditionally, to be tried civilly or by the military authorities, to which he consented.[20]

That evening Willcox provided McDowell with the details of the surrender of Sanchez and the other chiefs and the anticipated surrender of their bands. Willcox also told him that he had agreed to give the Indians who surrender a fair trial and good counsel. He then said, "My troops out since the 18th, must have full possession of the hostile country. Tiffany has instructions from his own department to turn over those who surrender and to cooperate with us."[21] McDowell passed this message to Sherman's AAG stating: "Please say to the General of the Army that Willcox now reports he does not need Mackenzie's forces at all."[22]

Later that night Willcox sent another message to McDowell. It was an attempt to get Sherman to understand the situation from his perspective.

> I thank you for your message concerning General Sherman's comments, and trust you will say for me what you know of the situation changing from day to day.
>
> At one time it appeared that Indian scouts could be enlisted in numbers to sufficiently reenforce the white troops of my own depart-

ment. Within two days after my troops were called to protect the Agency. No scouts could be had and troops from the outside were necessary, whosoever should command, and the reservation had to be closely watched. The rivers falling and rising changed the condition for reenforcing and supplying Apache from this side. Varying accounts have also been received of the attitude of the Indians coming into Cooley's ranche. My first wish for Mackenzie was to interpose between the Apaches and Navajoes. Next I wanted Bradley to communicate with Carr and get ammunition to him. Then I had to give up all idea of supplying Apache from this side and wanted Mackenzie to guard supplies, and thought whether he came with his cavalry was not so much a necessity of itself as to produce an overwhelming and lasting effect. Finally as the hostile numbers melted away I have asked for nothing but ammunition by Bradley. During all this time I have been constantly pushing my own troops towards the hostiles. Results speak for themselves and since my last dispatch of this evening it is unnecessary to say that I do not need Mackenzie's regiment at all.[23]

McDowell instructed his headquarters personnel to telegraph this message, verbatim, to Sherman. Unfortunately, for unknown reasons, it did not reach him.[24] Willcox did, however, send a copy to Pope, but, of course, he did not forward it to Sherman.

The next day, September 22, Willcox sent Lieutenant Haskell from Camp Thomas to the agency to accept the surrendered hostiles on behalf of the military. The following morning the five chiefs came in to the agency, accompanied by Nodeski and Casador (both of whom were Apache chiefs living at the agency and friendly with both agency and military personnel), as friends, to surrender to Haskell. While the chiefs met with Tiffany and Haskell their bands, composed of 60 men, 73 women, and 76 children, camped with Nodeski's and Casador's bands in a side canyon of the San Carlos River, about six miles north of the agency.

During their talk the chiefs said they would have all their men come in and surrender that day, with their arms, ammunition, and horses. At the completion of the meeting Tiffany and Haskell took the chiefs to Captain Stacey's headquarters (the agency schoolhouse) and placed them in confinement. Tiffany then reported that only seventeen agency and subagency Indians had not come in or were unaccounted for. He said they were probably in the White Mountains.

Meanwhile, Nodeski and Casador returned to their camp and told the men belonging to the five chiefs' bands to come down to the agency. That afternoon the men, who were very edgy, started out. While en route an Indian, seeing the agency police preparing to go on their usual guard duty, told the band members that the soldiers were coming after them. The frightened men returned to their camp and sent word they would surrender in the morning. That night most fled to the mountains north of the agency.

Tiffany was informed of their departure in the morning. He quickly notified the military. However, General Willcox did not have enough cavalry at his immediate disposal to send after them: all his troops, except one, were in the northern part of the reservation participating in his offensive operation. That evening Willcox sent messages to Carr, Price, and McLellan to move their forces to specific places north of the agency to prevent the hostiles from escaping to the remote areas north of the Black River. The previous evening he had sent a message to Sanford to move toward the agency with his command.

The next morning Tiffany's Indian police brought in eleven band members who had not fled. Rather than put them in the guardhouse, Tiffany, Haskell, and Stacey decided to let them camp at the agency. They were instructed to remain in the area. Tiffany had them watched by his reduced police force (many were away helping the military). It was hoped that this lenient treatment would calm those who had surrendered and encourage the others to give up. Also that morning Tiffany wired Willcox: "The hostiles who went out last night, I believe [did so] through fear, they not having been down with the chiefs to hear any of the talks, and perhaps not understanding what had been promised and which the arrested chiefs were precluded from doing by reason of being arrested. . . . These Indians appear to be alarmed and do not understand what the proceedings mean. One more of the hostiles has come in while writing this and I believe I can use these men to bring in the rest."[25]

The next day, September 25, forty of the departed warriors returned and surrendered to Tiffany. They were also allowed to camp wherever they desired on the agency. As a result they scattered with their families among the various Indian camps. On that same day Stacey and Tiffany talked to Sanchez. He agreed to identify the individual Indians who participated in the Cibecue battle and the ensuing hostilities—if he was released from the guardhouse. Tiffany quickly wired this information to Willcox. A short while later Tiffany sent Willcox another telegram about his conversation with Sanchez:

> Sanchez says that Arshay, cousin to medicine man, fired first shot at Carr's fight. Says George can tell you about killing on Apache road. George told him Yuclenn [Uclenny] and Altsasay [Alchesay] were in it; said he did not know that any of his men were in it or not, as they were scattered after the fight; says the medicine man must have been half crazy and got them in all this trouble. Also says Paradishe of Pedro's band told the Indian soldiers not to arrest the medicine man, Nock-a-dil-klen-ney [Nock-ay-det-klinne]. That Sergeant Mose laid on his face making out dead until after fight was over. Some of the Indians told him this. Says it was understood among Indian scouts before leaving Apache not to arrest the medicine man; Says he can give no information about horses and mules, they were distributed around, some lost their shoes off, became sorefooted and abandoned in the mountains. He brought one in with him.[26]

On the morning of September 26 Sanford arrived at the agency with his battalion. Shortly after his arrival he ordered that all the surrendered men be brought in, counted, and kept together. As they came in, he allowed them and their families to camp half a mile from the agency schoolhouse on the San Carlos River. Again, the Indians were watched rather than placed under guard.

The following morning, the twenty-seventh, Sanford met with Sanchez and the four chiefs. He reported after the meeting that the chiefs were "using all possible exertion"[27] to get their men into the camp. By that evening fifty-six hostiles had surrendered. They had given up ten government horses and two mules. Three of the horses were recognized as belonging to Hentig's troop. That evening Sanchez and the four chiefs were released and permitted to camp with their bands. By noon of September 29, sixty hostiles were in. They had turned in only nine old rifles, all of inferior quality. The authorities believed they cached their serviceable arms in the hills before surrendering.

Chapter 9

GEORGE AND BONITO
ARE ACCUSED

While the military and Tiffany were dealing with Sanchez and his allies, another situation was developing with George and Bonito and their bands. On September 16 George and his band came in to the subagency. Two days later he and some of his men went to Camp Thomas with Ezra Hoag, issue clerk at the subagency, for examination by General Willcox about the killing of Cowdon, the ranch hand killed at Phipps's Ranch. After the talk they returned to the subagency. Two or three days later, on September 20 or 21, Major Arnold, Willcox's AAAG, sent a message to Major Cochran at Fort Apache: "The General directs that you try to find out whether George or any of his band have been with the hostiles, and whether any of the murders committed on Apache Road and elsewhere were done by George and his band. Proof positive is wanted if it can be obtained."[1] Cochran replied:

> Have positive evidence that all of George's band has been with hostiles and that the murders committed near Seven-Mile Hill and Turkey Creek on August 31, were by his band and four of Bonito's band and Moseby, Gar, Marchilt and Skippy who formerly belonged to Eskilslaw's band. Gar killed citizen Cullen [Cowdon] at Phipps' ranche. Natchez of Bonito's band[2] and Tosechew of George's band had the two rifles of the soldiers killed near Seven-Mile Hill.

These Indians and nine of Cruse's scouts made the attack on the post Sept. 1st.[3]

Arnold then wired Tiffany: "The General desires the arrest of George and those of his band who were out at the time of the murders also of Bonito and those of his band who were out."[4] Tiffany replied: "I have reason to believe that Cochran is right about some of George's band and others I do not know the names of. Sanchez told me he believed some of George's band had been with attacking party on the post (Apache) and that Sanchez's women told him that George had a lot of money, gold and silver, he sent to Pedro's people near Cooleys."[5]

On September 23 Arnold notified Tiffany that a military force was being sent to the subagency to guard George and Bonito and their bands. Tiffany then informed Hoag, at the subagency, of the movement. Near the end of his message, he said, "If George and band and Bonito will not give themselves up so inform the military, and also send runner to me at once. Show no haste or anxiety but watch closely and secure George and their men who were out with them."[6] Hoag replied "that he thought there would be no trouble in doing so, and when the troops arrived he would communicate with them."[7]

That evening Capt. Alfred Theophilus Smith arrived at the subagency with Company I, 8th Infantry, and Clark's scout company. The next morning Lieutenant Haskell traveled from the agency to the subagency to join the force. Half an hour after Haskell left Tiffany received a message from Hoag expressing his worries about the situation:

The arresting of the chiefs at San Carlos [Agency] has created quite an excitement among the Indians here, all the circumstances connected with the arrest has been such as to create suspicion; first: the arrest of chiefs, second: the approach of troops, third: dispatches passing backward and forward, fourth and last: the hostiles all leaving make it impossible to arrest George and Bonito with the amount of troops here. [The hostiles that had come in to the agency with Sanchez and the four chiefs had left for the mountains the previous night.] Lt. Clark's scouts most of them belong to George's band and I don't know how they would act in case of trouble. [Brevet] Col. Smith is of same opinion as myself in regard to the matter.[8]

Tiffany immediately sent Hoag's message to General Willcox. The situation was indeed tense at the subagency. The rumors there indicated that the hostiles who had left the agency intended to fight. Smith spoke to George and believed he had one hundred armed warriors.

About when Hoag notified Tiffany of his concerns about arresting the Indians, Smith telegraphed Biddle at Camp Thomas to notify him that he felt his force was not sufficient to make the arrests. Biddle quickly responded: "Desist from all attempts to make the arrests until further orders. . . . Everything will be done to avoid precipitating hostilities with the Indians at the Subagency."[9] Also, Willcox, after receiving Tiffany's (Hoag's) message, sent a runner to the subagency with a message directing that the military operations there be suspended and the situation quieted.

Meanwhile, Haskell arrived at the subagency and talked with George and Bonito. Although they refused to surrender to the military force and go to Camp Thomas with them, they agreed to go there with Hoag, that evening, and give themselves up directly to General Willcox. Their men agreed to surrender and stand trial on the terms offered their chiefs—unconditional surrender with the promise of counsel and a fair trial.

That evening, at six o'clock, George and Bonito left with Hoag for Camp Thomas. About seven miles from the subagency George's horse fell and George injured his shoulder. He was carried back to the subagency in extreme pain. Hoag continued the trip with Bonito, turned him over to the military, and left for the agency to meet with Tiffany.

The next day Arnold wired Cochran: "Please send all evidence if any of Bonito's complicity in any of the murders near Apache and attack on post."[10] Cochran replied: "Hostiles say, he [Bonito] and three of his band assisted in the murders near this post also in attack on same."[11]

When Hoag arrived back at the subagency he found George recovered and riding a horse around his camp. During the afternoon of September 27 Arnold asked Major Sanford to see Tiffany about turning George and his men over to the military. In turn, Hoag informed George that he would have to go to Camp Thomas as he had promised Haskell. That evening George left for Camp Thomas alone, voluntarily and without a guard. Before he left Hoag gave him a note to carry to Willcox: "I send George, Coyotero Chief to report to you—told him he would probably have to remain some time at Thomas, but not in confinement. Hoping that this thing will soon be settled and all guilty parties be punished."[12]

That night George surrendered to the military at Camp Thomas and gave them the note. After Willcox read the message he was very dissatisfied with Hoag. He felt Hoag gave George a safeguard. Rather than hold George under Hoag's condition, Willcox told both George and Bonito they could return to the subagency if they promised they would deliver themselves up when he (Willcox) called for them. They promised they would. Consequently, on September 29, George left Camp Thomas and returned to the subagency. (Bonito returned either with George or on the previous day.)

Chapter 10

COLONEL MACKENZIE ARRIVES

Two forces were moving toward Fort Apache from New Mexico. The first force was composed of Troops I and K, 9th Cavalry, and Companies F and H, 13th Infantry, all stationed at Fort Wingate. It was carrying the surplus ammunition from the post (10,000 cavalry and 12,000 infantry rounds). It left Fort Wingate on September 11, marching over the road that ran to Fort Apache via the Zuni villages. As the force approached Arizona most high-ranking officers involved in the Cibecue aftermath, including General Willcox, erroneously thought Colonel Bradley was personally commanding it. Actually, Major James Judson Van Horn, 13th Infantry, was in command.[1]

The second force was Colonel Mackenzie's. It consisted of six troops of the 4th Cavalry and one company of the 15th Infantry. Mackenzie and his cavalry troops had marched from the Cantonment at Uncompahgre, Colorado, to Gunnison, Colorado, in early September in response to the initial reports of the Cibecue troubles. From there they took trains to Santa Fe, arriving on September 11. They then moved, via rail, to Fort Wingate. Between Albuquerque and Fort Wingate they were detained when one of their three trains had an accident. At Fort Wingate the infantry company joined them. They then marched along the Atlantic & Pacific Railroad to its terminus. From there Mackenzie planned to march to Holbrook,

Arizona, and then down the road, via Cooley's Ranch, to Fort Apache. It was ninety road-miles from Holbrook to Fort Apache.

On September 22, the day before Sanchez and the four other chiefs surrendered to Lieutenant Haskell, Mackenzie wired Willcox from the terminus of the railroad. He said he would be fifty miles from Fort Apache in two days and asked if he could "give any aid."[2] Arnold quickly responded: "Your dispatch received. The General desires me to say that the services of your regiment are not necessary as the hostiles are surrendering. He would like ammunition sent to Apache by some of Bradley's people."[3]

Willcox then notified General Pope, Mackenzie's superior, of his response to Mackenzie. Meanwhile, Pope was sending Willcox a telegram notifying him that Mackenzie's force and the force from Wingate were moving toward Apache. Willcox did not receive the message until the following day. He immediately wired Pope: "Your dispatch of 10 A.M. yesterday received at 10 this morning. There seems to be no reliability in the wires and Government business is pressed out contrary to law, for other business. I telegraphed you twice yesterday that Mackenzie was not needed. Please order him to his proper station. Arnold telegraphed him yesterday same effect as hostiles are surrendering and my troops occupy Cibicu region and Black and Salt Rivers. Please acknowledge."[4]

On receipt of this message Pope sent it up his chain of command to Sherman. Pope then wired Willcox that he had sent it and that Sherman had ordered Mackenzie to Apache.

The next morning Willcox was notified that the band members belonging to Sanchez and the four other chiefs had left the agency for the mountains. He was worried about another outbreak. At about the same time he learned Van Horn, not Bradley, was commanding the force en route to Fort Apache via the Zuni villages.

Willcox was concerned about the strength of Fort Apache as it was manned by only Company D, 12th Infantry, and he was ordering Carr farther away from it (toward the agency). He quickly sent Van Horn an update on the situation, via Cochran, and asked him to move into the fort with his command. In his message he said, "I heard from Mackenzie and telegraphed him his regiment would not be needed."[5] Willcox then sent a telegram to McDowell and Pope, notifying them that the band members had left and were "threatening a new outbreak" and that he had requested Van Horn to move into the fort. McDowell forwarded it to Sherman's AG.

The next day, September 25, Arnold wired Cochran. He asked him to deliver this message to Mackenzie: "The Commanding General directs me to inform you that there is no necessity for you to come into Apache. Telegraphed you 22nd not to come in answer to yours of the 22nd. What were your last orders and give dates. Bradley's troops under Van Horn can come into Apache."[6]

That afternoon Van Horn and his force arrived at Fort Apache. And late that evening Mackenzie arrived with Troop L, 4th Cavalry. The next day the rest of Mackenzie's command—Troops A, B, D, I and K, 4th Cavalry, and Company I, 15th Infantry—reached the fort. At about the same time McLellan and his force arrived there from the Cibecue battle site.

That day (September 26) and the next the military authorities and the newspaper correspondents in the Gila River valley were reporting that the Apache troubles were almost over. Most of the band members belonging to Sanchez and the four other chiefs had returned to the agency; George and Bonito and their bands had come in; and Pedro's men were at Cooley's Ranch and Fort Apache. The reports estimated that thirty-five hostiles remained in hiding on the reservation. This number included the renegade scouts from Lieutenant Cruse's company. One report said, "Those who are absent stay away more through fear than any desire to commit further depredations."[7]

In any event, shortly after Mackenzie arrived he wired Arnold a response to his latest telegram. Mackenzie said he had received Willcox's telegram of September 25 but not the one of the twenty-second and the "latest instructions regarding himself were of 21st from Genl. Pope saying: The General of the Army wishes you to push forward to Apache with all reasonable promptness and etc." and another on the same date stating, "If Genl. Mackenzie reaches Apache I want him to assume command of all troops in that quarter and proceed to punish or subdue the hostiles." Mackenzie concluded the message, "It is evident Genl. Willcox has not received similar orders. If I remain [I] deserve exact definition of my authority."[8]

At ten o'clock that night Willcox responded:

Col. Ranald S. Mackenzie. Courtesy National Archives.

It seems that the General of the Army has sent orders for you through General Pope not communicated to me. There should be no question between you and me but to execute the wishes of the General of the Army harmoniously. You will therefore assume command of everything in your quarter, viz., the District of Apache and proceed to punish or subdue the hostiles yet remaining out. Major Cochran will inform you of the status of the Indians in your neighborhood and you will report to me for further orders. I have ordered Gen. Carr down from the District of the Apache to subdue those hostiles who have retreated from their stronghold on the Cibicu to the reservation near San Carlos. Expecting Bradley at Apache whom I have been expecting since the eighth instant.[9]

The next day Mackenzie sent a lengthy message back to Willcox. First, he asked, "Under [the] instructions received which troops if any other than those at Apache . . . [do I] command"?[10] He then requested the further orders alluded to and asked the whereabouts of the hostiles. He also asked if he should send his wagon train back to the railroad for supplies. He concluded by saying that if his command is to remain, then he should know it at once. He also wired Pope: "Am assigned to District of Apache. Orders from Gen'l of [the] Army thro Gen'l Pope on 21st appear to place me solely under Gen'l Willcox's order. . . . Can I call on Bradley for supplies at end of railroad sending my wagon train to haul them? Is it decided that I am to remain here?"[11]

That afternoon Arnold answered Mackenzie's questions to Willcox:

The Commanding General directs that no other troops than those you bring and those you found at Apache are placed under your command at present. McLellan belongs to Biddle's command but will incidentally be of use to your Headquarters as he will keep the road from Thomas to Apache—unless you actually need him. Please order him to report to his District Commander. Carr is needed below where Tiffany reports most all the hostiles are now haggling about surrender. Your further orders are in connection with subduing and punishing the hostiles remaining in your quarter, to find and to get in all who are known to have been hostile or concerning whom there is any doubt. . . . The General thinks you had best wait a few days before sending in your wagons. The staff of the department is ordered to supply all troops at Apache. Meantime, we may hear from Washington something definite about your remaining or going away.[12]

He also sent a message to McDowell:

Notwithstanding my repeated despatches that [Brevet] General Mackenzie was not needed, but of which he was ignorant, he came into Apache last night with orders from the General of the Army to assume command of all troops in that quarter and proceed to punish or subdue the hostiles. Says if he is not needed he wishes to get back to New Mexico as soon as possible and asks for positive orders and an exact definition of his authority. Awaiting further instructions, I have placed him in command of District of Apache with orders to proceed to punish or subdue the hostiles in that quarter. I respectfully request at once an exact definition of his authority and my own.[13]

The next day, September 27, Willcox received a chastising reply from McDowell's AAG:

You say, Mackenzie came notwithstanding your repeated dispatches that he was not wanted. In answer to this I am directed by the Division Commander to say that one of the last dispatches received from you was that of the 24th instant to General Pope, asking that his troops under Bradley should be pushed to Apache. The Division Commander can well see that in answering your call, Genl. Pope should have decided for himself what troops he could best spare from his own command to reenforce yours; that it must necessarily lay with him to determine what particular force and what particular commander he should send. You ask an exact definition of his (Mackenzie's) authority and your own. On this point, I am directed to send you the following received heretofore from the General of the Army, now sent for your government:

Sept. 20th 81 the Genl. of the Army telegraphed Genl. Sheridan as follows: You may instruct Genl. Pope to hurry forward those supplies and troops and that if Mackenzie reaches Fort Apache I want him to assume command of all troops in that quarter and proceed to punish and subdue the hostiles. The Department Commander General Willcox is at Fort Thomas and assigned to the command by the superior orders of the President and his authority as such Commander must be respected.

In his telegram of the same date to the Division Comdr. [McDowell], the Genl. of the Army says Mackenzie's and Bradley's commands still belong to General Pope's department but the moment they come into Arizona, they fall under the Dept. command of General Willcox, only that when fighting is to be done, one officer must command and be on the spot.[14]

Sometime during the day Willcox sent a letter to Carr at his camp twelve miles north of the Agency.[15] It notified him that

Mackenzie had been assigned command of the District of Apache by virtue of his seniority and he (Carr) was on detached service and would receive orders direct from Willcox's Headquarters in the Field. The same day Mackenzie sent scouting parties out near Fort Apache to look for hostiles. Of course, since the remaining fugitives were few, and scattered and hidden, his efforts were unsuccessful.

The following morning, September 28, down in the Gila River valley, General Willcox was dealing with the situation with George and Bonito. He felt that once George returned to Hoag his safeguard would no longer be valid and he could arrest George without Hoag's restriction. His plan was to send Major Biddle to arrest George and Bonito and their bands. Overton was to report to Biddle at the subagency with Troops A and F, 6th Cavalry, at noon on the thirtieth. McLellan's battalion was also ordered to be there then. Biddle would then make the arrests. Also on that morning Arnold telegraphed Mackenzie: "The General finds it necessary to move McLellan to Sub-Agency. He directs you to guard the Apache and Thomas road as far as foot of Rocky Canyon road where Captain [Hugh Gibson] Brown, 12th Infantry, with company is stationed. A small detachment will be sufficient at present, and should there be any break at San Carlos which is not apprehended, will telegraph you. Also watch the Apache and San Carlos trail a short distance below the crossing of Black River."[16]

Later that day Mackenzie complained to Willcox that the order was breaking up his force and he had "no scouts by whom the watching of the country can be best done."[17] Perhaps Mackenzie would have understood the reason for the move if Willcox had told him of his plans to arrest the hostiles at the subagency. In any event, during the afternoon Willcox had Arnold respond to Mackenzie:

> The General considers that your command including Major Van Horn's must be used under the direction of the Department Commander for punishing and subduing the hostiles remaining out. This object can be more completely obtained by preventing the hostiles on the reservation from joining the hostiles in your district and reiterates the order sent you this morning. With all due respect to your views, it is not intended by the Dept. Commander to break up the unity of your command, but the duty of guarding the approaches to your district from below must be self-evident. It is

reported by the Indians who have surrendered that the renegade scouts and some of the hostiles who murdered the people on Apache Road are at Cooley's, or in that neighborhood, and that Uclenny is the man who broke the telegraph wire. He professes to be friendly but should be arrested and held until further orders. Alchersay [Alchesay] is also reported to have been with the hostiles.

Clark's company of scouts start this afternoon for Apache to report to you.[18]

Mackenzie replied to Arnold that he did not agree with Willcox's use of the troops and that he "[did] not believe Indians can be punished by scattering troops but by moving in a positive manner against them with a concentrated force, where they are known to be." Nevertheless, he indicated that he had complied with Willcox's orders.[19]

On that same day Arnold sent Mackenzie another message: "The Commanding General wishes to know what the understanding has been between the military and Pedro's people regarding their stay at Apache, and if there is any reason why they should not be required to bring in those of Cruse's scouts belonging to their bands on penalty of being removed to San Carlos."[20] Surely Willcox knew the answer to his last query. Eleven days earlier Carr had told him that to attempt to arrest the Indians at Fort Apache and Cooley's Ranch "would risk precipitating hostilities in the northern border" of the reservation.[21] In any event, the next morning Mackenzie responded: "Gen'l Carr was in command when Indians came in, there was a special understanding. They were placed in camp near post and permitted to gather their corn. Their chief Battatish [Bottalish] was sent to Cooley's yesterday. It is better to wait till his return before giving any orders. Battatish is acting in Pedro's place who is very sick, probably dying."[22]

Arnold replied, "Dispatch received. The Commanding General directs me to say that if you can find hostiles in your district you can and must go for them with all the force you need. The quicker the better."[23] Mackenzie then wired Willcox that he believed the hostiles were near the agency and "vigorous action [was not] necessary." He also stated that he did not know the state of affairs or the location of troops. He concluded his telegram by saying he expected to be ordered back to New Mexico.[24]

Throughout this period Willcox kept McDowell, Pope, and Mackenzie well informed of events. Pope was particularly attuned to the situation. In fact, he sent a message to Sheridan requesting that Mackenzie be ordered back to his department. Sheridan wired the request to Sherman's AG, Lt. Col. Chauncey McKeever, along with his own comment:

> The following dispatch is forwarded for the information of the General of the Army. As soon as the condition of Indian affairs at Apache will admit of it, I would like to have Mackenzie and his command return to New Mexico. Sept. 27th. Pope to Sheridan. Dispatches just received from Mackenzie at Apache. He was met before he got there by an order from General Willcox he was not wanted and forbidding him to come into Apache. He marched in under the orders of the General of the Army upon which General Willcox assigned him to the command of one of the small sub-districts into which Arizona is divided. I have therefore of troops belonging to this department eleven (11) companies at Apache where they are not wanted according to the repeated statements of the commanding officer of the Department of Arizona himself, leaving Wingate and the whole Navajo country stripped of troops and greatly delaying if not absolutely obstructing military changes and arrangements in this department heretofore agreed on and essential to the public interests. As my troops are wholly unnecessary at Apache, as they are needed in this department and as I am powerless to traverse the orders of the General of the Army, I have the honor urgently to request that Mackenzie be ordered back to this department or that I be authorized to order him back at once. There is of course much dissatisfaction not to say embarrassments induced by this condition of affairs.[25]

Sherman was away from his office when McKeever received Sheridan's message. McKeever immediately forwarded it to Secretary of War Lincoln. After reading it Lincoln instructed McKeever to send a message to McDowell directing him to "order, at once, Colonel Mackenzie's command and all other troops belonging to the Department of Missouri now in the Department of Arizona, to return to their respective stations in the Department of Missouri."[26] The message was sent to McDowell the following morning. Later that day McKeever retracted it:

[McKeever to McDowell] The General of the Army is this minute back from Cleveland and has seen my dispatch of this morning and *insists that General Mackenzie and his command remain at Apache, not limited to a district or post command,* but held ready to act according to circumstances. He wants you to ascertain and report to him (General Sherman) if all the Apaches have surrendered and are in custody. Have they delivered up the horses and mules they gained, and the saddles and equipments left by Colonel Carr on the ground. General Willcox [is] to remain in command of the department and see that General Mackenzie is supplied for vigorous action. As soon as General Sherman is satisfied that the Apaches are in fact subjugated and punished adequately he will order that command back to the Department of the Missouri. The Secretary of War has heard read the above dispatch, confirms it, and modifies his orders of this morning accordingly.[27]

McDowell sent this message to Willcox the next morning and asked him to provide the information Sherman requested. He also wired Sherman, reassuring him that Willcox understood his order for Mackenzie: "General Willcox is now acting under the order heretofore given by the General of the Army."[28]

At 5:00 P.M. Arnold notified Mackenzie of Sherman's message and added, "You will report whatever is needed for vigorous action and dispose of your command accordingly for this object."[29] Mackenzie immediately responded:

All reports received from yourself, Price, and other sources show Indians going south beyond limits of my district. I had sent prior to any instructions to endeavor to locate hostiles. My force has been much scattered by the orders of the Dept. Commander, five companies having been detached in compliance with his instructions of yesterday, three—two cavalry and one infantry to guard the road to Thomas, two cavalry to scout San Carlos trail to a short distance beyond Black River. If hostiles were in this vicinity in any force believe I would have heard of it before this. Think Major Sanford is correct, that they are among bands near Agency.[30]

Meanwhile, on that same day, September 29, Capt. Reuben Frank Bernard, the provost marshal over the prisoners at the agency,[31] informed Willcox that the hostiles who had surrendered there were not being held securely. Arnold responded, "Stacey reported today he had sixty prisoners in his charge besides women and children, but from your report it appears they are not yet under guard and they have not surrendered their arms. You will have them placed under guard and hold them as prisoners, if possible, and by all means secure arms, ammunition, horses, mules and equipments captured from Carr and remaining in their possession."[32]

Bernard planned his operation for the next morning—the same day Biddle was to arrest George and Bonito at the subagency. Later in the day Sanford, at the agency, sent a note to Carr, camped twelve miles north of the agency with his huge force: "If you can have your command here by soon after 7 A.M., it would be well, as the hostiles will be put under close guard at 9."[33]

At eight o'clock that evening Agent Tiffany, who had not been informed of the movements planned for the next day, wired Willcox:

> Have sent to camps today and find no hostiles out of hostile camp which is thoroughly watched by arrangement between [Bvt. Lt.] Col. Sanford and myself. Hoag sends me word he can no doubt have George's men to go to you at Thomas at any time you desire. Some hostiles that are desirable to have, dead or alive, I have ordered scouts to get if possible and kill if necessary, which meets Col. Sanford's approval. I believe this can all be done in a few days by the activity of Col. Sanford and myself cooperating with him. The only guns and animals formerly in possession of the hostiles are in corral and storehouse at disposal of senior officer.[34]

Irrespective of Sherman's order that Mackenzie and his force remain at Apache, at 9:45 that night Arnold wired Mackenzie: "The reality of hostile's surrender will be tested tomorrow at San Carlos, and at Sub Agency, 13 miles above San Carlos. The General [Willcox] has ordered them into custody. Sanford and Carr at and near San Carlos, Biddle will be at Sub Agency. Hold your command ready to move."[35]

At 9:35 the next morning Mackenzie notified Arnold that two of his 4th Cavalry troops were at the Black River and his other four cavalry troops were ready to move from Fort Apache. In the meantime McDowell had sent Sherman copies of messages he had sent to Willcox. At about the time Mackenzie said he was ready to move from Apache Sherman notified McDowell:

Your instructions to General Willcox are exactly right. Mackenzie's command has been hurried a long distance and must need rest. At Apache he is in good position for any eventualities. After he has had fair time to rest, and I am satisfied the hostile Apaches are prisoners, and that the moral effect intended by sending Mackenzie there has been fully accomplished, I will order him through you to return at leisure to his proper post. It would be well for the Apaches at the San Carlos Agency to realize that at any time the troops in Arizona can promptly be re-enforced from the north and east. Sooner or later some considerable number of these Apaches will have to be killed by bullets rather than by the rope.[36]

Chapter 11

MORE PROBLEMS FOR
GENERAL WILLCOX

The roundup of the prisoners at the agency went smoothly. Carr described the operation several weeks later.

> I had reveille sounded at 3 o'clock; but, owing to the impossibility of catching up the herd before daylight, I was only able to get packed and arrive close to the Agency, by nearly eight A.M. on the 30th.
>
> I halted just out of sight, and sent my Adjutant, Lieut. J. B. Kerr, Adjt. 6th Cavalry, in to the Agency. He could not find the Provost Marshal, who had not yet come up from camp, nor anybody to direct where my command should be posted; but saw Capt. Stacey, comdg. guard, and the Agent. They said that the hostiles would come under guard without trouble.
>
> The Adjutant observed the situation of the village of paroled hostiles and reported to me. I went forward a little till I could see it, and found that it was on the right of the Agency plain, near some bluffs and ravines. There were then some Indians on those bluffs looking at us, and I thought best to move my column back of the village; and did so, preventing any more from going out.
>
> As soon as those in the village saw who it was behind them (part of the command consisted of men whom they had tried to kill at Cibicu) they went and delivered themselves to Capt. Stacey Comd'g Guard at Agency. Some were at the beef killing, as it was issue day, and were found afterwards.[1]

Tiffany learned about the movement while it was occurring and immediately notified Major Sanford.

> I am afraid the movement being made this morning will have the effect to prevent the consummation of what we hoped viz: the speedy capturing and arrest of the hostile scouts and murderers who no doubt would have come in under former arrangements, and some of whom were already hiding near here to see if they could slip in. However I wish to assure you that no matter what my opinion in this respect may be, that in every possible way that I can render you assistance, or aid you by cooperation, I will do it with the best energy and means I have.[2]

After the roundup of the prisoners Carr camped his command about a mile north of the agency on the San Carlos River. The prisoners were confined in Stacey's headquarters, the agency schoolhouse. Only forty-five of the Indians were brought in; Na-ti-o-tish, his two brothers, and twelve other men had left the previous evening. Although Sanchez said they left to hunt stock, they remained in hiding on the reservation until the following July.

The military got two unexpected prisoners. The day before the roundup, Dandy Jim and Mucheco, two scouts who mutinied during the Cibecue fight (nos. 4 and 15, respectively) surrendered to Hoag, the issue clerk, at the subagency.[3] The next morning Mickey Free and another scout brought them to the agency and turned them over to Captain Bernard.

After confining the forty-seven Indians Bernard recommended to General Willcox that the prisoners be moved to Willcox. When the general learned that some had left the agency the previous evening, and not all who had surrendered brought in their arms, he agreed with Bernard and ordered him to bring them over the first leg of their journey, to Camp Thomas, thirty-four miles distant. Early the next morning, October 1, the prisoners were placed in irons and loaded into wagons. Shortly after 7:00 A.M. Sanford and his command (Troops G and I, 1st Cavalry, and Lieutenant Mills and his scouts) left with them for Camp Thomas.

The attempt to arrest George and Bonito and their bands at the subagency did not go smoothly. Major Biddle met McLellan's and Overton's battalions there about 11:00 A.M. He then met with George and Bonito. George asked to wait until the afternoon to surrender—after his people received their weekly rations. Biddle agreed. Hoag then told Biddle that Bonito would surrender without any trouble and that he would bring Bonito to him whenever he desired.

George did not show up when the time came for him to surrender. Biddle quickly moved his force to George's camp, where he found only women and children and three men. Biddle tried to find George's trail but was unsuccessful. Thinking that George and Bonito might have gone to Camp Thomas to turn themselves over to General Willcox, Biddle returned to Camp Thomas with his command.

George had fled to the nearby mountains with the approximately twenty-six men of his band. However, before he had departed, he and Bonito had gone to the Chiricahuas' camp, which was next to George's camp, and told them "the soldiers were coming and would murder their women and children."[4] At 10:30 that night about half the Chiricahua tribe fled the subagency.[5] Bonito[6] and four of his warriors went with them.

During the afternoon, while Biddle was at the subagency trying to make his arrests, Willcox telegraphed copies of some telegrams he had sent and received to McDowell for his information. Willcox included his message of the previous evening, September 30. After reading it McDowell had his AAG wire Willcox,

> I am directed by the Division Commander to say that your orders of the thirtieth to Mackenzie [to hold his command ready to move] are not fully to the effect contemplated by the General of the Army. The General of the Army has directed that Mackenzie shall have command not only of the troops he took into Arizona, but that he shall assume command of all troops in that quarter, and that he shall not be restricted to any district or post; your duty being to see that he is supplied for vigorous action. That one officer is to have command of all troops actively engaged and that this officer shall be Mackenzie.[7]

That evening Arnold tried to notify Mackenzie, by telegraph, of McDowell's orders.

> The Commanding General [Willcox] desires me to inform you that the seizure of the prisoners at San Carlos in hostile camps

effected without opposition. You will assume command at once of all troops actually engaged, without restriction as to District or posts and report your movements and what supplies you need for vigorous action against remaining hostiles.

Carr can be reached by telegraph [at] San Carlos. Price is due at San Carlos tomorrow. Sanford is at San Carlos receiving prisoners and sending them to the rear. Biddle is at Sub-agency with field telegraph operator.[8]

Before the message could be sent the telegraph line went down between Camp Thomas and Fort Apache. The telegraph operator returned the message to Arnold at 8:00 P.M. The next morning Willcox sent men out to repair the line. It would not be operational until shortly before one o'clock that afternoon. In the meantime, Hoag informed Willcox of the breakouts of George, Bonito, and the Chiricahuas. Willcox then asked Hoag to report the numbers of Chiricahuas and White Mountain Apaches that had left to both him and Mackenzie.

At 11:00 A.M. on October 1 Carr received several dispatches from Willcox. One said, "Hoag at subagency reports that George and Bonito left with their bands last night, probably towards old home and that Chiricahuas broke and went south. You will at once use your command in the most vigorous pursuit of these bands at once."[9] Another ordered Carr to forward an enclosed message to Mackenzie by runner at once, via the Apache Trail. Since it was open, Carr read it. It was the message ordering Mackenzie to assume command of all troops actively engaged in field operations against the hostiles, without restrictions as to districts or posts. A third dispatch was a telegram from Willcox directing Carr to report to Mackenzie for orders.

Carr immediately wrote a message reporting to Mackenzie and sent a runner to Fort Apache with it and Willcox's message for Mackenzie. In response to Willcox's message to use his command to pursue the hostiles at once, Carr sent Lieutenant Gatewood's scout company to the subagency to "look up and straighten out the trail or trails, if possible."[10]

During that day Carr received another dispatch from Willcox. It directed him to communicate his movements to Willcox's headquarters and to Mackenzie.

Before McDowell had placed Mackenzie in charge of all troops on the reservation, General Willcox ordered Lieutenant Colonel Price, who had just left the Cibecue region, to hurry to the agency as rapidly as possible and take command of it. Price reached the agency shortly after 7:00 A.M. on October 1, about four hours before Carr received Willcox's order to pursue the Indians who had broken out. On arriving Price telegraphed Willcox notifying him of his arrival. That afternoon Price received a telegram from Arnold directing him to report by telegraph to Mackenzie. At 2:40 P.M. Price sent the telegram reporting to him.

That evening Mackenzie sent a message to Arnold:

> I wish Carr to go to San Carlos Agency and take command. Price with his whole field command reporting to him. Carr to see that all hostile Indians that are there or come in are arrested, placed in double irons and sent to Thomas, or such place as you may wish and that he cause roll call of friendly Indians twice a day. Carr to take general charge at both Agency and Subagency till further orders. Will you please transmit the instructions to Carr as I do not know exactly how to reach him?[11]

Later that evening Arnold informed Mackenzie that Carr was still at the agency and his instructions had been transmitted to him.

About 2:00 P.M. on October 1, approximately three hours after Carr received orders to immediately send troops after the Indians who had broken out, General Willcox directed Lieutenant Overton, at Camp Thomas, to pursue the Chiricahuas with Troops A and F, 6th Cavalry, and Lieutenant Bailey's scouts. McLellan's force, also at Camp Thomas, had not rested since it had left Camp Thomas on September 17 for the Cibecue country as part of Willcox's offensive operation against the Cibecue hostiles. It was to join the pursuit the following morning, as soon as its horses were shod and its men were rested.

During the afternoon of the next day, October 2, Carr issued a written order directing Capt. William Miller Wallace to take Troops H and K, 6th Cavalry, and Lieutenant Von Schrader's scouts and pursue the Chiricahuas. The order also directed Captain Tupper, with Troops E and G, 6th Cavalry, and three Indian scouts, to scout the country north of the subagency for George and Bonito and their bands. The order also directed Capt. Thomas Wilhelm to march to the subagency with Company F, 8th Infantry, to provide additional support and pick up any hostiles who might be there. Of course, General Willcox was dissatisfied with Carr's slow response to his order to send troops at once after the Indians who had escaped.[12]

After the telegraph line into Fort Apache was operational the relationship between Willcox and Mackenzie worsened. About 1:00 P.M. of the day it was fixed, October 1, Willcox received a message from Mackenzie, dated the previous day, stating it was important for him to know if he was to remain at Apache. He said his grain and supplies were low, and if he was to remain, he needed to send wagons back to the terminus of the A&P Railroad to bring in more. At 1:40 P.M. Arnold responded: "Have you received last nights despatch ordering you to take command of all the troops actively engaged? Troubles have broken out from Subagency. Biddle ordered to report to you."[13] Willcox received another telegram from Mackenzie: "Is it true that Indians broke from reservation? What way have they gone?"[14]

At 1:45 P.M. Arnold replied to Mackenzie: "Biddle returned from Sub-Agency with his command late last night. Failed to bring in George and Bonito who fled and from depredations committed last night on the road between Sub-Agency and here it seems George's people or others are again on warpath. The Chiricahuas also broke last night from Sub-Agency. Have ordered Biddle and Carr to move troops to report their movements to you. Price at San Carlos today."[15]

Shortly thereafter Arnold received another message from Mackenzie asking if the officers in the field had been ordered to report to him. He stated that he would order his wagons to the railroad for supplies and that he needed a clear definition of his responsibilities as "two people cannot be in command."[16] Arnold responded: "Carr, Price and Biddle have been ordered to report to you. The orders you mention as given by Dept. Comdr. to Carr and Biddle were given before line was up to Apache. Sanford is escorting prisoners on the way here. He will be in tonight and will receive further orders from the Dept. Commander here, which I will communicate to you. With this exception, you are in command of all in the field."[17]

About then Mackenzie wired Arnold asking if there was any information regarding what direction George and Bonito had taken. At 2:15 P.M. Arnold replied: "Despatch received. Biddle ordered to report situation to you. I have just telegraphed you circumstances."[18]

Late that afternoon Biddle reported to Mackenzie for orders. He informed Mackenzie of the strength of each troop and company assigned to his district (the District of the Gila) and their present assignment. He also said, "Two of these Companies, A and F, Sixth Cavalry, are now in pursuit of horse thieves, supposed to be Chiricahuas. L and M Companies, Sixth Cavalry, are under orders from Dept. Comd'r to go somewhere, I don't know, under Captain McLellan. . . . Think Chiricahuas will make for Mexico down the Chiricahua range."[19]

Arnold wired Mackenzie: "The Dept. Comdr. [General Willcox] wishes to know your instructions with reference to Sanford's two companies when they become available to you. The prisoners cannot be kept here, nor safely sent down by the infantry. There is no cavalry whatever below and the Chiricahuas are believed to be moving in that direction. Sanford can be utilized by you from Willcox where he should be in two days and the prisoners put aboard the railroad. The prisoners are in wagons and with cavalry escort can be got to Grant in one day and to Willcox in another."[20]

Although all three district commanders—Carr, Price, and Biddle—reported to Mackenzie for orders on October 1, the relations between Willcox and Mackenzie continued to deteriorate. Late that afternoon Mackenzie sent a telegram through Arnold for Sherman's AG:

> It is evident to me that it will be impossible for me to act satisfactorily under Genl. Willcox. Am placed in command to an extent, but at the same time he is giving orders. Such a system will not work. The case is very difficult and it is hard for me to tell what is right. Genl. Sherman must settle the matter in some way. We now interfere very much with each other. If I am to be held responsible for the management of these affairs, which I have not sought and do not seek, I must have complete control of troops and thorough support of the Department Commander.[21]

Arnold showed the telegram to General Willcox, who had him wire Mackenzie: "The Department Commander directs that you forward immediately a full statement of the orders of which you complain and explain the manner in which the Department Commander's orders interfere with yours and in what manner your control of troops in the field has been prevented and in what respect you have failed to receive his hearty support. Answer fully and explicitly."[22]

Willcox added the following remarks to Mackenzie's telegram, all of which he forwarded directly to Sherman's AG, bypassing McDowell.

> My interference with Mackenzie is imaginary. No orders have been given to any under his command since he was heard from as having the field command. While the wire was down I ordered Carr and Biddle to look after the Chiricahuas and others. This morning Chiricahuas broke from subagency before Mackenzie could be notified. He was not heard from until one o'clock this afternoon. I did explicitly give him command of everything in the field, except Sanford's escort to the prisoners and I have consulted his wishes and am now waiting to hear from him about this. I will call upon Col. Mackenzie for an explanation of the statement in his despatch which, when received, will be forwarded with my views and wishes.[23]

That night Mackenzie replied to Willcox's request for an explanation, again routing his response through Arnold for Sherman's AG.

> I differed entirely from the Department Commander in his construction of my original orders from General Sherman. Today the Department Commander ordered me to assume control in the field and immediately notified me that he had ordered Carr to do something which I know not and Biddle and Sanford to do other things. Biddle notified me that McLellan and Rafferty have orders, but what he does not know. Two officers cannot get well along in that way. From the tone of your telegrams before I arrived and since believe that General Willcox does not wish me in his command and I would be doubtful of his support under the circumstances. I am going to take my command down the road towards Thomas tomorrow. I have indicated already what I think best.[24]

Willcox added the following comments to the telegram and again forwarded them with the telegram directly to Sherman's AG, bypassing McDowell.

> Herewith I send you Col. Mackenzie's explanation. I cannot see why orders received by me as Dept. Commander to subordinates while

wire to Apache was down and during a new outbreak of Indians should be ground of Mackenzie's extraordinary action in the midst of the campaign, especially as he was notified of such orders as soon as possible. His complaint of want of support is now narrowed down to a groundless suspicion owing to the anomalous relations in which the General of the Army has placed a field officer towards his Department Commander. Mackenzie, my junior, being ordered to command the troops and I to supply them. This extraordinary status is one I have suffered to exist solely in deference to the General of the Army. I feel constrained to say that being the Department Commander and senior officer I should be respected accordingly. I request that Col. Mackenzie be relieved from his anomalous position or relieved from duty in this Department.[25]

During the latter part of the day, most likely after Biddle saw Mackenzie's first telegram to Sherman's AG, Biddle sent Mackenzie another telegram: "There are 74 Chiricahuas, five of Cruse's scouts, 6 White Mts. Overton is after them with 60 men and ten scouts. I wouldn't count the scouts. I think the force too small to attack them. They are said to be in the Black rocks 10 miles south of Trumbull [Mount Turnbull] and 10 miles southwest of [old Camp] Goodwin. It's a strong position. McLellan will start for there tomorrow morning with 2 more companies. Even then the force would be too small, in my opinion, to give a victory."[26] Mackenzie replied: "Your report received. As the Dept. Comdr. knew of movements of McLellan, I have telegraphed to Dept. Hdqrs. about him and other troops to act with him."[27]

During the evening Arnold notified Mackenzie that Sanford's battalion had arrived at Camp Thomas with the prisoners and General Willcox was waiting for an answer to his telegram requesting Mackenzie's instructions for the battalion. Mackenzie answered: "Cannot Indian prisoners be sent [to Willcox, Arizona] in wagons, infantry escort? . . . [The] Commanding General had best order Sanford as he thinks best."[28] Mackenzie also said that he would start with his command the next day to find George and Bonito.

Later that night Arnold wired Mackenzie again: "As long as the prisoners are on our hands, it ties up at least two companies. The General has decided to get them to the railroad at once and as there is not sufficient infantry quickly available, Sanford will take them to [the] railroad; then to join McLellan, Rafferty and Overton in pursuit of [the] Chiricahuas under such instructions as you may have for them."[29]

Mackenzie then sent a message to Willcox stating that he wished Sanford's force to join Overton's, McLellan's, and Rafferty's and punish the Chiricahuas on completion of his duty with prisoners. Sanford "must arrange for joining Capt. McLellan before leaving Camp Thomas," he added.[30]

About seven o'clock the following morning Sanford's force left Camp Thomas for Willcox with the forty-seven prisoners. About then Arnold wired the chief quartermaster for the Department of Arizona, Lt. Col. Henry Clay Hodges, who was at Willcox personally supervising the shipment of supplies: "Make arrangements with railroad to transport 47 Indian prisoners by railroad to Tucson. If possible, have train at Willcox ready for immediate transmission upon their arrival, which will be tomorrow evening the 3rd."[31]

That same morning General Willcox left Camp Thomas with his staff. His decision to leave the area then appears to have been made suddenly. No historical records mention the movement before its occurrence, except telegrams Arnold sent to Benjamin at Whipple Barracks, to Hodges at Willcox, and to Mackenzie "Commanding in the Field" just before they departed, announcing they were leaving for Fort Grant that morning.[32]

General Willcox left Camp Thomas shortly after Sanford's force departed, following the same road. His party caught up with Sanford's battalion around noon. A couple of hours later the group reached Cedar Springs—a stopping place twenty miles from Camp Thomas and midway between Thomas and Grant. They found a woman, two men, and a boy barricaded in a house. They learned from them that the Chiricahuas had attacked some freighters nearby and the fight had ended within the past few hours.

The attack was disastrous. The Chiricahuas killed six of the seven freighters and then plundered their wagons. They left the scene after their lookouts spotted Willcox's entourage moving toward the Springs. About three miles south of the station the fleeing Chiricahuas cut the telegraph line into pieces three and four feet long at several places, leaving the posts north of Grant without telegraphic communication with the outside world. A short while

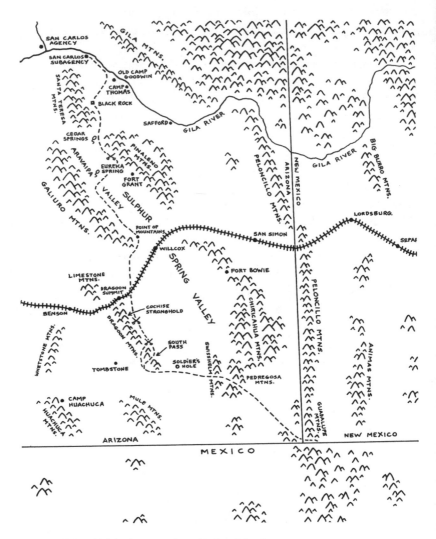

Route of the Chiricahuas as they fled to Mexico

later they killed a settler who was returning to Cedar Springs from Grant. At approximately 2:00 P.M. they slew four military repairmen who had been sent out from Grant to repair the telegraph line. They then set up an ambush for the military.

Shortly after Willcox reached the Springs Overton and his battalion arrived. The general immediately sent Sanford after the Chiricahuas with Troop G, 1st Cavalry, Overton's force, and Mills's Indian scouts. About 3:00 P.M. Sanford's command fell into the Chiricahua ambush. The troopers fought the Indians into the night. After dark some Chiricahua men left the area with their women, children, and stock. The remaining warriors occupied the troops until the main band was safely away. They then left the battle site. Although the military expended an enormous amount of ammunition during the fight, no Indians were known to have been killed. One soldier was killed, and three were wounded.

When Sanford realized the Chiricahuas were gone he took his command to Grant to spend the night. During the night the Chiricahuas camped near the eastern slopes of the Galiuro Mountains, ten to twelve miles from the battleground.

During the battle Willcox and his party took a roundabout way to Fort Grant, via Eureka Springs. They did not reach Grant until 3:00 A.M. Willcox needed to report a decisive victory to Sherman. About half an hour after he arrived at the fort he wired McDowell:

> Sanford with Bernard, Overton and Glass; 3 companies had hard fight today lasting all afternoon and till 9 o'clock at night, the Indians retreating across the Arivayva [Aravaipa] Valley towards the Gulura [Galiuro] Mountains. Fight occurred between Thomas and Grant and about fourteen miles from Grant. Encountered Juh's[33] whole force outnumbering us, they began the attack and were driven up mountain side. Graham range [Pinaleno Mountains]. Our loss small, one soldier killed, four [three] wounded.
>
> Got my Cibicu prisoners through to Grant safely.[34]

The report was exaggerated. The military was not outnumbered. The Chiricahuas' withdrawal to the mountains was both a fall-back strategy and a result of the military's offensive drive.

The morning after the fight Willcox's subordinates asked Capt. Henry Carroll, at Separ, New Mexico, with Troops F and H, 9th Cavalry, to move his force to Willcox via the Southern Pacific

Railroad. They hoped Carroll and his men would arrive in time to intercept the Chiricahuas before they crossed the Southern Pacific tracks.

Meanwhile, Willcox telegraphed General McDowell's AAG asking the general to send the soldiers he was holding in reserve in the San Francisco area to Willcox Station: "Please push down what troops you can rapidly. Juh is strong and means mischief. I will push on to Willcox. Wire cut between here and Thomas, but sent couriers to Mackenzie, who is coming to Thomas."[35] In response McDowell sent the force, which was composed of three small 4th Artillery batteries, armed as infantry, and two troops of the 1st Cavalry. The train trip to southeastern Arizona required three days. General Willcox also made plans to have enough railroad cars ready on his arrival at Willcox Station to move all his cavalry to the most effective point along the railroad tracks to engage the hostiles.

Also during that morning Willcox received Sherman's response to his first direct telegram, in which Mackenzie had complained about him and he had complained about Mackenzie. The response was written by Sherman's AAG: "The General of the Army says your dispatch should have been addressed to the Assistant Adjutant General of the Division of the Pacific. He further desires me to say that he is awaiting an answer from General McDowell to a dispatch inquiring about the actual condition of affairs in Arizona. When he has that answer from General McDowell, he will give orders as to Colonel Mackenzie quick enough."[36]

That afternoon General Willcox left Grant for Willcox, twenty-seven miles away, with his staff, Sanford's battalion, and the prisoners. Overton's battalion left for the settlement a short while later, taking a roundabout route. Sanford, who became ill during the Cedar Springs fight, stayed at Grant to recuperate.

Before General Willcox left Grant Deputy U.S. Marshal A. F. Burke wired him from Willcox, Arizona, asking when and where the Indian prisoners would be turned over to civil authorities. Burke said he was waiting to make arrangements for their safekeeping. General Willcox replied, "Status of Indian prisoners will have to be defined before turning any over to Civil authorities."[37]

Willcox also received a message from McDowell asking him to telegraph the "number of prisoners, where held, number at each place, number and custody of scouts, [and] number of women and children."[38] (Sherman had asked for this information several days earlier.) Willcox responded: "Prisoners 61. 47 at this point, 2 of them scouts. One scout at Agency under charge of Col. Carr.[39] 13 prisoners at Apache. Number of women and children not exactly known, will exceed 200, at Apache and Agency. Not considered prisoners."[40]

McDowell did not forward this information to Sherman until two days later. When he did, he also said that ten horses and two mules had been recaptured but he had not received a report about the number of saddles and equipment.

About dawn on the day after the Cedar Springs battle the Chiricahuas left their campsite heading southeast, along the foothills of the Galiuro Mountains. As they approached Point of Mountains, a small settlement about seven and a half miles west of Willcox, they killed a settler. When they reached the abandoned settlement shortly after noon, they camped at the corral.

Carroll's train arrived at Willcox about eight hours later—less than twenty-four hours after the Cedar Springs battle. General Willcox's party reached Willcox at 9:15 P.M., after being caught in a severe rainstorm that swept across the region. The forty-seven prisoners were quickly loaded on a special train and taken to Tucson. The train left Willcox at 11:00 P.M., guarded by a detachment of Company A, 8th Infantry, under Captain Brayton, and Capt. Clarence Mitchell Bailey's Company D, 8th Infantry.[41]

On arriving at Willcox General Willcox established his field headquarters at Norton and Stewart's store. His plan was for Carroll's battalion, with Mills and his eighteen Yuma scouts, to proceed on Carroll's train to Dragoon Summit, at the north tip of the Dragoon Mountains, twenty-one railroad miles southwest of Willcox. They were to intercept the hostiles if they crossed the tracks near there. Bernard's and Overton's battalions were to stay at Willcox until it was known where the Chiricahuas crossed the railroad tracks. They would then move by train to that point, where they would debark and pursue them.

Late that evening, probably after the rainstorm abated, the Chiricahuas left Point of Mountains. They moved along the foothills of the Galiuro Mountains to the southern end and then headed almost due south throughout the remainder of the night toward the eastern slopes of the Dragoon Mountains. They crossed the railroad tracks shortly after daylight—before Carroll's force could intercept them. At 9:00 A.M. Carroll left the summit and headed down the eastern side of the Dragoons in pursuit.

During the morning Bernard prepared his command (Sanford's and Overton's forces less Mills's scouts) to leave Willcox. His train left the town at 10:40 A.M. On their arrival at the summit, about 11:20 A.M., they joined the chase.

Early that afternoon Carroll found the Chiricahuas camped in a canyon just south of Cochise's stronghold. He quickly laid plans for a surprise attack. While he was moving part of his force south of their encampment, his scouts fired their guns, spoiling his plans. As he started to chase the fleeing Indians, Bernard came up and joined the pursuit.

The six-troop force fought a running skirmish with the Chiricahuas for approximately seven miles along the foothills of the Dragoons, until about dusk, when the Chiricahua rear guard turned into the range and climbed its slopes. The main band was then speeding through the South Pass, a gap through the mountains. When Bernard reached the place where the guard turned, he deployed his force to prevent them from moving back down that side of the range. Carroll's battalion and some 1st Cavalry troopers dismounted and moved toward the guard. The two opponents skirmished until nightfall. Three 9th Cavalry enlisted men were wounded in the skirmish.

After dark the Chiricahua rear guard moved down the west side of the range and headed south, picking up the trail of their main band. They followed it southerly, then easterly, around the southern end of the range.

Bernard's force did not realize the Chiricahuas had left the mountaintops until the following morning. They then decamped and followed them. During the afternoon a severe thunderstorm swept over the area. That evening Bernard took his command to Soldiers Hole, a popular stopping place in the Sulphur Spring Valley, to spend the night.

Chapter 12

THE GENERAL LEAVES THE FIELD

On October 2, the day of the Cedar Springs battle, Colonel Mackenzie left Fort Apache for the Gila River valley with seven cavalry troops and half of Clark's scout company. About noon of the next day Major Arnold sent a couple of messages to Camp Thomas for Mackenzie. The first message was a copy of Willcox's telegram to McDowell's headquarters asking for more troops from California. The second message, addressed to "Colonel Mackenzie, Commanding in the Field," informed him of the Cedar Springs fight. It also stated that General Willcox would be moving Bernard's and Overton's battalions to Willcox for further action against the Chiricahuas "as they move south."[1] Since the telegraph line between Grant and Thomas was still down, the messages were sent by courier.

The telegraph line between Grant and Thomas was repaired at about 9:30 A.M. on October 4. Shortly thereafter General Willcox, then at Willcox, sent Mackenzie another message informing him of what had happened since he left Camp Thomas.

Major Biddle, at Camp Thomas, made several attempts to notify Mackenzie of the fight before Mackenzie reached Thomas. All were unsuccessful. On Mackenzie's arrival there, shortly after noon on October 4, Biddle informed him of the battle, the details of the breakouts, and the status of the pursuit. Well aware that he was in charge of field operations, Mackenzie decided to place Major Sanford in charge of the efforts to subdue the Chiricahuas. About 3:30 that afternoon, while the running fight on the east side of the Dragoon Mountains was starting, Mackenzie sent the telegram ordering Sanford to take command of the operations against the Chiricahuas, through General Willcox's headquarters at Willcox.

> You will take general control of the troops in pursuit of the Chiricahuas. From advices from Adjutant General of the Department there are two companies of the Ninth under Carroll, two companies of the Sixth and two companies of your own regiment under either yourself or Bernard, followed by two companies of the Sixth under McLellan. There are also two companies of the Sixth under Wallace. You can show this telegram as your authority. I shall leave this matter to you with great confidence and best wishes.—Signed R. S. Mackenzie, Colonel.
>
> Will Assistant Adjutant General [Arnold] please transmit to Major Sanford? Signed: R. S. Mackenzie, Colonel.[2]

When the message arrived at Willcox's headquarters it was shown to Willcox. He immediately wired Col. John Cunningham Kelton, McDowell's AAG, informing him of the status of the pursuit. The last sentence of his message asked, "Please telegraph me who is in command."[3] Willcox also had Arnold respond to Mackenzie: "Dispatch received. Department Commander directs me to inform you that he is here in person directing operations. Sanford sick at Grant. You will report what portion of the troops can be spared from your quarter."[4]

Mackenzie quickly replied. He asked Arnold what Willcox meant by "my quarters," then stated he "has before asked [the] limits of his authority, but received no decided information."[5] Later on October 4 Mackenzie wired Arnold again, stating that ten troops of cavalry were already pursuing the Chiricahuas.

Surely General Willcox knew that Mackenzie's troops, the closest of which were in the Gila River valley, were too far north to be useful in the pursuit. The general's telegram did, however, affect a large military operation Carr had under way.

Carr planned to capture George and his band and totally disarm all the Indians at the subagency since "there were about 180 Coyotero or White Mountain Apache warriors [there] affiliated and sympathizing with those about Fort Apache."[6] He planned his operation for that night, October 4. Hoag had agreed to try to lure George to the subagency before dark and then telegraph the results. Carr would then surround the place during the night with his large force of cavalry and infantry.

That afternoon, at 4:10, Carr received a telegram from Mackenzie giving him Capt. Edward Miles Heyl, 4th Cavalry, with four 4th Cavalry and two 9th Cavalry troops. Mackenzie closed the telegram thus: "If you are not sure you are strong enough, delay till he [Heyl] has arrived. There is nothing like having enough men."[7] Heyl and his cavalry were then coming down the road from Fort Apache. Carr decided to delay the operation until the next morning so Heyl could be included, and sent two Indian runners to notify Heyl of his plans. Carr's expanded force would be huge, sixteen companies and troops.

That evening George came in to the subagency, met with Hoag, and agreed to bring in his band. Meanwhile Mackenzie received Willcox's telegram asking what troops he could spare. Mackenzie then wired Carr: "Suspend operations at present and report what force you can spare to go after Chiri's. Gen'l Willcox has assumed direction of affairs in the South in person; and calls on me to know what troops can be spared."[8]

Mackenzie then notified Arnold that he could spare no troops but had telegraphed Carr to find out if he could spare any. That night, at 8:45, Arnold sent Mackenzie another telegram: "The Department Commander directs me to say that you need not send any more companies after the Chiricahuas. . . . He says also that if you take care of the hostiles around the reservation, he will look after the Chiricahuas down here. Report condition [of] affairs at San Carlos."[9]

Carr had already canceled his operation. He had done so when he had received Mackenzie's message. However, many of his troops had already left their stations. Although he stopped the forces with him, he could not notify Heyl or Tupper in time. During the morning their forces moved into their positions, partially surrounding the subagency. Fifteen of George's warriors surrendered, but George and four or five of his men escaped. They had slipped away during the night after an Indian from the agency informed George of the intended movement against him.

Also on October 4, Willcox received a response from Sherman's headquarters regarding his second complaint/countercomplaint telegram: "The General of the Army declines to act upon a dispatch from you sent direct to the Adjutant General of the Army in violation of regulations and orders."[10]

That night Willcox resubmitted the telegrams properly, through his chain of command. McDowell added his comments on the package before sending it to Sherman:

> In a dispatch of the 1st instant General Willcox says Biddle and Carr sent troops [after the Chiricahuas] and report to Mackenzie today "commanding in the field."
>
> It is possible if not entirely probable that Mackenzie's views were taken before the telegram of the thirtieth had been received by Willcox [McDowell's telegram which bluntly told General Willcox that Mackenzie was to have command of all troops actively engaged in the field operations].[11] The latter's orders given to meet the outbreak of another band in another quarter when the communications with Mackenzie were momentarily interrupted cannot fairly be held to be an infraction of the orders of the General of the Army. But in the meantime each officer has feeling against the other, each is dissatisfied with their official relations and each appeals to the General of the Army to terminate them. There being no question as to the facts and orders being those of the General of the Army, I submit the case to his best judgment only calling attention to the fact that since Willcox has had Mackenzie's reinforcements he has called on me for more troops, which I sent him yesterday. He is not therefore in a condition in his own judgment to dispense with Mackenzie's troops if he is with their commander.[12]

During the evening of October 4, at about the same time Hoag was meeting with George, Willcox routinely forwarded Mackenzie's telegram (placing Sanford in charge of field operations against the Chiricahuas) and his response (informing Mackenzie that he was personally directing the operations against them) to McDowell for his information. The next day McDowell's AAAG responded bluntly:

> The Division Commander notices that to an order given by Mackenzie from Thomas to Sanford at Grant sent through your headquarters you return answer that you at Willcox, are in person directing operations,

and you ask him what portion of his troops he (Mackenzie) could spare. In this the Division Commander says you are surely not complying with the orders of the General of the Army which orders have been communicated and reiterated to you, and which you show you have received and understood. You must do as the General of the Army orders and leave the active operations exclusively in Mackenzie's hands. This must be done at once and he notified.[13]

Later that day Willcox replied:

Dispatch received. On my way down here from Camp Thomas we struck the hostiles at Cedar Springs and have followed them continuously and with success from that point to the mountains near southern border. Sanford was left sick at Grant, but is here and reports for duty tomorrow when I will turn over charge of field matters to him. He was designated by Mackenzie, who will thus and by previous orders have complete charge in the field. I leave for Fort Lowell tomorrow.[14]

Willcox also notified Mackenzie:

Two companies of cavalry coming from California have been ordered to disembark at Benson to follow-up Chiricahuas. They are due there before noon. Sanford will report for duty in the morning and then you are by this means and orders heretofore given, left in complete command of all operations in the field. Have sent you latest intelligence from Bernard. Three companies of foot artillery will be at Willcox tomorrow afternoon, reporting to Sanford. You will make frequent reports of the situation to Dept. Headqrs. which will leave here for Fort Lowell tomorrow at two P.M.[15]

The next day General Willcox and his staff took the afternoon westbound train to Tucson. The general left Lieutenant Haskell at Willcox. Sanford had requested that Haskell stay to assist him. General Willcox remained in Tucson for the remainder of the Chiricahua campaign.

The day before General Willcox left Willcox Sherman responded to McDowell's telegram forwarding the complaint/countercomplaint telegram:

Your dispatch of last night embodying several from General Willcox, in Arizona, is received. Colonel Mackenzie, with his specific command, was ordered to Arizona to punish the Apaches for their attack upon Colonel Carr's command. The dispatches from General Willcox, Department Commander, were then so conflicting that I ordered Mackenzie's command to be marched to Fort Apache, and held entire so as promptly to be returned to New Mexico when called for, as it has been earnestly by General Pope, and approved by General Sheridan. New complications, as expected, have now arisen in Arizona, which make the presence of Mackenzie's command still more necessary, and as his troops belong to another division, it is my office alone to make the necessary orders which are:

Colonel Mackenzie will report to and receive orders from the department commander, General Willcox, in Arizona, while serving in that department. General Willcox will be ordered and instructed by you to give immediate command of the operations in the field against the hostile Apaches to Colonel Mackenzie, with control of such of his own troops, and of the necessary stores as are in that quarter, and will support him by all the means at his command to subdue the hostiles in that region, and the moment this is done to relieve Colonel Mackenzie, by an order in writing, when the latter will return to his proper command by easy marches.[16]

The next day McDowell's AAG sent Sherman's telegram to General Willcox. General Willcox responded just before he left Willcox. He pleaded his case directly to Chester Allan Arthur, president of the United States, completely bypassing his chain of command (McDowell, Sherman, and Lincoln).

I am assigned to command of Dept. of Arizona by the President of the United States. Upon the late Apache outbreak, I took immediate measures to place my troops in position to crush it and they were successful. While this was being consummated, I was relieved from all command of troops in the field in that quarter by a junior officer and I appeal to you against this injustice and use of authority on the part of the General of the Army.

After this outbreak was quelled by me, another tribe, the Chiricahuas, broke out, going south near me, murdering and robbing. I collected the troops in my vicinity and under my orders they successfully attacked the enemy and are still routing and pursuing them. In the midst of this new and successful campaign, I again received peremptory orders to turn over all my forces in the field to a junior. My position as Dept. Commander has been violated when I am on full and vigorous duty in the field, exercising the powers conferred upon me by the President, who alone can designate a General to supersede me in command. I therefore appeal to your excellency direct, neglecting the usual channels of communication because the case is urgent. I ask that I may be relieved from this ignominious position in the eyes of my troops, the army, and the country.[17]

President Arthur showed Willcox's telegram to Sherman, who replied,

You were kind enough to show me the dispatch of Colonel and Brevet Major General Willcox Commanding the Department of Arizona, which dispatch was in the motion of an appeal from my orders touching the conduct of military affairs in reference to the recent outbreak of the Apache Indians belonging to the San Carlos Reservation.

The beginning of this outbreak was by the firing on Colonel Carr's command on Cibicu Creek—40 miles from Fort Apache on the 30th of August resulting in the death of Captain Hentig 6th Cavalry and six men. Colonel Carr retreating by night to Fort Apache to which place the Indians followed him and threatened the post. General Willcox took measures to suppress this outbreak calling for reinforcements of General McDowell, his own Division Commander and of the Military Department and Division of the Missouri. General Pope at Santa Fe with the sanction of General Sheridan ordered Colonel Mackenzie of the 4th Cavalry, with troops from Uncompahgre and Fort Wingate. The distance is great and the country particularly difficult and as these troops approached Arizona from the northeast they were struck by conflicting reports. General Willcox at one time saying reinforcements were not needed but again calling for them.

Inasmuch as this particular force belonged to another command and the scene of operations near the line dividing General McDowell's and General Sheridan's Divisions, the orders necessarily emanated from a command superior, myself. They were exhibited to Mr. Lincoln, Secretary of War, who approved—and as he is now absent I herewith submit a copy of those orders which are in my judgment not only lawful and proper but absolutely necessary to ensure successful action in the part of Colonel Mackenzie. He is an officer of peculiar energy and fitness for the task of subduing and punishing these Apaches.

These outbreaks have been in the past years almost as regular as the seasons and besides the murders and robberies with which they are always attended, they paralyze the industries of that whole quarter of our country including two most important transcontinental railroads. The Apaches have a sufficient reservation and are maintained by the U.S. there in—but they will not stay and on the slightest pretext break out and commence murdering and stealing. I believe Colonel Mackenzie under existing orders will so punish them that we shall have no more such outbreaks. It is not a question of personal honor, but of national necessity.

When the end is reached, if General Willcox still thinks he has been wronged, I will advise that a Court of Inquiry investigate and report all the facts so that the President may act understandingly.[18]

Ten days later the adjutant general of the War Department wrote a letter to General Willcox: "I am directed by the Secretary of War to inform you that the President declines to entertain your appeal until it shall have come before him through the regular military channels."[19] Because the letter was mailed it was not received at Willcox's headquarters until about November 5. Willcox did not resubmit his appeal through his chain of command. By that time Mackenzie and his troops were relieved from their duties in Arizona and had left the territory.

On the day General Willcox left Willcox for Tucson, Mackenzie, unaware of the dispatches during the past few days between Willcox, McDowell, and Sherman, sent another telegram of complaint to Sherman's AG:

General Willcox deals with me in a remarkable manner. On the first he ordered me to assume control in the field and directions were given me in a series of telegrams to give orders for Sanford, who was escorting prisoners to railroad, to go into effect on completion of that duty. Instructions for him were sent to AAG Dept, with the request that he transmit them. On the 4th on my telegraphing Major Sanford, the AAG telegraphed "Dispatch received. Dept. Comdr. directs me to inform you that he is here in person directing operations. Sanford sick at Grant. You will report what portion of the troops can be spared from you quarter," and in another dispatch of same date, referring to the Dept. Comdr., he telegraphs, "He says also that if you take care of the hostiles around the reservation, he will look after the Chiricahuas down here. Report the condition of affairs at San Carlos," and in dispatch of 5th he says "Sanford will report for duty in the morning and then you are by this means and orders heretofore given, left in complete command of all operations in the field." Under the circumstances I am, while trying to do as well as I can, in a very false position.[20]

The telegraph operator mistakenly wired Mackenzie's telegram directly to Sherman's headquarters, bypassing both Willcox and McDowell. Sherman must have realized Mackenzie was unaware of the higher-level correspondence because his only response was to ask McDowell to inform Mackenzie "he has given all the instructions in the matter referred to by Colonel Mackenzie that he considers necessary."[21]

From the time the troops met the Chiricahuas near Cedar Springs until General Willcox turned over field operations against the Chiricahuas to Sanford, Willcox kept Mackenzie, as well as McDowell, fully informed of the events and movements of the troops against the Chiricahuas. The day after General Willcox left Willcox, Haskell sent him a telegram bringing him up to date. General Willcox forwarded it to McDowell verbatim. McDowell's AAG, Colonel Kelton, replied. He said it was not clear to McDowell where the troops south of the railroad were in relation to Mackenzie. He also asked if Mackenzie knew of the facts and if the movements mentioned by Haskell were ordered by Mackenzie. He then stated, "There should be no question about this."[22] Willcox simply replied, "These troops are under Mackenzie's command and he must know the facts reported by Bernard and telegraphed by Haskell, as he, Mackenzie, ordered Sanford to assume command of the troops acting against Chiricahuas, before I left Willcox. Haskell was left with Sanford, at Sanford's own request."[23]

McDowell was not convinced that Willcox would not interfere with Mackenzie's efforts to command the troops in the field. On October 10 he ordered Kelton to go to Arizona on "public business." Privately, he told Sherman that Kelton was "to see that the service there was in all respects in conformity with the orders of the General of the Army."[24] Publicly, his visit was called "a tour through Arizona."[25]

On October 13 Kelton arrived at Tucson and met with General Willcox. He then moved to Camp Thomas and visited Mackenzie. He found that General Willcox had completely relinquished command of the forces in the field to Mackenzie.

Major Sanford's first day as commander of the field operations against the Chiricahuas (October 6) was busy. He took command of the operations and issued orders in the morning, although General Willcox and his staff did not leave the area until the afternoon. During the afternoon Sanford sent McLellan's battalion down the west side of the Chiricahua Mountains to try to intercept the Indians before they crossed the border. That night the train from California arrived at Willcox with Capt. Henry Wagner's cavalry and the artillery batteries. Sanford quickly ordered Wagner to proceed to San Simon, Arizona, by rail with his battalion and then "go with all possible despatch"[26] down the eastern side of the Chiricahua Mountains after the hostiles. Despite the efforts of McLellan and Wagner, the Chiricahuas easily crossed into Old Mexico. Captain Bernard had the best chance to catch the Indians but dallied too long at Soldiers Hole.

After Sanford took command of the field operations against the Chiricahuas and General Willcox left for Tucson, Sanford kept Mackenzie well informed. Mackenzie, in turn, kept General Willcox informed. Both fully cooperated with each other in the performance of their respective duties. There were no more exchanges of hostile telegrams between the two men.

Other than the spat with General Willcox, Mackenzie's stay in Arizona was uneventful. On the day General Willcox left for Tucson, Mackenzie left Camp Thomas and went to the subagency. The next day he traveled to the agency. There he met with White Mountain, San Carlos, Tonto, Yuma, Maricopa, and Warm Springs chiefs to determine the state of affairs of the reservation Indians. Mackenzie told them the troops would protect the friendly Indians but would inflict severe punishment on any who caused trouble; only the guilty Indians need fear the presence of troops. Mackenzie found the situation quiet at both the agency and the subagency. The senior military officers in the Gila River valley, the agent and the issue clerk, told him that a large military force was not needed at either place. Mackenzie returned to Camp Thomas the night of October 10. On October 12 he sent a message to General Willcox's AAG:

There is now no large band of Indians against which it is necessary to use troops. The Chiricahuas with a few White Mountain Indians, reports show, have gone to Mexico and we may expect a good deal of trouble with their raiding parties, similar to that in New Mexico from Victoria's band. A large number of the hostile White Mountain Indians have been arrested and more than sixty are now in the guardhouse at various points. There is a small number not to exceed fifty; hiding in scattered parties about the country. These parties can probably be caught through the Indians in the course of a few months. It is my belief that the Sixth Cavalry and four companies of the First are quite sufficient of that arm to deal with the present or prospective situation in the territory. It is important that the companies of the Fourth and Ninth regiments go without delay to their proper stations. The companies of the Fourth have been absent many months, some having been in the field eighteen in the past two years and need a thorough refitting and recruitment which can only be got at a station and the same is true to a degree of the Ninth. I would like to be informed in the next few days of the decision of the General on this matter as my train will be back from the railroad on the sixteenth and if I do not require it to move the troops should send it back again for supplies, for winter is coming and it is to my mind very important to get troops who have been out so long to their proper stations. The matter of the Chiricahuas will take time to settle and can easily be arranged by cooperation with Mexican officials— that of the White Mountain Indians by steady management extends over quite a period of time.[27]

Before Willcox relieved Mackenzie and his troops from duty in Arizona McDowell asked Sherman for reassurance that the decision was Willcox's responsibility. Sherman provided him with the assurance. On October 17 General Willcox issued Field Orders No. 32, assigning many of his units and most of the units McDowell sent to Arizona to posts and stations within the territory.[28] The field orders strategically placed them to guard against incursions by the hostiles into Arizona, to promptly respond to any new outbreaks, and to show a strong military presence at the reservation to discourage more Indian troubles. In addition, the field orders disestablished the military districts set up during the previous month and directed Mackenzie and his force back to the District of New Mexico.

During the morning of October 18 Mackenzie left Camp Thomas, via Fort Apache, to return to his department. On that same day General Willcox and his staff moved back to Willcox, reestablishing his Headquarters in the Field there. Less than a week later General Pope issued Standing Order 216, which transferred the Fourth Cavalry to New Mexico and named Mackenzie commander of the District of New Mexico.[29]

About a month later General Willcox sent 2d Lt. Elon Farnsworth Willcox (his son and aide) to Mackenzie to assure him that he would cooperate with him in the future regarding plans and operations against the hostiles and to obtain his promise for cooperation. On December 1 Lieutenant Willcox reported to his father:

> I find General Mackenzie very willing and anxious to cooperate with you with reference to any hostile Indians, and he assures you that any of your troops sent into his District will remain intact as far as possible.
>
> . . . General Mackenzie thanks you for sending your Aide to him and says that he will be glad to hear from you at any time, and that he will furnish you all useful information in his power.
>
> . . . I assured him of your cooperation with him.[30]

The batteries, companies, and troops from California were gradually withdrawn from Arizona and returned to their proper stations. By the end of 1881, of the twelve units that McDowell had sent in response to the Cibecue affair and the Chiricahua campaign, only Troops C and M, 1st Cavalry, remained in the territory. On April 16, 1882, Troop C returned to its station, Fort Bidwell, California, completing the withdrawal.

Chapter 13

FIND THE "GUILTY" APACHES!

On September 8 Scouts 10 and 14, two of Cruse's mutinous scouts, surrendered'at San Carlos. Several days later General Willcox asked Tiffany to send them to Camp Thomas. On September 17 Tiffany hitched up a wagon and left for the post with Scout 14. Scout 10 was too sick to make the trip. En route Tiffany stopped at the subagency. There he picked up Eskiticha, also known as Skippy (Scout 8 in Cruse's mutinous company).[1] About noon that day, while Hoag was eating dinner, Skippy had come in and surrendered to him.

At Camp Thomas Tiffany turned the two men over to Willcox. The general confined them in the guardhouse and questioned them. Apparently they convinced him of their innocence; during the morning of the nineteenth Willcox released both from imprisonment and temporarily assigned them for duty with Lieutenant Clark's Company C, Indian scouts.[2]

Eight days later Clark's company, including Scouts 8 and 14, left Camp Thomas for Fort Apache. Willcox and Biddle had second thoughts about letting the two men go with the company, and the next day Biddle sent a courier to Clark with a message to send the two back to Camp Thomas.

Scout 14 is not mentioned again in contemporary documents. He probably returned to Camp Thomas with Skippy and then went back into hiding. Skippy, however, stayed with the military. They

retained him at Thomas, probably as a casual, and used him to carry dispatches.[3] Scout 10, who had remained at the agency, is not mentioned again either. He probably went back into hiding after escaping or being released.

Dandy Jim and Mucheco, who had surrendered on September 29, were taken to Willcox with the forty-five prisoners rounded up on the thirtieth. At Willcox they were loaded onto a train and taken to Tucson. They arrived there at 4:00 A.M. on October 4. The Indians, handcuffed or shackled in pairs, were then loaded into large army wagons and taken to Fort Lowell and confined.

Shortly after Sanford left San Carlos with all the prisoners, two more Apaches surrendered to Tiffany. Dead Shot, another of Cruse's mutinous scouts, gave up during the morning of October 1. He was immediately put in irons and confined under guard.[4] Arshay, who surrendered on October 7, admitted being a participant in the Cibecue fight and firing on the troops. He said Dead Shot was a leader in the fight.

Two days later Mackenzie had Skippy, who was still at Camp Thomas, rearrested and put in the guardhouse in irons. Mackenzie then notified Major Arnold of the rearrest, stating "[There is] positive evidence in possession of Lt. Kerr and Col. Carr to convict him, which I am sure C.G. did not know."[5] Shortly thereafter Skippy, Dead Shot, Arshay, and another Indian prisoner were taken to Fort Lowell and confined with the other Cibecue prisoners.

Apache bucks hung for the murder of Captain Hentig. Buehman Photo, Tucson, Arizona. On October 4, 1881, Henry Buehman and his assistants went to Fort Lowell and photographed all the Cibecue prisoners at the fort. The October 20, 1881, *Arizona Star* states that Buehman took four photographs. One was of Sanchez, "the murderer of Captain Hentig, by himself"; another was of the "two deserter scouts," Dandy Jim and Mucheco. Note the similarity between the chair and background here and in the photograph of Sanchez (fig. 20). Both photographs were probably taken at the same session. The above caption is on the back of the original photograph. If this photograph was indeed taken at Fort Lowell on October 4, then the caption was written later and is incorrect. Only Dandy Jim was eventually hanged. Courtesy Special Collections, University of Arizona Library.

George lingered close to the subagency after his breakout, apparently afraid both of surrendering and of leaving the reservation. In fact, the day after he left Hoag told the military, "George is lying out across the [Gila] river and wants to come in."[6] The fifteen men of his band who surrendered during the partial surround of the subagency on October 5 were immediately taken to the guardhouse at Camp Thomas. On the sixth, Biddle appointed Capt. William Scott Worth provost marshal over the Indian prisoners at Camp Thomas and directed him to "investigate the charges that may be preferred against each or all of them."[7] Two days later Worth said he found nothing against them and recommended their release. His recommendation, however, was not heeded.

During the next few weeks George and his remaining renegades hid from the military, reportedly near Ash Creek, committing no depredations. Mackenzie tried to find them. On October 9 he ordered Carr and his five 6th Cavalry troops—Troops B, C, D, E, and G—and two Indian scout companies to move to Fort Apache via Ash Creek. He directed Carr to send out scouting parties while en route to hunt for them and other scattered hostiles. During the trip Carr sent out detachments under Lieutenants Stanton and Craig. They thoroughly scouted the country for thirty to forty miles east of the Apache Road. All attempts to find George were unsuccessful. Finally, on October 30, George and six of his men came to the subagency and surrendered to Hoag. They were taken to the agency and then to the guardhouse at Camp Thomas.

General Willcox received both pro and con information about the participation of Alchesay, Bottalish and Uclenny in the hostilities around Fort Apache. On September 30 Mackenzie wired the general from Fort Apache: "Interpreter [Hurrle] says that he first supposed Indians named [Alchesay, Bottalish, and Uclenny] were engaged in outbreak is sure now they were not. George's band tried hard to involve them in it. Major Cochran knows Mosby tried [to] roundup stock belonging to [a] citizen. Alchesay prevented it, is now at post. Uclenny at Cooley's. Major Cochran [is] satisfied wire was cut by George's people. Interpreter investigated matter thoroughly."[8]

On the day that Worth said he could find nothing against the fifteen members of George's band he reported that there were sufficient grounds to believe that Alchesay, Uclenny, and Bottalish

Üclenny
1st Sergeant Ind. Comp.

Battafish
Sergeant. Ind. Comp.

Mose.
Sergeant. Ind. Comp.

Moschy
Private Ind. Comp.

Frederick Darley Ogilby and four Apaches. As a captain, Ogilby commanded Fort Apache from October 1874 until his death at the fort in May 1877. Courtesy White Mountain Apache Tribe Heritage Program, Fort Apache, Arizona.

killed the people on the wagon road near Fort Apache and that several other Indians, who he named individually, were with them at the killings. Worth recommended that all be arrested. Worth probably received his information from George's men.

Five days later, on October 13, Mackenzie directed Carr to make the arrests:

> If you desire, rather to entrust it to another officer than to execute it yourself, as you intimated to me at San Carlos, I will send Capt. [Adna Romanza] Chaffee with his company to execute under your instructions, in which case he must have every possible assistance.
> . . . I cannot express to you too strongly the importance I attach to these arrests, and have given much thought to the subject before directing.[9]

And five days after that Carr's forces swept through Pedro's villages and arrested nine Indians, including Alchesay, Uclenny, Bottalish, and Esketeshelaw.[10] They and a few other Indian prisoners were taken to the guardhouse at Camp Thomas.

On November 13 Mosby and Mazill came in to the subagency and surrendered to Hoag. About three weeks later Tiffany arrested Gar. All three were placed in the guardhouse at Camp Thomas. Before Tiffany turned Gar over to the military, he questioned him in the presence of Hoag, Sterling, and other men. He then reported,

> Gar says he was in the attack at Fort Apache that Balottish, Alchesay and Uclenny were the leaders, he was with them. That he, Gar, killed W. [Johnny] Cowden at Phipps' house, that there were five of them, George, [and three others whom he specifically names] beside himself, that they told him he must kill Cowden and that George gave him the pistol and he (Gar) killed him with it. That they were going there when they heard the shots on the road at Seven-Mile Hill, and went around and found Balottish, Alchesay, Uclenny and Bonito; that Balottish said he had shot the two men on the wagon with one shot and got thirty dollars off them and gave the money to Chuay, Balottish's brother-in-law, that Uclenny said he killed one man who tried to get back to the post.
> . . . He also says that Es Kite se law [Esketeshelaw] . . . [and four other Indians whom he specifically names] who are in the calaboose [guardhouse] at Thomas have done nothing.

That he and the men who tried to kill the soldiers at the fort and who did the killing should be punished and that he is one of them, and tells the truth.[11]

Benjamin sent a copy of Tiffany's report to Carr for his information. Although Tiffany believed Gar was telling the truth, Carr did "not credit [Gar's statements] . . . much."[12]

Since the four captured scouts were enlisted soldiers, the military tried them by court-martial. It convened at Fort Grant in mid-November 1881. Sergeants Dandy Jim and Dead Shot and Corporal Skippy were quickly found guilty of violating various Articles of War and sentenced to death by hanging. They were then kept in prison awaiting confirmation of their sentences by the president. Private Mucheco received a dishonorable discharge and was sentenced to confinement at hard labor for the term of his natural life. He was sent to Alcatraz prison, in San Francisco Bay, then a military prison, to fulfill his sentence.

On the day Sanchez and the four other chiefs surrendered to the military Willcox asked McDowell to obtain the views of the law officers of the government about some legal arguments of his, which, if sustained, would allow all hostiles involved in the Cibecue battle and aftermath to be tried by military commissions. The AAG of the War Department responded five days later. He said the message was submitted to the secretary of war, "[who] is of opinion that the question should not be formally raised; that while regularly enlisted Indian scouts are within the jurisdiction of courts martial just as are all enlisted men, those Indians who commit murder or take life when not engaged in actual battle with troops should be brought to trial before civil tribunals."[13]

Willcox talked to Tiffany about the matter. Tiffany reported the talk to the commissioner of Indian affairs:

I have the honor to report that on November 1st I started for Willcox for an interview with General Willcox in accordance with telegram from him.

The interview was on account of the status the Indians which were turned over to him by me occupied in the way of the law. He stated none but the scouts who were enlisted in the Apache company and who turned against the soldiers in the Cibicu affair could be tried by court martial, and he wished to know if I favored the balance being sent to the Indian Territory. I told him I did not, as among those in confinement there were innocent ones, and that from what I learned, many of them only fired back after the soldiers had opened an indiscriminate fire on the Indians at Cibicu; that I had but little doubt there was great sympathy with the medicine man; that the medicine man had great influence among them; that the move of the soldiers towards Cibicu was not suspected, and they could not have a preconcerted arrangement. That if Sanchez and others were to be punished, it would be better to send them to some prison such as Alcatraz for a year or two.

He told me he had reported that he thought best to send them to the Indian Territory. I would respectfully suggest that to do that would be in my opinion more cruel than to confine closely in a prison, and I am not in favor of it for many reasons. I told him that I thought those who had committed murder such as at Moody and Middleton's Ranch should be tried and if identified should be convicted and hung; and to punish those who were only suspected and not proved guilty would be unjust. I think if those guilty can be individualized and punished for being individually guilty, it would have a good effect and make them careful how they transgressed, also that if a man was cleared who did no wrong, it would establish the fact that justice would be done them and thus encourage obedience. I am fully aware the sentiment of the general community is not educated up to this point, but I know these Indians are farther advanced towards civilization than credit is given them for.[14]

About one week later Willcox wired McDowell asking if "it is intended to send White Mountain Apaches to Indian Territory."[15] One week after sending that message Willcox again telegraphed McDowell: "Please urge answer from Washington to my dispatch recommending White Mountain prisoners to be sent to Indian Territory, and urge some action adequate to the outbreak, trial by Courts or banishment in order that the criminals shall not escape punishment altogether."[16]

Willcox had officers with the prisoners at Fort Lowell write reports to hasten a decision. Captain Stacey wrote his on December 4:

I have the honor to invite your attention to the Apache prisoners at this post: these men have been in confinement since the last of September, most of the time in irons. At the time of their surrender I was present at San Carlos. When they came in it was upon the condition that they should be tried, and the guilty parties punished. Sanchez, one of the principal men among the prisoners, called my attention to this matter a day or two ago, and requested to know when they would be tried. I could, of course, give him no information upon the subject.

If there is any law that will reach their cases, or any court having jurisdiction, I recommend that they be brought before it for trial. If, on the other hand, they cannot be tried and the Government is determined to hold them in custody, I recommend their removal to some place where they can be allowed more liberty than they can have here consistent with their security.[17]

Ten days later Captain Brayton wrote:

I have the honor to state that the Indian prisoners at this post are becoming very restless and stubborn under their long and close confinement. Sanchez their main chief, complains daily that they have not been treated justly, that they were told when they surrendered they would be tried, if found guilty, punished, if not, they would be released, and is persistent in claiming that the promise should be kept. They have now been in the guardhouse at this post over two months, handcuffed, two and two, a necessary precaution (more and more apparent everyday) on account of the small number of men composing the garrison, and the large number that would be required for guard were the irons taken off. I have had a talk with Sanchez this morning and through him the Indians have requested me to represent their case to the Commanding General and ask that they be released and sent back to their families, or tried at once as promised them.

I agree with the Indians that they are entitled to have some disposition made of their cases.[18]

Willcox added his endorsement: "I would most respectfully urge prompt action in regard to their disposition according to the circumstances of the respective classes of cases."[19] He then forwarded the reports to McDowell, who sent them to Sherman.

On December 10 Capt. Harry Clay Egbert, the acting judge advocate general for the Department of Arizona, submitted his report on the Cibecue affair.[20] Three weeks earlier, on November 19, Willcox had directed him to investigate the killings of the civilians during the Cibecue aftermath by Indians other than the scouts and to determine, if possible, the individual Indians involved.

Egbert was a logical choice for the assignment. On September 22 General Willcox had ordered him to move to Camp Thomas for duty on the trial of the Indian prisoners. On his arrival on September 25 he began to familiarize himself with the information already collected about the hostilities. When Willcox's AAG sent the message to Egbert, Egbert was presiding as judge advocate for the court-martial of the mutinous scouts. Their trials were almost finished. He probably had more knowledge of the entire Cibecue affair than anyone else in the department. Regardless, his task was not easy. His report named, in many instances, the individual Indians believed to have been involved in each act of hostility. It was quite comprehensive. Nevertheless, near its end, he concluded, "The numbers of the hostiles must always remain uncertain."

Egbert said the most prominent Indians in the Cibecue battle, besides the scouts, were Sanchez, Ne-big-ja-gy, Na-ti-o-tish, Indaschin, Es-ke-al-te, Tobo-ka-sin (Sanchez's brother), and Arshay. Egbert also presented what he learned about the activities of the Indians after the fight. He said that at early dawn on the morning after the battle the hostiles who fought Carr's command went down to his abandoned camp. They found the flour, canned goods, saddles, aparejos, and other equipment of the pack train that the command left behind. They collected the items they did not want to keep into a large pile and set it on fire. They then dug up and mutilated the bodies of the dead.

After the hostiles finished pillaging the campsite, twenty-one of them moved west to Cherry Creek. While most of this party depredated in the Pleasant Valley region, some attacked the Middleton Ranch. After finishing there they drove their stolen horses over to Cedar Creek.

According to Egbert the group consisted of four Indians from Sanchez's band, six from Es-ke-al-te's, two from Indaschin's, and nine from the bands of Na-ti-o-tish and Ne-big-ja-gy.[21] The most conspicuous Indians in the party were Na-ti-o-tish and Ne-big-ja-gy. Na-ti-o-tish commanded the group and assigned the duties during the attack on the Middleton Ranch; Ne-big-ja-gy also participated in the attack on the ranch.

On the day the twenty-one men left the Cibecue battle site, a second party, which included nine of the mutinous scouts, left the battleground in the opposite direction. They followed the troops to Fort Apache and participated in the attack on the post.

Egbert believed four bands of Apaches were involved in the attacks around Seven-Mile Hill: Bonito and his "small Chiricahua band of four men"; George and his band numbering about twenty-six men; six White Mountain Apache outlaws; and part of Pedro's band.[22] The extent to which Pedro's band had participated in the hostilities around Fort Apache could not be determined with any degree of certainty. Egbert listed seven members of his band, including Bottalish, Alchesay, and Uclenny,[23] whom he believed participated in the killings at Seven-Mile Hill. He then stated that the only evidence regarding these killings was conflicting Indian testimony.

Indeed, it was conflicting. Egbert based his belief on Tiffany's interview of Gar and the statements of other Indians. Bottalish, Alchesay, and Uclenny, however, denied being present. They said George and his band told them the killing was done by George and three of his men, whom Bottalish and Alchesay individually named, and by Mosby, Mazill, Gar, and Bonito.

Although Pedro's principal men were seen several times during the day of the killings, August 31, it was not enough to establish their innocence. About 8:00 A.M. on that date Pedro, Mosby, Alchesay, Bottalish, and other Indians came to see Major Cochran at Fort Apache. They professed their friendship and said they wanted to camp on the parade ground "so as to be safe from bad Indians."[24] Cochran had little confidence in them but decided to take them at their word. He told them they could not camp on the parade ground but pointed out to them a place where they could camp. It was at a high point northeast of the post on the other side of the White River. He told them to move to it at once. They went away promising to do so the next day.

They soon had second thoughts. When Carr returned to Fort Apache, about three o'clock that afternoon, they were pondering whether to come in to the post. Cooley, who had come in to the fort on hearing from an Indian of Carr's fight and that his command was surrounded and would be massacred in the morning, was then talking with them. After a long discussion the band members decided not to move to the post.

Owens, the mail carrier, was killed that afternoon, at about one o'clock. Later that afternoon or in the early evening the soldiers and

Pedro, 1873. In 1872 Pedro visited Washington, D.C., with other Apaches. This costume is the one he wore during the visit. Photo by Timothy H. O'Sullivan, Courtesy Museum of New Mexico, Negative No. 148298.

the Mormons were killed at Seven-Mile Hill. Cowden was killed in the evening. That night Pedro's men sent their women and children to Cooley's Ranch, about forty miles north of Fort Apache. According to Egbert, the hostiles involved in the killings at Seven-Mile Hill spent that night at Phipps's ranch house.

The next morning Cooley sent Mose out on a horse behind Alchesay to advise Pedro's band. Egbert said the hostiles who stayed at Phipps's place arrived at one of Pedro's camps, about two miles from Fort Apache, at 8:30 that morning. After a long talk they separated. Eighteen or twenty of them went north; thirty-two remained.

Egbert reported that the parties concerned in the attack on Fort Apache later that day were George's band, the small band of renegades under Mosby; nine of the mutinous scouts among whom were Yank, Mickey, Dandy Jim, Dandy Bill, and Sabatto; and "most probably" the majority of Pedro's band. He believed the Indians who charged toward the fort during the fight, then dismounted and opened fire, were the thirty-two men who remained at Pedro's camp earlier that morning.

Back at the Cibecue battle site, after the two parties had left (one for Pleasant Valley and the other toward Fort Apache), the remaining Indians stayed there another day. They then moved to near the point where the White and Black rivers joined the Salt River. Their plan was to march to the agency and attack it after gathering what allies they could on the reservation. Egbert said they expected the remainder of the White Mountain Apaches at the subagency, the Chiricahuas, and possibly the Tontos at the agency to join them.

George's and Mosby's bands met them at their rendezvous. About one hundred fifty men gathered there. Most of Pedro's band, if not all, did not join them. They stayed at Cooley's Ranch and were friendly toward the whites. According to Egbert, they were discouraged by the attack on Fort Apache and probably persuaded by Cooley.

Before the group could move south to the agency the Black River rose to a high level, preventing them from crossing to the other side. They were detained on its north side "for some days," during which time they became disheartened and doubt and dissension prevailed in their councils. In fact, many became so demoralized that they left the group. Some, including George, decided to move south to the subagency and quietly take refuge among the camps of the friendly

Indians there; others decided to go north and slip in among Pedro's
Indians. Eventually, about sixty warriors remained. They had previously sent their families in to the agency. "After long and anxious
consultation" they decided to surrender.[25] This was the group led by
Sanchez.

Near the end of his report, Egbert said,

> Excepting the confessions of Gar there is no available evidence
> against any of the Indians who committed the murders on the 7-Mile
> Hill, unless Indian testimony can be received. Under these circum-
> stances it is not easy to see how a conviction could be obtained in
> the civil courts.
>
> . . . I would recommend that the leaders in the outbreak and the
> participators and accessories in the murders be confined at Tortugas[26]
> or whatever other military prison may be considered more available,
> and that those not prominent in the Cibicu fight be moved to the
> Indian Territory.
>
> This would break the prominence of the White Mountain tribe on
> the San Carlos Reservation and be a most salutary warning to the
> remaining tribes.[27]

Willcox endorsed Egbert's report: "The views of Captain Egbert as
to final disposition of the prisoners are concurred in, in order that
these Indians may not escape punishment."[28] He forwarded the report,
with his endorsement, to McDowell, who sent it to Sherman.

On December 20 the post surgeon of Fort Lowell, Dr. Levi
Force, notified Departmental Headquarters there was a "prevalence
of pneumonia among Indian prisoners at [the] post; two have died."
He attributed the disease to the small breathing space in the guardhouse. Dr. Force warned, "If something is not done to improve their
condition, mortality among them will greatly increase."[29]

On Christmas Day McDowell notified Willcox that on the twelfth
of that month Sherman had instructed that the Indian prisoners who
were not scouts be turned over to the civil authorities or remanded
to the custody of their agent. McDowell closed his telegram by
stating, "Considering the stringent conditions under which these
prisoners are now confined you will, of course, act without delay."[30]

Willcox did not think Sherman and McDowell understood what
would result from the order. The next day he notified McDowell,

If Indian testimony is not admissible before civil courts, the only Indians subject to trial by said courts are the two who killed Moody and Turner at Pleasant Valley. That was in Yavapai County, and the civil authorities here are willing to receive them. They will be turned over at once.

Remanding Indians to the custody of the Agent is the same as setting them at liberty. The Indians engaged in the murders at Turkey Creek and etc., and those prominent at Cibicu, are in my hands and segregated. If I set them at liberty, I know it will be contrary to the views of the General of the Army and of yourself, and of the country at large. I have recommended a disposition of them. See my endorsement approving Egbert's printed report, and I earnestly ask favorable action on that disposition. Meanwhile I will relax prisoner's confinement as much as will be safe.[31]

On that same day McDowell, who had studied all the documents he had received on the Cibecue affair, wrote,

The salient feature shown in these reports is the request of the Indian Agent Tiffany to Colonel Carr "to arrest or kill or both" a medicine man of the White Mountain Apaches, who had become prominent among his own people and the neighboring bands of Apaches by pretending to be able to raise the dead.

This Indian had, however, committed no crime. It was not for any overt act, but for what he said—or it was said he had said—not for anything done but for something feared, and this request of the Indian Agent was so far sanctioned by General Willcox that he gave Colonel Carr orders August 7th and August 13th to arrest him.

. . . I ask attention to the report of the Acting Judge Advocate of the Department of Arizona [Egbert's December 10 report].

. . . I do not concur in his and the Department Commander's recommendation as to the disposition to be made of the Indians, except those who are liable to trial by court martial, many of whom have been so tried.

As to the Apaches—not scouts—who have surrendered or have been apprehended and who were concerned in the Cibicu fight, their offense consists in our attempt to rescue an influential man of their tribe who, whatever he may have been to them—as demagogue, quack, pretender, fortune teller, swindler, or simply fanatic, had committed no act of hostility on the whites.

They have suffered a long imprisonment, have lost all their horses and ponies, their year's supply of standing corn and cached stores, and, except those who have killed soldiers or citizens not as an act of war and who should be tried by the civil courts, I recommend they be sent back to the agent and allowed to cultivate their lands as heretofore.

And in respect to the scouts who have been tried by court martial and in whose cases the proceedings are understood to have been sent to Washington, I cannot but think that, while they are without doubt liable to the pains and penalties declared by the Articles of War, the fact that they were ignorant of those Articles and of the extent of the crime they committed, should go to their favor, and that only those who may have been convicted of killing their officers or companions be condemned to death. The others might be sent away in perpetual exile and such other punishment as may be thought necessary.[32]

McDowell sent his note up his chain of command. He did not send a copy to General Willcox.

On January 10, 1882, Egbert reported the names of each Indian prisoner and the acts of hostility each was thought to have committed. He said all the evidence was from Indians. He concluded his report as follows:

The above facts have been collected from a large quantity of confusing and conflicting statements—some taken by me personally—some received by telegraph and by mail. Most of the Indians have more than one name and as many of the statements were entirely hearsay and many others so dimly connected with the participators through the medium of my informants, as to be little stronger than hearsay, I feel very doubtful, (for the above reasons and also because it will be very difficult to make the Indians testify consistently and freely) of the probability of a conviction of many of the prisoners before the civil courts. The facts are sufficiently established to amount to a reasonable certainty in the mind of any one examining them extrajudicially; but that is a very different matter from a conviction in due course of law.[33]

The next day Willcox reported to McDowell:

Referring to your telegram of twenty-fifth December, and my answer, all the scouts in our hands have been tried by court martial; three (3) other prisoners can be tried by civil authorities on white man's evidence. Against twenty-eight (28) other hostiles, there is nothing but Indian testimony, which the Judge Advocate [Captain Egbert] does not consider reliable and not likely to stand under cross-examination, and against these and the remaining hostiles—thirty-six (36) in number, the only tangible evidence is the fact of their presence at the Cibicu affair, and subsequent coming in to surrender. Please notify me by telegraph of any action taken on [Brevet] Major Egbert's report of December 10th, taken in connection with this and my last telegram on the disposition of these hostiles. I am still holding the prisoners as segregated, waiting reply to my telegram of December 26th, and recommendations therein contained.[34]

While Willcox was attempting to convince the decision makers to send the Apaches away from Arizona, he was trying to catch the hostiles and renegade scouts who remained hidden on the reservation. They were evasive. On October 21 Stanton and Darr arrived at Fort Apache from a scouting mission to the head of Ash Creek. They found no recent signs of the hostiles. Four days later 1st Lt. Edward Everett Dravo and his Troop D, 6th Cavalry, and Gatewood's scout company left the post on a long-range scouting mission. On their return on November 5 Carr reported to Willcox,

> Lieutenants Dravo and Gatewood just returned. Scouted by way of Medicine Man's village as far as Cañon Creek. Scouts killed two outlying Indians near there. Crossed to south side of Salt River and returning this way found a trail not previously known, crossing Salt or Black River, East of mouth of Cibicu; followed it and found on it north of Black River tracks of two more Indians with one squaw and one child. Dravo sent his scouts in pursuit, who overtook and killed the two males, one named Sah-huh of Sanchez band, and brought in the squaw and child. Lieutenant Dravo and his command have travelled over an exceedingly rough region and have acted with commendable energy and skill.
>
> This course, although painful to contemplate is according to existing orders and is the only one to effectually drive the outlying hostiles to surrender.[35]

As early as September 21 Tiffany had notified Haskell that the renegade scouts might be with Pedro's band at Cooley's. The officers at Willcox's field headquarters also suspected at least some were there. Sanchez also said they must be at Cooley's. On September 22

Arnold notified the commanding officer of Fort Apache that Departmental Headquarters would pay $30 for each scout brought in. The Indians at the fort and Cooley's did not turn in any under the offer.

In October both Captain Chaffee and Tiffany received information from Tiffany's spies and runners that the renegade scouts were being aided by Pedro's band at Cooley's Ranch and near Fort Apache. In late October Chaffee reported that he believed Cooley's Ranch was a rendezvous for the fugitives and said that if his suspicions proved true he would ask General Willcox to arrest and move all the Indians at Fort Apache and Cooley's to San Carlos. He said he believed the renegade scouts "go in and out at Apache and Cooley's whenever they wish."[36]

Chaffee asked Willcox for approval to hire two scouts to act as spies to try to learn the situation with the renegade scouts and Pedro's band and, if possible, ascertain the whereabouts of the renegade scouts. Willcox gave him the approval. Chaffee sent the two scouts, one of whom was Mickey Free, up to the area. On their return to San Carlos Chaffee reported, "Scouts sent to Apache and Cooley's report twelve of deserted Indian scouts are in the White Mountains east of Apache, also a camp of five squaws on White River about 8 miles east from post. They assist scouts and are visited by some of them every night; also report man employed as Sawyer, name not learned, is selling ammunition to Indians. This information was obtained from squaws in camp near Apache."[37]

Willcox asked Arnold to transmit a copy of Chaffee's report to Carr "for [his] information and action as he may deem necessary to capture or kill the [renegade] scouts" and to tell Carr that the "Indians professing to be friendly around Apache and Cooley's must be told to move to the reservation unless scouts are [soon] caught."[38] Arnold transmitted the report to Carr with the ultimatum for Pedro's people. Carr was incensed. His reply is summarized in the military records.

> Cannot communicate [General Willcox's ultimatum] with Indians without interpreter. Post interpreter is at Grant as witness. Telegram is bulled and has to guess at meaning. Presumes C.G. does not take for gospel everything Mickey Free, a notorious liar, says. If Capt. Chaffee's scouts can find whereabouts of revolted scouts they should be able to arrest them. Has sent several scouts in direction of

White Mountains but all report no signs. Sent expedition this morning to go to the Bonito, turn to the left and strike the east fork about 13 miles from Apache and then circle to the north. They may strike squaw camp. Absence of packers and guides interferes greatly with operations. Can not believe report that Sawyer Jessup is selling ammunition. Does not like Capt. Chaffee sending spies in his neighborhood without reporting to him what they are there for. Don't care to be criticized by Indian spies.[39]

Over the next several days Carr and Benjamin seriously discussed the removal of Pedro's band. On October 19 Carr sent him a telegram transmitting his views and those of Captain MacGowan, the provost marshal in charge of the prisoners at Fort Apache, on the renegade scouts and the removal of Pedro's band to the agency. Carr said, "The Indians [Pedro's band] cannot comply with ultimatum."[40] Three days later Willcox had his AAAG notify Carr, "The Department Commander directs me to say that as it appears that the removal of the Indians is questionable, you will refrain from executing the orders given, either to notify or remove them until the matter is more carefully considered in the light of future policy. The first object is to secure their cooperation and interest [in] the capture of renegade scouts. This is a military necessity."[41]

On December 5 Tiffany interviewed Gar. He then reported the conversation:

Gar further says "that a good many of the scouts would have come into the Agency but Mose the first Sergeant of the Apache Scouts would not let them, telling them I would kill them right off and they must not come."

Gar says "that the scouts and their women go nights to near the Post Apache and he Mose gets them tobacco, flour and etc., that it would be no use for him to send scouts word to come in here [to the agency], as Mose would not let them come, and that Mose tells these scouts all that is going on."[42]

On being informed of Gar's statements Carr said he did not "believe that Mose [was] guilty of the crimes accused."[43] Tiffany, however, again thought Gar was telling the truth and was certain "Pedro's band and Cooley's Ranch [had] been the harboring vicinity of renegades."[44]

On December 10 Egbert reported that sixteen of Cruse's mutinous scouts remained in hiding on the reservation, eleven of whom belonged to Pedro's band. In the last months of 1881 Carr sent out scouting parties under Lts. William Stanton, Henry Peoble Kingsbury, Frederick Grady Hodgson, and John Brown Kerr to hunt for the outlying Indians. A couple of the parties found their trails, but none found the fugitives. A few days before Christmas a party commanded by Kerr found a hostile camp that had been abandoned for about three weeks. When Kerr returned to Fort Apache, two days after Christmas, he informed Carr that he had no idea where the hostiles or renegade scouts were located. Hodgson had informed Carr similarly when he returned from a scouting trip five weeks earlier.

Carr reported that during Kerr's December scouting trip the Indian scouts crossed the trail of the hostiles several times without noticing it, and thought there might have been communication between the renegades and the scouts. He suggested that the army pay White Mountain Apaches for assisting in the capture or killing of the hostiles. He also suggested hiring spies to help locate their camps.

Chapter 14

GENERAL WILLCOX IS
TRANSFERRED

On January 19, 1882, Willcox reported that 68 Indians were being held for the hostilities associated with the Cibecue battle and its aftermath: 41 at Fort Lowell, 24 at Camp Thomas, and 3 scouts at Fort Grant. The next day Tiffany wrote to Hiram Price, the commissioner of Indian affairs:

> I notice in the newspapers that Genl. Willcox recommends, "That the Indian prisoners now in his charge, captured by the U.S. troops, except the mutinous scouts, be sent to the Indian Territory and to the Tortugas."
>
> If this be true, I most respectfully state that Genl. Willcox has no Indians in his care or possession captured by U.S. troops.
>
> The Indian prisoners are those who surrendered to me, or were taken by my scouts and turned over by me to him, under the direct promise and stipulation that they should have a fair trial and good counsel, and you have the papers among those I sent the Department from San Carlos.
>
> To do as he recommends would be a breach of good faith on the part of the Government or the Military, and one to which I as their Agent cannot consent without the most earnest protest.
>
> I consider that to accede to Genl. Willcox's recommendation, without complying with the terms upon which the Indian prisoners gave themselves up, would be a breach of the National faith—a blot

upon the Government, and it would produce a feeling of mistrust among the Indians that it would be difficult to overcome, if it ever could be.

I cannot understand how Genl. Willcox under the circumstances can so far forget himself as to make such an unjust suggestion.[1]

Price sent the letter to the secretary of the interior, Samuel J. Kirkwood, recommending "that if it has been decided that there is no authority of law for the trial of the Indians in question by the military, the Hon. Secretary of War be requested to direct their transfer to the U.S. Indian Agent at San Carlos Agency."[2]

Meanwhile, Willcox continued to argue for his recommendation:

> The legal obstacle to disposition of prisoners by trial by civil courts is that they are prisoners of war, and there is a want of competent evidence to identify and convict the hostiles of crimes, as we should have to depend upon unfriendly Indian testimony, which cannot be trusted and has not the sanction of an oath. There is no known obstacle to their disposition as heretofore recommended by me, viz: banishment. And this is the only safe course. If they are returned to the Agency, I shall require an additional regiment of troops.
>
> These prisoners are the bold spirits of their tribes. They would return to their reservation as embittered enemies of the whites and heroes of their nation, let off from crimes and hostilities without punishment. The reservation would be entirely unsettled and will break out on small provocation. I propose to move the troops in the neighborhood of San Carlos against the Chiricahuas expected at any moment. The removal of these prisoners would set the troops footloose and nothing else will.[3]

The day after Willcox sent this letter forward, Kirkwood sent Tiffany's letter, with Price's recommendation, to Robert Lincoln, the secretary of war. Lincoln immediately instructed Sherman to turn over to Tiffany the Cibecue prisoners who were not mutinous scouts. Tiffany received the prisoners from Camp Thomas on March 2, 1882, and the Lowell prisoners on March 8.

On January 31, 1882, President Arthur confirmed the sentences of the scouts. He ordered that their execution by hanging occur on March 3, 1882, between the hours of 10:00 A.M. and 2:00 P.M. About a week later the meaning of the president's action was explained to the scouts. Shortly thereafter one tried to escape. Capt. William L.

Dandy Jim. Photo by Henry Buehman in the late 1870s. Courtesy Special
Collections, University of Arizona Library.

Foulk, the provost marshal in connection with their execution, reported the incident:

> During the night of the 10th of February 1882, or morning of the 11th of February 1882, Dandy Jim managed to sever his shackles with the aid of an iron hook or staple which he had pulled out of the boards of his cell, and a piece of a razor which he had managed to get possession of. At reveille he asked permission to go to the sink, which was accorded him. As he gained the door of the guardhouse he made a determined and vigorous jump or leap and ran off at a rapid pace towards a ravine near the post and the mountains. He was closely pursued by the sentinel, the corporal of the guard and the corporal in charge of the guard, they firing at the prisoner as he ran. After he had gained a distance of perhaps 500 yards or more, a shot from one of the corporal's guns struck his left arm below the elbow and very soon thereafter the prisoner was overtaken and brought back to the guardhouse, very much exhausted from the loss of blood and excitement produced by his rapid running. The surgeon was immediately sent for and the wound dressed. The wound was principally a flesh one, the bone however was grazed by the bullet as was afterwards discovered, from the fact that a very small piece of the same was found in the discharge from the wound.[4]

On February 22 Major Benjamin, Willcox's AAG, informed the commander of Fort Grant that the three scouts would be hanged there. Eight days later Foulk, the chaplain, and the interpreter visited the scouts. A reporter for the *Arizona Star* who was at Grant for the hangings wrote,

> The prisoners were interviewed today by the Post Commander and Chaplain Mitchell, through an interpreter, and were advised of tomorrow being their last day on earth. They appeared to be reconciled to their fate, and said that if it could not be avoided the sooner they would go the better. Dandy Jim is the only one upon whom the sentence has a dampening influence. He is young and robust and consequently dreads the awful fate awaiting him. The gallows, which have been constructed at some distance from where the prisoners are confined, was placed today immediately in front of the guardhouse [about 30 yards from it], and as the prisoners looked through the iron bars it loomed up before them in all its horror. After seeing it Dandy Jim declined to partake of any food, but Dead Shot and Skippy made light of it by laughing and mimicking at the

manner at which they should die by the rope. They have no fears of the hereafter and say their hands are clean, meaning innocence, and if nothing can be done for them in this life they are prepared to die. Every precaution has been taken to carefully guard them. Two troops of cavalry have arrived here as additional force, in the event of any occurrence. The execution will be conducted with as little demonstration as possible.[5]

The prisoners were given all they wanted to eat and dressed in clean clothes. The next morning they ate little of their breakfast. They did not look toward the gallows. After breakfast Skippy asked how many hours he had to live. When told, there was a "marked effect on his appearance."[6] Foulk reported the events later that day:

At 11 o'clock A.M. 3rd March 1882 I went to the guardhouse in company with the chaplain of the post, and interpreter; were also present two reporters of the press. The iron shackles were taken off the prisoner's legs, and light ropes substituted, their arms were tied loosely.

About 12 o'clock the troops having formed in the order previously recited in front and near to the place of execution [three troops of cavalry, one company of infantry, and two companies of Indian scouts], the prisoners were conducted from the guardhouse on to the platform of the gallows [smiling and showing no signs of fear]; and the ropes were immediately placed around their necks. [A series of orders and telegrams relating to the court-martial and hangings were then read] . . . after which the interpreter informed each prisoner in succession that they were at liberty to make any statement they desired.

And in reply Dead Shot spoke as follows: That he was going to where he would meet his friends that had gone before him; that he had suffered a good deal in this world and he would soon get rest; that since he first met the white people he has been wearing good clothes, plenty to eat and now he was to pay with his life for the white man's kindness to him: that Dandy Jim and Skippy were his relatives (the former his nephew and the latter his cousin): that he had done no wrong as he had gave himself up to the Agent at San Carlos, and if he done wrong he would not surrender.

Dandy Jim spoke as follows: That he was not well and could not talk much; he had to die as there was no help for him. If he begged for his life people would laugh at him and he didn't want that.

Skippy spoke as follows: Said it was not right to hang him an innocent man; that the sun was going down and God would take care of him.

The prisoners having nothing further to state [shook hands with everyone on the platform], the Chaplin offered up a fervent prayer to the all wise Providence in behalf of the condemned men, after which caps made of black muslin were adjusted over their heads, faces and necks, their arms more closely tied; and at one o'clock P.M. a trap door in the platform of the gallows closing from underneath the same and on which the prisoners stood was sprung open and down by the executioner and the prisoners were thereby suddenly suspended by the neck and executed by hanging—death being produced seeming almost instantaneously—Dead Shot and Skippy died without a

Fort Grant, 1892–95, looking east, from the north end of the parade ground. The commanding officer's quarters is at the end of the trees on the far right. From left to right: the guardhouse (the guard is in front), the quartermaster's storehouse, the adjutant's office. Courtesy U.S. Army Military History Institute.

struggle, Dandy Jim showed some little signs of life for a minute or less. After the prisoner's bodies had remained hanging by the neck for twenty minutes or more they were taken down one at a time, examined by Post Surgeon J. B. [Joseph Basil] Girard, Asst. Surgeon U.S. Army, and A.A. Surgeon [M. F.] Price, (the latter on temporary duty at the post with Capt. Chaffee's command) who finding life extinct, pronounced them dead; and the prisoner's bodies were placed in order of examination into neatly made coffins, and the lids of the same fastened over them.

The troops forming the battalion were then dispersed in regular order to their respective quarters or camps. Immediately after which the bodies were conveyed in a Government wagon in charge of the Provost Sergeant, guard, and police party to the place of burial near the post cemetery, and there the remains were properly interred in graves made in advance of the execution.

. . . A large concourse of citizens from the surrounding country, settlements, and elsewhere were present and witnessed the execution all of whom conducted themselves with the utmost decorum, not even a voice was heard among the entire assemblage while the order of ceremony was in progress.[7]

Many years later Thomas Cruse said,

I have always regretted the fate of Deadshot and Skippy. The former was the sage of the Indian company, the latter our clown and wag. I doubted at the time if they had intentional part in the firing upon us. It seemed to me that they were swept into the fight by excitement and the force of evil circumstances.

. . . Suicide was virtually unknown among the Apaches, but on the day that Deadshot was hanged at Grant, his squaw hanged herself to a tree on the San Carlos Agency.[8]

While the scouts had been imprisoned at Grant, on the night of February 3, the San Carlos police captured Scout 11 of Cruse's mutinous company. Dr. Stanley D. Pangburn, acting agent in Tiffany's absence,[9] questioned him and then reported, "I learned that nine other renegades of that company are and have been in the vicinity of Cooley's ranch and that they receive their means of subsistence from that place. He [Scout 11] also states that they will not come in and surrender themselves as long as there is a possibility of their being punished. In his capture here, he fought desperately for liberty, plainly showing that it is not their intention to be easily taken."[10]

Scout 11 was taken to the guardhouse at Camp Thomas.[11] In June 1882 he was tried by general court-martial at Fort Grant. He received a dishonorable discharge and was sentenced to confinement for eight years at Alcatraz.[12]

A month after the three scouts were hanged Sherman visited the agency while on a tour of Arizona "to see the actual condition of affairs"[13] in the territory. While there he telegraphed Secretary of the Interior Kirkwood:

Colonel Tiffany,[14] your Agent here, holds as prisoners 67 White Mountain Apaches, who surrendered on account of the Cibicu Affair

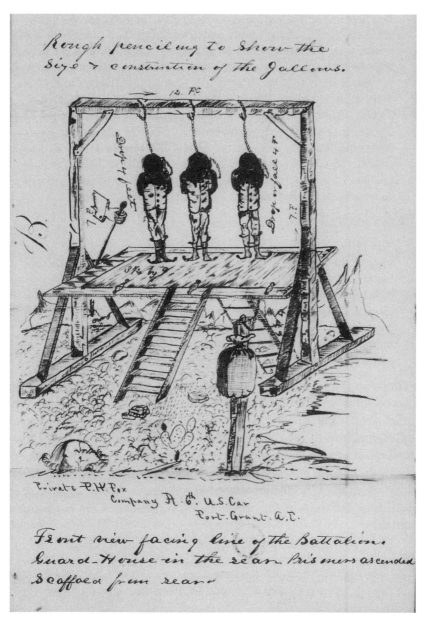

The hanging of Dead Shot, Dandy Jim, and Skippy. Sketch by Private Patrick H. Fox, Troop A, 6th Cavalry. It accompanied Captain Foulk's report on the hangings. Courtesy National Archives.

last September. They are here with all their families leaving astray all their horses, cattle, sheep and everything they possess in the northern part of the reservation. Some of the prisoners have been tried and executed, a few more may deserve trial and punishment, but the mass should be allowed to return to their homes to collect their stock and to get ready for their corn. I am convinced that Col. Tiffany knows all the facts and all the parties and should be allowed discretion to set at liberty such as are not guilty of murder, perfidy or robbery, and that the guilty parties should still be held or be delivered over to the Civil Court of the Territory. We have just held [a] long talk and I am convinced that there is no danger of repetition and that substantial justice will result.[15]

Kirkwood then notified Price:

The discretion asked for Agent Tiffany is a very large one; but in view of the great delay that seems inevitable in having a trial before the courts, he had better be instructed to discharge the least implicated, reserving for trial those accused on good grounds of the worst crimes. Perhaps such course may tend to hasten the action of the courts as to those not liberated. Instruct Agent Tiffany, as above indicated, and write to [the] Governor of Arizona, informing him and urging him to hasten, if possible, the trial of those still detained.[16]

That day the Commissioner wired Tiffany, directing him to act in accordance with the secretary's instructions. Tiffany immediately released all but fifteen of the sixty-seven prisoners. A day or two later, on April 8, 1882, four of the fifteen escaped when they broke and ran after being taken from the guardhouse for "a call of nature."[17]

Both the U.S. attorney general and the governor of Arizona Territory asked the U.S. district attorney for Arizona, James A. Zabriskie, to hasten the trials of the prisoners. Nevertheless, it did not happen quickly.

Meanwhile, the Chiricahuas had returned to the United States. First they visited Na-ti-o-tish on Eagle Creek.[18] On April 19 they moved near the agency, killed Sterling, and left with Chief Loco and his band of Warm Springs Apaches.[19] Eight days later they were back in Mexico.

Sherman was frustrated. In response to the raid he telegraphed Lincoln suggesting that New Mexico be added to the Department of Arizona and Mackenzie be promoted to brigadier general and placed in command of the department. He also recommended that the 7th Infantry be switched with Willcox's 12th Infantry. His recommendation was not acted on.

Willcox knew he had another problem. About six weeks after the Chiricahua raid he wrote to Sherman, through McDowell:

> I have the honor to invite attention to the fact that some seventeen of the revolted scouts are still at large and supposed to be harboring in the White Mountain fastnesses, somewhere within the limits of the San Carlos Reservation, and where it is a delicate matter for the troops to scout. In addition to these scouts, there is a small band that never came in after the Cibicu fight, and probably the Indians who recently broke guard and escaped from San Carlos Agency. Captain MacGowan estimates them at about forty bucks [Na-ti-o-tish's band]. . . . Unless they took part in the late outbreak [the Chiricahua raid at the subagency], . . . they seem to have kept quiet, but their presence is a standing menace to the people in that section of the country and a nucleus for renegades.
>
> It is believed that by offering a reward for the capture of the scouts, other Indians might be induced to hunt them down, as by this time they must be tired of harboring and feeding them. The reward of thirty dollars is not enough, but if fifty dollars each could be added, the amount eighty dollars, would probably suffice.
>
> The scouts are well armed; and those who have joined them— Gar and others, are among the boldest as well as the worst of the band.
>
> If a reward could also be given for their capture, it might result in bringing them in, also the reward should be paid dead or alive, as the danger attending their capture would be very great. The one captured near the Sub Agency fought desperately.
>
> If $2500 from the Contingent Fund of the War Dept. could be placed to the credit of my Chief Quartermaster to be disbursed under my orders, I believe these Indians could be captured or forced to surrender.[20]

The War Department refused Willcox's request. Five weeks later Na-ti-o-tish and his warriors went on the warpath. During the morning of July 6 they ambushed John Colvig, the new San Carlos chief of police, at the subagency, killing him and three of his Indian policemen.[21] While they were in the area thirteen men of Sanchez's band joined them. Na-ti-o-tish then had about fifty-four men.

Indian police at the San Carlos Agency guardhouse, 1880. Courtesy U.S. Army Military History Institute.

During the next several days they swept northwest, shooting settlers and stealing stock. Troops were sent after them from Forts Verde, McDowell, and Apache, Whipple Barracks, and Camp Thomas. When Na-ti-o-tish and his warriors had started their rampage, they stole several horses, including "a pony that was the apple of Sanchez' eye."[22] Sanchez and seven Indians voluntarily joined the troops sent in pursuit from Camp Thomas.

Several troops met the hostiles at Chevelon's Fork (north of General's Spring, on Black Mesa). The ensuing battle, known as the Battle of Big Dry Wash, was disastrous for the Indians. Although

many escaped through the woods, sixteen were killed. Na-ti-o-tish and two of Cruse's mutinous scouts were among the dead. Some escapees returned to the reservation and hid among their friends. Eight days after the battle Major Biddle, then at Fort Apache, reported that he was sure escapees were being harbored by the Indians living near the fort. He suggested that the friendly Indians be ordered into Fort Apache or sent to the agency at once so he could send out scouts to "kill everything out there." Biddle also suggested that Pedro, at Forestdale, "be notified that Indians found one mile from his camp would be killed on sight."[23]

Willcox wanted the renegades. Acting agent Pangburn offered the assistance of his Indian police. Maj. Andrew Wallace Evans, the commander of Fort Apache, however, reported, "In my opinion, troops cannot act on the reservation where doubtless some of the hostiles are concealed without danger of bringing on a general war. It is a very delicate matter. . . . Moreover, it would be almost impossible to find the concealed parties."[24] Nonetheless, Willcox pressed for more information as to the probability of bringing on a general war by attempting to carry out Biddle's suggestions.

But Willcox's tenure in Arizona was ending. Three days before the Battle of Big Dry Wash, on July 14, the adjutant general of the army issued General Orders No. 78. The orders assigned Brig. Gen. George Crook commander of the Department of Arizona and directed Willcox to report with his regiment for duty to the commanding general of the Department of the Platte.[25]

After Willcox was notified of the transfer of his regiment, he saw an Associated Press newspaper dispatch: "The occasion for the transfer however seems to be in the fact that affairs in Arizona have been in very bad condition for the past year, and the Department has come to the conclusion to make an improvement there. Secretary Lincoln said today that he was determined to stop the Apache raids and disorders in that Territory and to send an experienced and energetic officer to do the duty."[26]

Willcox immediately responded: "Had my recommendations to have a military agent placed at San Carlos and my urgent request to have the Cibicu prisoners sent away instead of being released, been granted, I do not believe any further troubles would have happened on the reservation."[27]

Sherman simply replied,

The existence of the San Carlos Apache Reservation in the very center of Arizona, subject alone to civil control, i.e., no control at all, and the liberation of the Cibicu prisoners have been beyond his control for the effect of which he is in no manner responsible. I am well satisfied that Genl. Willcox has done his best, and that the troops have been brave, zealous and prompt to move and fight— little by little the Apaches will cease to trouble the Government, or any on earth, and each year their spasmodic efforts to regain their liberty to murder and steal will diminish and disappear. These

Apaches know Genl. Crook, and fear him. Therefore his assignment to the command of the Department is wise and right. No reflection is thereby cast on Genl. Willcox, who has done his best, and that is all that was expected of him; or should be expected of any Army Commander.[28]

Just before Willcox and his regiment were to move to the Department of the Platte, they were ordered to the Department of the East.[29] A few days later, on August 31, Willcox reported that in addition to the five mutinous scouts tried by court-martial, several were reported killed by the San Carlos police, others were killed in battle, and "it is believed that but eleven are alive of the whole company, some sulking in the White Mountains and other parts of the San Carlos Reservation, or about Fort Apache, harbored and concealed by their friends in the tribes. The difficulty, as reported by various commanding officers at the fort, seems to be to get at them on the reservation without stirring up a general war."[30]

Chapter 15

GENERAL CROOK TAKES OVER

General Crook assumed command of the Department of Arizona on September 4, 1882.[1] A week later he left Whipple Barracks with Capt. John G. Bourke, his aide, and Assistant Surgeon John Oscar Skinner to hold talks with the reservation Indians. First he went to Fort Apache, where Corydon Cooley and Severiano joined him as interpreters. Near there he met with Pedro,[2] Alchesay, Uclenny, Mose, and about forty-six others. Crook asked them to tell him everything that had happened since he had left nine years before.

The Indians complained that the military officers and agents had treated them badly. They also said they had not understood what the officers and agents wanted of them and had no confidence in them. Regarding the Cibecue troubles, Pedro said,

> There came a Commanding Officer—a man with large whiskers all over his face (General Carr). He sent for me. I was lame and could hardly walk, but I went up to his house from my place over yonder. He said, "I am going out on a campaign." I said: "Why? There are no bad Indians in the country. Why should you want to make a campaign now?"
>
> When he said that he was going on that campaign, I told him that the Indians had permission to plant on the Cibicu, the Carrizo, over by that hill (pointing) and in other places and that they were all contented. They all had passes and were planting corn and had cattle

in plenty and were very contented. I asked him why he wanted to go out and make a campaign against them. When he made that campaign, all that the Indians had was destroyed, their corn cut down, their cattle driven away.

. . . When I asked him why he was going on that campaign and told him that when I was in Washington the President had said that we were all good Indians and all at peace, he looked at me in a very foolish way and just snickered—but did not reply. The interpreter Charlie [Charles Hurrle] was there, but I could get no information out of him.

Then I came right back to my house and saw the troops starting through that pass (pointing to west) and that's all the satisfaction I got.

Then I sent this Indian, Not-sin, to overtake General Carr and ask him what he was going for, and General Carr said that he was going out to the Cibicu to arrest the Indian who was having all that dancing. Ba & kee klin-in [Nock-ay-det-klinne]—the Doctor. At this I was not alarmed because I knew that there was then no trouble with the Indians and that they were all good. Then Major Cochran told me that he had received word from the Agent at San Carlos that all the Apaches had to go down there and he said: "Pedro, you had better go back to your own corn fields over at Forestdale." This was after General Carr and the soldiers had left for the Cibicu.

When Severiano brought us in word of the fight at the Cibicu, everybody was much excited and I thought best to take all my women and children up to Cooley's house. When the Commanding Officer Major Cochran told me about the message from the Agent at San Carlos, I intended starting for my corn fields, but when I heard of the fight, I thought best to go up to Cooley's house. This thing is all past now and I have said all I want to say about it but I have something else I want to talk about. I don't understand this thing. I am getting to be a very old man now. I have always done what was right. Often, when I have wanted a little fun, I have sent word to all the women and children to come up and have a dance; other people have done the same thing; I have never heard that there was any harm in that; but that campaign was made just because those Indians over on the Cibicu were dancing. Why is this change?

Another Indian, probably Uclenny, then spoke.

I have always been a friend of the soldiers and now, in this Cibicu affair, I have suffered without cause, and I am sorry to say that I have been in the guardhouse for (5) five or (6) six months, and all because I tried to be a friend of the whites and to benefit them. Cooley went with me when I went to General Carr and offered him my services. General Carr told me to go back to Cooley's house and try to find out all I could about the Apaches who were out. I did so. After all that, he sent out in the night and had me arrested and I was in the guardhouse for (6) six months, at the San Carlos and at Camp Thomas.

Alchesay then said,

Uclenni [Uclenny] and I were doing all we could to help the whites, but we were both taken off by General Carr and put in the guard-house. All that I have ever done has been honest. I have always been true and obeyed orders. I made campaigns against Apache-Yumas, Apache-Tontos, Pinalenos and all kinds of people, and even went against my own people.

Next Mose spoke.

General Carr sent for me and told me that he wanted me to go to the Cibicu, to tell the Indian Doctor that he, General Carr, wanted to see him. The Doctor wasn't at home, but another Indian told me that the Doctor would come into see General Carr in six (6) days. When I told this to General Carr, about (3) three days afterwards, he, General Carr, went to the Cibicu with the soldiers. When we got to the cross-ing of the Carrizo Creek, General Carr gave the Indian scouts (20) rounds of ammunition apiece. When we got over to the Cibicu, General Carr sent me with another Indian over to where the Doctor had some corn planted. The troops got there almost as soon as I did and just as I had begun talking with the Doctor. When I told the Doctor that General Carr had sent me after him, he made no reply, but eat with his head hanging down. When I took the Doctor down to General Carr's camp, I sat down and he set down alongside of me. A soldier came up and began punching the Indian soldiers and telling them to "ugashe" (go away). Then General Carr's cook began firing at the Indian soldiers; we had hardly reached the camp, when this happened. I was up on the bank with the Doctor. General Carr and Captain Hentig were down in a little ravine close to me, but I couldn't see them. The next thing after that shot was fired, the Indian and the white soldiers began firing at each other. The other Indian soldiers ran into the brush, but I staid where I was. I was sitting alongside of the Doctor. The first shot fired at the Doctor didn't hit him; the second shot wounded him. I laid down behind a pile of aparejos. The Doctor was hit in the head and fell without a word. I got behind the aparejos. That's all I saw. I could hear the Doctor breathing.

I came back with General Carr and the troops. General Carr came to me and said (3) three times: "Good! Good! Good! You are going back with us to Camp Apache."

When they gave the Indian soldiers cartridges at the Carrizo, an officer asked me, "whose friends are you? Are you for us or are you going to help the Indians at the Cibicu?" There was nothing said by the Indians. I didn't hear them say a word about fighting the troops.

After the Doctor was killed, the troops left there and marched all night to get back here. I couldn't tell how many Indians were in the fight. I was with the soldiers.

There were (4) four or five chiefs there, but I don't know how many men they had. When I arrested the Doctor, he was alone.

All the white soldiers from the post were out there. I heard the Indians say that the General (Carr) took the troops from here to make war on them, but that they (the Indians) didn't want war. If they wished, they could have killed all the soldiers in that rough country.

I was one of the first soldiers enlisted and have been a soldier ever since. I saved my money and put it into stock and had a good deal of property. It looks to me as if General Carr went out there just to destroy everything.

The Indians and whites both stole all I had—now I haven't got anything.

The conference then broke up. Before Crook left Fort Apache he questioned several whites living there, including Lieutenant Cruse. Crook moved his camp to the Black River, fifteen miles away. Eleven renegades, many of them former scouts from the Cibecue battle and some individuals from the previous day's meeting, came to his new campsite to talk. Crook said to them, "I want you to speak about what you know of what happened at the Cibicu." First, Kulo, a former scout, spoke.

I started away from Camp Apache with the soldiers and when we got over to the crossing of the Carrizo ammunition was given to us. Then an officer asked us, "are you going to be for us or against us? At the time that question was asked us, we had confidence in the officer in charge of us. The Captain with the long beard—General

Carr. We answered that we had confidence in him and would be for him.

After that Moses [Mose] here, (i.e. Cut-mouth Moses, then 1st Sergt of the Scouts) detailed myself and Chili here, (pointing to one of the ex-scouts) to go over and notify the Doctor Baxka klin-ni [Nock-ay-det-klinne], that the soldiers had come to arrest him.

When we got over to where the Doctor [was], the soldiers came right behind us. When the troops came down to where the Indian Doctor was, Moses and the Indian soldiers took the Doctor and went with the troops down to where they were to make camp. While they were unloading the mules, General Carr's cook had a fire built.

The cook fired a shot at us and we all started to run away from him and ran to the packtrain and aparejos which were in the milhouse near the stream. As we ran in there, the white soldiers opened fire upon us. After the firing on both sides had lasted a little while, we scattered and went off in parties of 1,2,3 and 4. After we scattered, I saw no more of that body of soldiers. We were all much frightened and worried because those officers had treated us so badly.

We have been out ever since and have not shown ourselves to any officers, because we have been afraid after the treatment received then. Alchesay came and told us that you (General Crook) were here and we have come in, trotting all the way.

I don't know of any Indian being killed except the Doctor, but I have heard that there were several Indians wounded.

I don't know how many white soldiers were killed, the white soldiers got back to Camp Apache before we did and I then learned from Indians living near there, that some of them had been killed. I didn't go to Apache myself; I went up to the headwaters of the Carrizo, near where Severiano had his cattle, but I learned from Indians living near the post what I now tell you. We didn't want a fight with the soldiers; the fight was unexpected by us, as, up to that time, the soldiers had been our good friends. When the firing began, we ran away to hide and get out of range.

Several other former scouts then spoke.

Charlie. What kind of a man was that officer [General Carr]? What could he have been thinking of? What had he put in his head that he should suddenly act that way? Everything seemed to be going on all right and much to his satisfaction. Here we were his soldiers. I have been a soldier since I was a boy—and he said he was content with us. He never said a word against us—either to us or the interpreter and yet he suddenly turned around and treated us in that way. What kind of a man must he be? We had had many other Commanding Officers before he came—they were all good men and treated us well; and so too did this man until this time. What was the matter with him? He never gave us a reason; he never said a word to us. We used to be his soldiers and if he wasn't satisfied with us he used to punish us; he used to put us in the guardhouse for not finding water on the trip—that was all right, we expected that, but we can't understand why he should treat us as he did at the Cibicu.

Charlie repeated, almost in words, the statement of Moses and Kulo concerning the distribution of (20) twenty cartridges to each Indian scout at the crossing of the Carrizo and the questions then asked them.

I was with the party under Moses that arrested the Doctor and brought him down to the soldier's camp; there was a big crowd of white and Indian soldiers and women and children all close together. I went to the corn field, got some green corn and was making bread out of it when the firing commenced.

I don't know who commenced the firing; I ran off with the other Indian scouts when they scattered. I started down Cibicu Creek; when I got a way, below, an Indian came to me with a woman and said there had been fighting, the Doctor had been killed and some white soldiers; how many he didn't know.

I only know of the Doctor being killed on the Indian side.

We didn't want to fight the soldiers because they were our friends—we were all of that opinion. I wasn't in that party, but one of the chiefs of the Cibicu when all were running away, found a mule loaded with ammunition. We have been waiting for some one to come here in whom we could have confidence. Many of our people blame the soldiers. I am glad to see you. I have told you the truth.

Saunni (an ex-scout and son of one-eyed Miguel). I have just the same thing to say that the others have said and I have the same opinion of that officer at the Cibicu. I think that there was something wrong with his head. I know that his cook fired the first shot and then the soldiers opened fire upon us and we ran in every direction.

Comanche (ex-scout). Reported the same story almost as Moses and the others, but could not say who fired the 1st shot as he was eating his dinner when the shooting began.

Ziddi-ku (ex-scout). I saw the cook; I was standing close to the woodpile where he was, near the aparejos. I saw the cook fire the

1st shot with his pistol, and almost as quick as anything the white soldiers grabbed their guns and began shooting at the Cibicu Indians who were near the Doctor and then the fight commenced. I saw but one Indian shoot—the Indian who killed Captain Hentig. I was right close to Captain Hentig when he was shot. The Indian who shot him was Han-she.

Nagataba, Ahane, Comanche, Nita and Ize-di-ku [Ziddi-ku] at this point admitted that they had been present in the fight of July last on the top of the Black Mesa [the Battle of Big Dry Wash]. Natalish [Na-ti-o-tish], so these five Indians said, came to them and told them that the Indians of his band had taken their families away from the San Carlos and he wanted them to go with him. This Indian, Natalish had charge of all the Carrizo Indians on the San Carlos. The trouble began between Sanchez and Natalish. Natalish told these five (5) Indians that the whites were going to kill all the Apaches and that the soldiers would fire on them just as they did on the Cibicu and so he persuaded them to go with him. They were in the fight on the Black Mesa where they lost 15 or 16 killed; men, women and children and (11) eleven wounded. They left after the fight and did not know whether any of the wounded died or not. Down in Tonto Basin, they said that there were (2) two Indians killed and (2) two wounded, one of whom died afterwards.

Alchesay then said,

I want to say a few words. I am very well satisfied with everything that has been said and done here this evening. These Indians are not to blame. There has been so much said and done that they hardly know what to do, but there are bad Indians of the Cibicu band at the San Carlos Agency. I am glad of this talk. I have understood all you have said to me.

These Indians are not to blame; they have been forced into this thing by the way in which they have been treated. I have given you my hand and you have given me yours. If you knew everything as well as the Indians do I don't think that you would blame them.

Alchesay also complained about not having a good interpreter for a long time. He said Severiano was a good one. Near the end of the meeting Crook spoke.

I have heard all that you have said and I think I understand you. It is believed by the white people that these Indian soldiers turned against the white soldiers at the Cibicu; when white soldiers do such a thing as that we always kill them. The whole matter seems to be wrapped up in a good deal of mystery and confusion. Each side has a different story. The promptness with which you have come in here makes me think you are telling the truth as you know it.

I don't do things halfway; I either do one thing or the other. I want all those who have Government guns to turn them in and those who have not, to hunt them up and return them. When they do that, we'll wipe out the past and commence on a scrubbed floor, on a new basis. In a short time, I'll send an officer up to Fort Apache to enlist soldiers as we did when [Brevet] Major [George Morton] Randall[3] was here; and I'll expect these soldiers to control all the Indians, just the same as they used to do. They must report everything that is going on, so that the guilty may be punished and the innocent may not suffer with them. That officer will report directly to me; of course, if he don't suit, I'll send another and keep on doing it until I get one who will suit. You will know when that officer arrives and you can turn your guns into him. That's all I've got to say.

Crook then moved his camp to a point four miles north of the agency on the San Carlos River. At noon on September 26 he met with Indians from tribes living near the agency and subagency. Most of the leaders, including Sanchez, complained about not receiving enough necessities and rations and other issues. The chiefs who had been moved to the agency and subagency several years previously under the Indian Bureau's plan to consolidate the Indians expressed dissatisfaction with their location and the desire to move their bands back to their homelands. They said they would forgo rations to do so.

Later in the afternoon Crook met with Indians involved in the Battle of Big Dry Wash. Manuel did the talking.

The agent gave us permission to plant on the Cibicu and gave us hoes and spades to work with. Our crops were fine. I don't know why the soldiers were sent up there unless our fine crops made the Agent mad. All Mexicans and Americans raise corn; take pleasure in raising it. After he had found out that we were raising corn, why did that fat agent send out soldiers after us? What had we done? We had an abundance of everything; had planted corn, watermelons, muskmelons, beans, everything. We couldn't understand why the Agent should always be sending men up to see what we were doing; their horses always trampled down our fields of corn. Up where we planted was an open road; no stolen horses ever found their way in there; we never did anything wrong; then why did the Agent send soldiers in there?

If the commanding officer of Camp Apache wanted to arrest the Doctor why didn't he send out and do it? He could have done it without any trouble. But he brought out soldiers with him to make a campaign, and they began firing on us. Of course, some of our people fired back, but who wouldn't? We couldn't understand why the soldiers should treat us in that way. We had always been their good friends. After that fight, we came down here to the Agent, who was our Captain. But he too was very unkind to us and we were afraid that he would fire upon us also. The Agent said, "Go away." I said, "I want to remain here where I belong; why did you let that officer at Camp Apache make war upon us? We are your people— you are our commanding officer. We want to stay here." But he said:—"go away; go off to the mountains." I told the Agent I hadn't done anything wrong. I hadn't gone on the warpath. I hadn't stolen anything. I wanted to stay here where I belonged. But he took me, tied me all up, tied my hair, put irons on my feet and hands and put me in the calaboose. I haven't done anything wrong, at least, I don't think I have.

Three days later Crook, still at the same campsite, met with eight Indians "who had been in the various engagements with troops." Only two Indians spoke. An Indian called Nodiskay (probably Nodeski) said much the same thing that the chiefs had told Crook three days earlier. Tubukasinda said,

Lately, every day, every night, since the Cibicu, we have been told all sorts of things; we were to be put in the guardhouse, have our arms taken from us and be sent away from this country. A man would be suddenly put in the guardhouse without any cause and then let out again without any explanation. We couldn't make out what was meant by such treatment.

We had permission to go over to the Carrizo to plant; we had a splendid field of corn; we had over (100) one hundred cows.

Over on the next creek, Cibicu, we had over (200) two hundred cows, and a great many mares and young colts and another fine field of corn—we were getting to be very rich.

When that Captain came out with the soldiers from Fort Apache— General Carr—he let his soldiers turn their horses in upon our corn and it was all destroyed; our cows were killed or stolen, and the same with our mares.

It looked to us as if the Americans didn't want us to work and didn't like the idea of having us make our own living; and as if they wanted to destroy all we had and drive us out on the warpath. After the trouble on the Cibicu, we never had any peace; first, one man would come and tell us that we were going to be put in the guardhouse; then another would say that we were going to be arrested, disarmed and taken far away to another country.

And in this way we were very much excited and didn't get any rest; so we thought it better to go on the warpath at once and have the business ended. We thought it would be better to die fighting in the mountains than to die in this place.[4]

From his camp near the agency, Crook then notified McDowell that he had met with the Indians.

I learned to my own satisfaction that the Indians are so firmly of the belief that the affair of the Cibicu last year was an attack premeditated by the white soldiers, that I am convinced any attempt to punish one of the Indian soldiers for participation in it would bring on a war.

Without wishing to express an opinion upon that affair, I have no doubt from what I know of the Indians and the country in question that, if the Indians had been in earnest, not one of our soldiers could have gotten away from there alive.

Of course, afterwards, it was perfectly natural for the Indians who had lost friends and relations, to commit the depredations, which they did in the vicinity of Fort Apache.

When I first met the Indians, I found them sullen and distrustful, and it was only with much difficulty that I got them to talk with me. After breaking down their suspicions, by railing at them and shaming them for not trusting me who had always been straightforward with them, they finally came around and talked freely with me.

They all agreed that affairs could not well be worse; that one officer of the Government would tell them one thing and another something else, until finally they lost confidence in everybody, and not knowing whom or what to believe, lent a credulous ear to every story which Mexicans, or other irresponsible parties throughout the country concocted.

They were constantly told that they were to be disarmed and then they were to be attacked, as at Cibicu; the interpreters were incompetent and some of them prejudiced and probably as a consequence of this incompetency and prejudice innocent Indians had been ironed and put in the guardhouse.

No one knew when his turn would come and they were fast arriving at the conclusion that they were all to be killed anyhow, and that they might as well die fighting as in any other way.

I have but very little doubt that in a very short time there would have been a general outbreak, and when we consider the hundreds of exposed ranchmen and prospectors throughout the country, in which they would depredate, the deplorable consequences of such a contingency may readily be imagined.[5] Furthermore, I became satisfied from the explanations the Indians made, that all the troubles of the past season, terminating in the engagement on the summit of Black Mesa, in July last, were but an outgrowth or a culmination of the ill feeling engendered at the Cibicu.

. . . There are now no hostile Indians out, excepting the Chiricahuas who have taken refuge in Mexico.[6]

Tiffany had resigned as San Carlos Apache agent on June 30, 1882, because of his health. He had been at San Carlos little since the previous December. On September 1, 1882, three days before Crook assumed command of the Department of Arizona, Tiffany's successor, Philip P. Wilcox, took charge of the reservation.

In late September the eleven remaining Cibecue prisoners were taken to Tucson to appear before a grand jury. They arrived there on October 1, and the jury examination began on the second. On the sixth the grand jury completed its investigation and discharged them, concluding "there was no evidence before the jury to implicate these prisoners in any crime."[7] The prisoners were taken back to San Carlos and released.

On October 8 Crook, not knowing the prisoners had been discharged, wrote a confidential letter to Zabriskie, the U.S. district attorney for Arizona, in Tucson:

In accordance with suggestion contained in telegram received from Marshal Tidball,[8] I take the liberty of writing a few lines to express an opinion upon the merits of the case, (now being prosecuted by you) involving the Indian prisoners lately taken from the San Carlos Agency to Tucson.

As you must be aware, I have for some weeks been among the Apaches, looking carefully into everything pertaining to their condition and endeavoring to ascertain what grievances, if any, they could adduce in palliation of their attitude of hostility. I find them all so firmly convinced that the affair at the Cibicu, and as a consequence, most of the troubles which followed in its train, was an attack premeditated on the part of the soldiery, that I am sure any punishment inflicted for participation in that encounter will bring about a war which will be destructive to the growing interests of this Territory and New Mexico.

Where all are equally implicated, the singling out of a few for trial will impress the Indians as an unjust and cruel discrimination, especially when the uncertainty of the testimony upon which you have to depend for conviction, is taken into consideration. The Apaches insist that one of the young men hanged last spring at Fort Grant had taken no active part in the troubles—that he hadn't fired a shot and that his life was sworn away by heated, ignored and mendacious witnesses.

You will, I am confident, perceive that the situation is one of extreme delicacy and that my administration will be very seriously embarrassed unless the Apaches can be made to feel that they are to be trialed upon a basis of exact and even-handed justice, treated with kindness when they deserve it and not punished without sufficient cause. It was upon such a groundwork that I provided when last in command of them and it is upon the very same foundation that I intend to operate during my present detail.

I look for the assistance and cooperation of all who have the real advancement of the Territory at heart and especially for that of Government representatives like Marshal Tidball and yourself, whose influence can strengthen or tie my hands, according as it may be exercised.

I do not want to be understood as saying that the Indians deny any of their acts of hostility, but they claim, as above stated, that the conduct of the troops at the Cibicu and of Agent Tiffany at all times forced them to the outbreak, of which all the consequent atrocities formed a part in their code.

They are now anxious to be at peace and I know them too well not to feel assured that they mean what they say.[9]

At about that time Crook asked Agent Wilcox to let the agency Indians live wherever they wished within the boundaries of the reservation. Wilcox agreed to do so under the condition that those who moved away from the agency become self-supporting as soon as possible. He also agreed to give them rations and supplies until they could gather their first crops the following fall; however, they had to pack them out to their camps.

On November 2, 1882, Crook met with the agency Indians and informed them of the agreement.[10] That month some of the Cibecue and White Mountain Apaches moved back to their homelands. Gradually, more Indians moved northward, particularly the relatives and friends of the ones who had already moved. As summer approached and the Gila River valley got hotter, more moved. By October 25, 1883, 180 men and about 720 women and children, mostly Cibecue and White Mountain Apaches, had transferred. Some had not received rations since July and were self-supporting. Crook visited many of their camps in October and then reported, "They are now thoroughly contented and satisfied."[11]

After assuming command of the Department of Arizona Crook decided to end the efforts to capture the remaining renegade scouts. They soon lost their fear of reprisal and rejoined their bands. On May 24, 1884, Crook sent a message up his chain of command asking for the release of the two scouts who were confined at Alcatraz Island because of the Cibecue troubles:

> At best, the condition of affairs then prevailing [in the Department of Arizona in 1881] was so chaotic and the stories told of the whole business so conflicting that I am constrained to ask that clemency be now extended and the sentence remitted in the above cases, and that these prisoners be returned to their own people.
>
> I am sure that such action will have a happy effect upon their relatives, who have unceasingly petitioned for their release, and who by the vigor and energy with which they are applying themselves to farming, are showing themselves worthy of favor from the government.
>
> If these prisoners were guilty of the offences charged, other members of their tribe were equally so. The Apaches can see no justice in our singling out these men for punishment, especially when they believe and assert that they were the party assailed.
>
> For my own part, from the evidence gathered since coming again into Arizona, I am convinced that the trouble should never have occurred.[12]

Less than four weeks later the acting secretary of war directed that the two scouts be released. On June 19, 1884, the adjutant general of the army issued Special Orders No. 142, which called for their release on receipt of the orders. They were immediately returned to the reservation.

Sanchez returned to the Cibecue–Carrizo Creek region, probably during November 1882. He was not involved in any significant troubles thereafter. According to the historian Harold B. Wharfield, in 1887 Sanchez and several Indians "were sent to Washington to visit President [Grover] Cleveland. There the Apache were presented with medals, called upon government bureaus and toured the city. They returned to the reservation with glowing stories of the sights seen and great cities."[13]

Pedro remained a chief for about two and a half years after the Cibecue affair. On March 1, 1884, Lieutenant Gatewood reported,

> Monday I am going to Forest Dale [Forestdale] to depose old Pedro as chief and put in someone else, probably Alchesay. As it is now, no one is really responsible, Pedro is so old and deaf and feeble that he can do nothing with them [his band members]. They sneak off the reservation and buy arms and whiskey from the Mormons, and it is almost impossible to get them to report on each other. But if there is a chief with get up, he can be calaboosed for not reporting those who do wrong which will have a tendency to check their going off.[14]

Alchesay did indeed succeed Pedro, probably as a result of Gatewood's trip. Eventually Alchesay became a principal spokesperson for the Cibecue and White Mountain Apaches. As such, he made several trips to Washington, D.C., to confer with the president and Indian Bureau officials.[15]

In the decades following Crook's return to Arizona many Cibecue and White Mountain Apaches enlisted as scouts and faithfully served the military. Except for isolated fights involving small numbers of individuals, there were no more conflicts between the military and the two tribes.

Chapter 16

CONCLUSION

In a supplement to his annual report for 1881 General Willcox wrote, "The immediate cause of the attack on Colonel Carr was the arrest of the medicine man. The remote causes are unknown, as no grievance had ever yet been complained of by the White Mountain Indians; but it is possible that this attack and the subsequent one on Fort Apache were made under the inspiration of the medicine man's prophesying that the white men should be cleared out as soon as the corn was ripe, which time had nearly come."[1]

Obviously, Willcox did not conduct a thorough investigation into the cause of the battle. In fact, there was no serious attempt to determine the cause beyond Crook's questioning of Apaches and whites in September 1882. Nevertheless, much can be gleaned from the many contemporary documents.

The situation that led to the Cibecue affair was described in the introduction to this book. The direct cause of the battle was the lack of meaningful communication between the military and the Apaches, particularly between the military and Nock-ay-det-klinne himself, during the weeks preceding the battle. Before the fight both the military and the Indians were alarmed. The Indians were "disturbed by idle, mischievous, and false reports; were apprehensive of danger from the troops; uneasy and restless."[2] The nearby military was affected similarly. Nothing suppressed or quelled the rumors, suspicions, and fears of either side.

Careful study of the archival telegrams, letters, and reports suggest that two instigators fueled the anxieties of both the military and the Indians.[3] Surely they were Charles Hurrle, the post interpreter, and his Apache girlfriend.

Hurrle was born in Germany, and his parents were German. He enlisted in the U.S. Army when he was twenty-one years old and was assigned to Troop E, 6th Cavalry. Recruit Hurrle arrived at Camp Verde, Arizona, where Troop E was stationed, on August 4, 1876. Ten months later, in early June 1877, the troop was transferred to Camp Apache. Apparently Hurrle learned the Apache language through mingling with local Indians.

Private Hurrle was discharged, on the expiration of his term of service, on May 4, 1881. He went to live with a young Apache prostitute named Hannah who was well known to the soldiers at Apache. Apparently Hurrle had been close to her for a while. In August 1882 he said he had "kept an Apache woman" for about three years.

Hurrle was hired as the interpreter for Fort Apache beginning on July 1, 1881. He claimed to understand the Apache language well. During Carr's inquiry Cruse said Hurrle "has the reputation of being the best interpreter in the country."

Dan L. Thrapp, in his book *General Crook and the Sierra Madre Adventure*, concludes that Hurrle may not have been proficient in the Apache language. He also explains the complexities of the Apache tongue and the difficulties that white men can have with it. Thrapp bases his opinion on a report by Carr which said that while arresting Nock-ay-det-klinne at his village, Mose sometimes repeated and explained to Nock-ay-det-klinne Hurrle's translations.[4]

Quite possibly Hurrle had boasted of his knowledge of the Apache language to comrades at the fort, and some, not knowing any better, believed him. While Carr and his command marched down Cibecue Creek after arresting Nock-ay-det-klinne, Na-ti-o-tish, obviously not trusting Hurrle's translations, came up to Carr and asked, through Hurrle, if Severiano could be the interpreter for Nock-ay-det-klinne. Carr said Severiano could be, if he would come in to Fort Apache. Thirteen months later Alchesay complained to Crook about their interpreter (Hurrle) and suggested Severiano for the position.

Al Seiber, a highly regarded chief of scouts during the Apache Wars, knew the Apache tongue. He did not think Hurrle was a capable interpreter. He said the Cibecue Creek battle "was caused by misinterpretation through ignorance, the interpreter not knowing enough of the Indian language to make a close bargain with a squaw."[5] Unfortunately, he did not explain what he meant by that statement.

Hurrle was the individual who informed Carr that Nock-ay-det-klinne said the dead Indians would not rise until the whites left, which would occur when the corn was ripe. In mid-August 1881 the Indians around Fort Apache said Hurrle's female companion was behind the circulation of the reports "about the killing and driving off [of the] white men" and "there is no such talk and has not been [any]."[6] Seventeen months later Carr said Hurrle's girlfriend "was simply an unchaste young squaw who could be trusted while well watched" and "was the principal source of the reports of the hostility of the neighboring Apache tribes."[7]

It was in mid-August 1881 that the information that Fort Apache was to receive a "big cannon" and reinforcements was quickly spread among the Indians living in the region around the post. At the same time the rumor that the Indians would be attacked and moved off the reservation was also circulated. Carr tried to find out who started this story but could not. He realized someone on his staff was leaking confidential information to the Indians. It was being promulgated almost immediately. Hurrle was a member of Carr's inner circle and thus privy to the information.

On August 22 Pedro and Uclenny told Carr that they had learned that the whites were upset with Nock-ay-det-klinne. Carr had been very careful not to alarm the medicine man. The two Indians said Hurrle's girlfriend first spread this information, but Carr did not believe them. He thought it was Mose.

What kind of a person was Hurrle? Would Hurrle, knowing that the Indians did not want him as their interpreter, excite them to make them believe he was on their side and to keep them from complaining about him so he could keep his high-paying job?[8]

Would he do the same with the military? Would he compulsively tell boastful lies? Quite possibly. During Carr's Court of Inquiry in August 1882 Hurrle falsely recollected an event to make himself appear favorably and important. When Carr questioned him, he admitted the truth.

On September 25, 1882, a couple of days after Crook visited Fort Apache and met with Pedro's band and the renegade scouts, Bourke sent a telegram to Lt. Col. George Wheeler Schofield, then the commanding officer of Fort Apache, from Crook's camp on Aliso Creek.

> A party of Apache squaws has just reached this camp much worried by a report made to them by your Interpreter [Hurrle] to the effect that it was General Crook's intention to put the Indians, now with him, or with whom he has been in conference, in the guardhouse at San Carlos or Tucson. As such reports and all useless and senseless remarks of same character have a most mischievous effect, General Crook directs that you order your Interpreter to be more exact in his statements. He wishes no threats made to Indians and none put in the guardhouse, or otherwise punished, without orders from himself.[9]

Later that day Schofield replied:

> Your dispatch by hands of squaw received. I think what the squaws you mentioned told you grew out of a talk I had with Mose and Alchesay who are subpoenaed as witnesses, before Court at Tucson, or they have been misinterpreted.
>
> I told the two they must go as witnesses, or they might be punished, or put in prison. They seemed to understand it, and Hurrle says they did.[10]

The next day Hurrle telegraphed Crook: "There must be a misunderstanding. I did not tell any Indians or anybody that they would be put in the guardhouse only that they would be punished if they were summoned to attend court and refused to go. Alchesay and Mose were summoned. I'll bet a thousand dollars that I did not say anything of the [kind]."[11]

Crook then wired Schofield directing him to inform Hurrle that "he will communicate with Alchesay, Mose, and other Indians only through you, and not on his own responsibility." Crook concluded his message by stating, "I have just seen U.S. Marshal. Alchesay and Moses will not be sent away from Apache or otherwise disturbed without further orders from me."[12]

In early October Hurrle showed up in Tucson. He had resigned from his position and was leaving the territory for the east. While in Tucson he blatantly lied to a federal grand jury and to the editor of the *Arizona Star* about Tiffany. Hurrle's false claims, along with the doings of a few other men who were biased against Tiffany and out to get him, caused the then former agent great embarrassment, inconvenience, and expense. Hurrle later admitted he had lied.

Present-day historians can only speculate about Nock-ay-det-klinne's motives, thoughts, and doings during the few months before the battle. Most of the information that the whites received about him were rumors that were never authenticated. Was Nock-ay-det-klinne's influence declining just prior to the Cibecue battle? Questions such as this one will also never be answered with any certainty. Some conclusions, however, can be reached. That the Cibecue Apaches were at their homes with their crops and families when Carr marched to the Cibecue suggests they were not then ready for war and probably did not know the troops were coming until they were en route. The proximity of the ambush point to their village may be another indicator of their surprise at Carr's visit. The attempted ambush before Carr's arrival at their village shows that the decision to fight was made before Nock-ay-det-klinne's arrest.[13] Certainly the Apaches considered it a major intrusion for outsiders, such as Carr's force, to travel to their village to whisk away an important member of their tribe, someone they relied on for their well-being.

What were the chances of a general uprising during the Cibecue affair? Several knowledgeable people commented on this afterward. One officer said, "The Navajoes showed no sort of purpose to be troublesome nor to join the White Mountain Apaches, nor, indeed, did any other Indians in Arizona or New Mexico."[14] Another stated, "There has never been, nor has there been any likelihood of any general outbreak among the Arizona Indians."[15] During Carr's Court of Inquiry, Captain Egbert reported similar views:

> The White Mountains and their cousins, the Coyoteros were largely effected. These two tribes stand together. In the time of Cochise, the war chief of the Chiricahuas, that tribe was supreme in eastern Arizona, and the White Mountains sent a contingent when he

called on them in his raids on the Tontos and others, but the feeling between White Mountains and Chiricahuas is now, and long has been an unfriendly one. True, Bonito, who is a part Chiricahua, with his band of four men, was engaged in the affair, but Agent Tiffany reported the result of his anxious examination to be that the warlike leaders of the Chiricahuas were all quiet, and their subsequent outbreak is due to other causes. The Tontos, usually unfriendly to the White Mountains, were for a time somewhat inclined to listen to the medicine man, but Mr. Tiffany reported that they had given up the affair, and the official evidence is abundant that they were not in the conflict, and that they offered their services in a body to fight the White Mountains, as soon as the Cibecu affair was known.

As for the Apache Yumas, Apache Mojaves, and especially the San Carlos Indians proper, whole bands of whom had been destroyed in the Crook Wars with the active assistance of the White Mountains, they laughed at the Medicine Man, and have been zealous in the maintenance of peace by forcible measures.

It will therefore be seen that a general war was a most improbable, if not impossible, affair except in the light of a large part of the Indians being engaged on our side, if needed, and that the disturbance, which I have no doubt was real and active, existed only among the White Mountains, and part of the Coyoteros, and Bonito's little band.[16]

In his annual report for 1882 McDowell openly defended Willcox's and Carr's handling of the events after the Cibecue battle. Nevertheless, he believed Willcox had acted illegally by ordering the arrest of Nock-ay-det-klinne. Earlier he had said that in accordance with the Act of Congress of June 10, 1834, C. 161, S. 18, section 2152, Revised Statutes, only the president had the authority to order a military force to make the arrest and "in this case the Agent, instead of sending his Indian police to arrest the medicine man within his own jurisdiction, for any offense of which he was accused, asked the military authorities to do so, and the Department Commander, most unfortunately ordered his troops to make the arrest."[17] Willcox, who had practiced law during a break in his military career, argued with him about its applicability, but could not persuade him to change his mind. McDowell forwarded a report containing his belief to Sherman. However, it was ignored.

Shortly after the Cibecue affair the long-standing spat between Willcox and Carr erupted into a vicious feud. It resulted in Willcox filing charges and specifications against Carr and asking that he be tried by a general court-martial. Many of the charges and specifications concerned the Cibecue affair. A court of inquiry was held to render an opinion about some of the accusations. It found they should not be made the subject of trial by court-martial. Their feud, however, did not end until May 1883.

NOTES

Introduction

1. See Grenville Goodwin, *The Social Organization of the Western Apache*, for a detailed description of the social organization of the Western Apache.

2. In 1875 Cooley established a ranch near present-day Show Low, Arizona. It became a popular stop for travelers. Cooley knew the Apache tongue well.

After Col. Ranald S. Mackenzie arrived at Fort Apache in late September 1881, which will be discussed in a later chapter, Willcox's acting assistant adjutant general (AAAG) warned Mackenzie, "Look out for Cooley—his reputation is not considered good." During the Cibecue aftermath Cooley strongly supported Pedro and his band. National Archives (NA), Record Group (RG) 393, Letters Received (LR), Dept. of Ariz. (DAZ), 1881, No. 3672, Arnold to Mackenzie, Sept. 28, 1881.

3. Many historians of the Apache Wars call the White Mountain Indian Reservation the San Carlos Indian Reservation. Technically, there was no reservation named San Carlos until 1896—ten years after the Apache Wars ended.

On May 26, 1872, Brig. Gen. Oliver Otis Howard, peace commissioner, issued an order that abolished the Camp Grant Reservation (which was set aside for the San Carlos Apaches and the southern White Mountain bands) and extended the boundaries of the White Mountain Indian Reservation to the south and west to embrace a portion of the Camp Grant Reservation. He called this extension the San Carlos Division of the White Mountain Indian Reservation. An executive order was issued on December 14, 1872, enacting Howard's recommendation. It again designated the new addition by that name.

The agency built within the extension to administer its affairs was called the San Carlos Agency, but the reservation remained the White Mountain Indian Reservation until 1896, when it was divided into two separate reservations, the Fort Apache Indian Reservation and the San Carlos Indian Reservation.

Nevertheless, most San Carlos Agency agents of the 1870s and 1880s called the White Mountain Indian Reservation the San Carlos Indian Reservation. The various Interior Department and Indian Bureau officials and military officers used both names. Often the same individual used one name and then the other.

4. The Yavapai were not Apaches; they belonged to the Yuman tribe.

5. Petone was a son or brother of Pedro (present-day historians do not know which).

6. Letter from Maj. A. J. Dallas to Gen. Oliver Otis Howard, Appendix P, Annual Report of the CIA, 1872, as quoted in Davisson, "New Light on the Cibecue Fight: Untangling Apache Identities," 434.

7. NA, Records of the Bureau of Indian Affairs (BIA), LR, 1881, No. 16849, Tiffany to Commissioner of Indian Affairs (CIA), Sept. 9, 1881.

8. In October 1876 about 800 White Mountain Apaches were at the subagency and about 1,000 Cibecue Apaches were at the agency.

9. Annual Report of the CIA to the Secretary of the Interior for 1881, Report of Tiffany, Sept. 6, 1881, 10.

10. NA, BIA, LR, 1881, No. 16849, Tiffany to CIA, Sept. 9, 1881.

11. See Lori Davisson, "New Light on the Cibecue Fight: Untangling Apache Identities," for a detailed discussion about the Cibecue and White Mountain Apaches and the events that caused them to be so affected by Nock-ay-det-klinne.

12. It is impossible to define the term "Coyotero Apache." From the time the first explorers came into present-day Arizona through the nineteenth century the term has been applied to many different Apache groups and bands. During the Apache Wars there was no consistency among officers, the various agency officials, and so on, as to which Apache group was being called Coyotero.

13. See James T. King, *War Eagle: A Life of General Eugene A. Carr*, for an account of the inimical relations between Willcox and Carr.

Chapter 1. Trouble on the Reservation

1. Historians know little about Nock-ay-det-klinne's life prior to the Cibecue troubles. Most information about him is from memoirs of soldiers who were stationed in Arizona during the Apache Wars. Scholars have questioned the accuracy of virtually all this information.

Nock-ay-det-klinne, also known as Bobby-ti-klen-ni, was described in 1875 in a report by Post Surgeon L. Y. Loring from Camp Apache: "Bobby-ti-klen-ni, about fifty years of age, is an honest sober man. He is chief of the largest subtribe which may be accounted for by his generosity and mildness. He controls his people with a steady hand, and is impartial in his dealings with both white man and Indians. At one time he was hostile, but is now well affected towards the Government." L. Y. Loring, Surgeon U.S. Army, Camp Apache, A.T., "Report on Coyotero Apaches," January 11, 1875; quoted in Dan L. Thrapp, *General Crook and the Sierra Madre Adventure*, 4. This may be the most accurate early information on Nock-ay-det-klinne.

2. Tiffany was appointed White Mountain Indian Reservation agent in March 1880. He arrived at San Carlos on June 1 and resigned twenty-five months later, on June 30, 1882. The Indians called him "Big Belly" because of his obesity.

3. John G. Bourke, an army officer who studied Indians while serving as an aide to George Crook, said Nock-ay-det-klinne "drilled the savages in a peculiar dance, the like of which had never been seen among them. The participants, men and women, arranged themselves in files, facing a common center, like the spokes

of a wheel, and while thus dancing hoddentin [the pollen of the tule, a variety of the cattail rush] was thrown upon them in profusion." Bourke, "The Medicine-Men of the Apache," 505.

4. For a biography of Sterling, see Dan L. Thrapp, *Encyclopedia of Frontier Biography*, Albert D. Sterling, 1365–66.

5. Cibicu and Cibecue refer to the same creek. The first is the early spelling; the latter, the present-day spelling.

6. NA, RG 75, BIA, LR, 1881, No. 18075, Incl. 3, Tiffany to Sterling, June 20, 1881.

7. NA, BIA, LR, 1881, No. 12492, Tiffany to CIA, July 11, 1881.

8. Ne-big-ja-gy was also called Ka-clenny and Es-keg-i-slaw.

It was difficult, of course, for outsiders to identify these multinamed Apaches, but the problem was more complex than that. Soldiers and agency officials wrote and spoke the Apaches' names phonetically. Since the Apache tongue contains sounds different from the English language and is difficult for whites to repeat, there were many pronunciations and spellings. To overcome these difficulties some Apaches were given simple Anglo or Spanish-based nicknames. Many are used herein.

9. Annual Report of the CIA to the Secretary of the Interior for 1881, Oct. 24, 1881, 8–9.

10. NA, BIA, LR, 1881, no. 16849, Tiffany to CIA, Sept. 9, 1881.

11. NA, M689, 5843AGO1881, Carr to AAG DAZ, Nov. 2, 1881, App. A, Carr to AG DAZ, Aug. 1, 1881.

12. NA, RG 153, Carr Inquiry, 1882, Exhibit 4, Carr to Tiffany, Aug. 8, 1881.

13. NA, M689, 5843AGO1881, Carr to AAG DAZ, Nov. 2, 1881.

14. Sam Bowman was often employed in various positions by the army in Arizona during the Apache Wars. Britton Davis, an army lieutenant who knew Bowman well, said Bowman "was part Choctaw Indian, a faithful and courageous man." Davis, *The Truth about Geronimo*, 36.

15. NA, RG 153, Trial of Enlisted Men at Fort Grant, A.T., 1881, Trial of Sgt. Dead Shot. Hereafter cited as Trial of Dead Shot.

16. NA, M689, 5843AGO1881, Carr to AAG DAZ, Nov. 2, 1881, App. E, Tiffany to Carr, Aug. 9, 1881.

17. Carr is referring to Alcatraz Island in San Francisco Bay. The island was then a military prison.

In 1884 Gen. George Crook employed the same solution for a similar situation. He arrested the Chiricahua leader, Ka-ya-ten-nae, and shipped him off to Alcatraz for allegedly inciting his followers to defy authorities.

18. NA, M689, 5843AGO1881, Carr to AAG DAZ, Nov. 2, 1881, App. F, Carr to Tiffany, Aug. 10, 1881.

19. When Clum established the San Carlos Subagency in 1875 he hired Ezra Hoag to work there. The Apaches called Hoag "Crooked Nose" because of the shape of his nose. He was well liked by all the Indians.

Hoag got extremely intoxicated at times and gambled heavily at Maxey, a small settlement adjacent to Camp Thomas. In July 1882 an investigation of the management of affairs at the agency implicated him in a ring that was stealing Indian goods from the agency and shipping them to a store owned by Jerome B. Collins in Maxey.

After Hoag and his cohorts were accused of the wrongdoing, acting agent Stanley D. Pangburn notified Hoag that his services were no longer required. Hoag left at once for "Thomas or Mexico." Pangburn said that before he left, Hoag admitted to him that he had been involved in the theft. The investigator could not find that Tiffany, who had been on the East Coast most of the time since the previous December, had any involvement or knowledge of the stealing.

On October 1, about two months after Hoag's departure, the subagency was closed and its buildings abandoned, primarily because of the wrongdoings. The Indians who had received rations from the subagency then moved their camps about seven miles from the agency buildings and received rations from the agency.

20. NA, BIA, LR, 1881, No. 16849, Tiffany to CIA, Sept. 9, 1881.

21. NA, M689, 5843AGO1881, Carr to AAG DAZ, Nov. 2, 1881, App. H, AAAG DAZ to Commanding Officer (CO) Fort Apache, Aug. 7, 1881.

22. Ibid., App. K, Carr to Tiffany, Aug. 13, 1881.

23. NA, BIA, LR, 1881, No. 16849, Incl. 1, Tiffany to Biddle, Aug. 13, 1881.

24. NA, M689, 5843AGO1881, Biddle to Tiffany, Aug. 13, 1881.

25. Indian Bureau inspectors tried to audit each Indian agency at least twice a year.

26. In mid-July 1881 Nana, a Warm Springs Apache, crossed into the United States from Mexico near Fort Quitman, Texas, with his followers. They spent the following five weeks raiding extensively across southern New Mexico Territory. They then returned to Mexico. Stephen H. Lekson provides an excellent account of this raid in *Nana's Raid: Apache Warfare in Southern New Mexico, 1881.*

27. NA, M689, 5843AGO1881, Carr to AAG DAZ, Nov. 2, 1881, App. N, Tiffany to Carr, Aug. 14, 1881.

28. Ibid., App. O, AAG DAZ to Carr, Aug. 13, 1881.

29. In 1881 the summer rains started on July 1. On July 26 the Gila River was no longer fordable. Within a few days a raft was built, on orders of the commander of Camp Thomas, to transport the people who were traveling over the Apache Road across the river. The raft operated at the point where the Gila ran within a couple hundred yards of Camp Thomas.

In mid-August 1881 it rained for eight consecutive days. Four inches of rain were recorded at Fort Apache during that period. The Gila River overflowed its banks, washing away the subagency buildings and all the gardens and crops of the Yuma, Mojave, and Tonto Indians.

30. Another telegraph line ran from Camp Thomas through the subagency to the agency.

31. Although the telegraph line into Fort Apache was down, the post was not totally isolated from the outside world. Thomas Owens, a regular mail carrier between Camp Thomas and Fort Apache, traveled to Apache twice during mid- to late August. On the first trip he left Camp Thomas on August 19, after being delayed a few days by the high waters in the Gila, and arrived at Apache on August 24. On his second trip Owens left Camp Thomas on August 28 and arrived at Fort Apache on the thirtieth—after Carr left for the Cibecue. He traveled with two mules, one of which was a pack mule.

During this period throughout the military hierarchy, telegrams were followed up with a "mail copy." Owens regularly carried the mail copies being sent to and from Fort Apache. However, on his first trip, since the mail had been made up during the morning of August 15, he did not carry a couple of important mail messages, including Biddle's notifying Carr that the two cavalry troops could not reach him.

Some Mormons with a wagon also traveled from Camp Thomas to Fort Apache during mid- to late August. They crossed the Gila River on the nineteenth and arrived at Fort Apache on the twenty-fifth. When they arrived they reported that the troops to be sent to Fort Apache were at Camp Thomas waiting for the waters of the Gila to go down.

32. NA, BIA, LR, 1881, No. 16849, Incl. 1, Tiffany to Carr, Aug. 14, 1881.

33. It is likely that the telegraph line was down only at the Gila River. The commanding officer of Camp Thomas was responsible for maintaining and repairing the line from there to the center of Rocky Canyon, the halfway point between Camp Thomas and Fort Apache. The commanding officer of Fort Apache was responsible for the other half of the line. A repair crew out of Apache had checked their portion of the line shortly after it went down.

34. NA, M689, 5843AGO1881, Biddle to AAG DAZ, Aug. 17, 1881.

35. NA, RG 98, CS, DAZ, 1881, no. 1282, Benjamin to Biddle, Aug. 18, 1881.

36. NA, M689, 5843AGO1881, Biddle to AAG DAZ, Aug. 19, 1881.

37. Welford C. Bridwell was also known as Clay Beauford. While a sergeant in the 5th Cavalry during the Apache campaigns in the winter of 1872–73, he earned the Medal of Honor for outstanding service. He served as chief of the San Carlos police from 1874 to 1877. For a biography, see Thrapp, *Encyclopedia of Frontier Biography*, Bridwell, 168.

38. NA, M689, 5843AGO1881, Biddle to AAG DAZ, Aug. 20, 1881.

39. Ibid.

40. NA, M689, 5843AGO1881, Tiffany to Biddle, Aug. 20, 1881.

41. Ibid., Biddle to AAG DAZ, Aug. 21, 1881.

42. NA, RG 98, CS, DAZ, 1881, No. 1313, Benjamin to Biddle, Aug. 22, 1881.

43. NA, M689, 5843AGO1881, Biddle to AAG DAZ, Aug. 24, 1881.

44. During their meeting Not-chi-clish told Carr that he had lived near Fort Apache for the past fifteen months with the permission of the agent. He said he had not drawn rations during the last ten months and was self-supporting. Hurrle then informed Carr that Santo stayed near Fort Apache during the summer months and returned to the agency for the winter. Not-chi-clish had about 75 people in his band; Santo had about 115.

45. NA, RG 153, Carr Inquiry, 1882. Hereafter cited as Carr Inquiry.

46. NA, M689, 5843AGO1881, Carr to AAG DAZ, Nov. 2, 1881, App. B, Orders No. 125, Aug. 17, 1881.

47. Carr Inquiry.

48. Trial of Dead Shot.

49. Because of a knife slit that disfigured his mouth, Mose was also called "Cut-Mouth Mose." In August 1881 John Bourke said he was "a young Apache [who] . . . used to be one of General Crook's scouts and performed very effective service in the campaign which broke the back-bone of Apache hostility in 1872–3. He was one of the first to be enlisted." Bourke Diary, Vol. 45, 2067.

50. Carr's assumption about the validity of Nock-ay-det-klinne's "Indian police story" was correct. During that period Tiffany did not send his police to see Nock-ay-det-klinne.

51. NA, BIA, LR, 1881, No. 18075, Incl. 3, Sterling to Tiffany, June 20, 1881.

52. NA, BIA, LR, 1881, No. 12492, Tiffany to CIA, July 11, 1881.

53. As late as 1910 Navajos traveled to San Carlos and Fort Apache to trade with the Apaches. They usually exchanged blankets for buckskins and woven baskets.

54. NA, BIA, LR, 1881, No. 16849, Tiffany to CIA, Sept. 9, 1881.

55. At this time Bourke was on detached service pursuing his ethnological interests among several of the Indian tribes in the Southwest. Bourke left Fort Apache for Fort Wingate and Santa Fe on August 29, 1881.

56. Bourke Diary, Vol. 45, 2069.

57. NA, RG 153, Trial of Enlisted Men at Fort Grant, A.T., 1881, Trial of Private No. 15. Hereafter cited as Trial of Pvt. No. 15.

58. Bourke Diary, Vol. 45, 2070.

59. Trial of Dead Shot.

Chapter 2. An Ambush Fails

1. NA, RG 153, Trial of Corporal Skippy, 1881. Hereafter cited as Trial of Skippy. In November 1881 four of Cruse's scouts were court-martialed for mutiny during the Cibecue battle. Nine months later a court of inquiry examined certain charges and specifications that General Willcox filed against Colonel Carr concerning the battle. The documentation from these cases provides much of the material for this chapter and the next.

2. NA, M689, 5843AGO1881, Egbert to AAG DAZ, Dec. 10, 1881.

3. Ibid., Carr to AAG DAZ, Nov. 2, 1881, App. P, Carr to AG DAZ, Aug. 13, 1881.

4. NA, M689, 5845AGO1881, Carr to AAG DAZ, Nov. 2, 1881.

5. The five officers were Captain Hentig, 1st Lts. Carter and William Stanton, 2d Lieutenant Cruse, and Assistant Surgeon McCreery. Hentig was the commander of Troop D; Stanton commanded Troop E; Carter was the regimental quartermaster for the 6th Cavalry and the acting adjutant general with Carr's force; Cruse commanded Company A, Indian scouts; and McCreery was a 1st lieutenant in the Medical Corps. (During this period assistant surgeons held the rank, pay, and emoluments of a 1st lieutenant of cavalry for their first five years of service and that of a captain thereafter.)

Most of Cruse's scouts had enlisted on June 6, 1881. Two were not taken on the trip to arrest Nock-ay-det-klinne (one was in the guardhouse for stealing ammunition, and the other was sick).

Each scout was assigned a number between one and twenty-five. The first five numbers were assigned to the sergeants, the next four to the corporals, and the rest to the privates. Of the sergeants, Mose was number 1, Dead Shot was 2, Dandy Bill was 3, Dandy Jim was 4, and Chapeau was 5. According to Cruse's enlistment report of June 30, 1881, their ages were 40, 42, 26, 28, and 24, respectively.

6. Carr Inquiry, Carr to AG DAZ, Aug. 29, 1881.

7. It was generally known that Nock-ay-det-klinne was to be arrested, although Carr had tried to keep it secret. Carr had received the dispatches from Departmental Headquarters and Tiffany about arresting him on August 15. He had then queried his officers, the interpreter, the scouts, and other "trusted" individuals regarding how to make the arrest. He warned each to keep the knowledge that the medicine man was to be arrested to himself. Two days later Carr wrote, "I learn today that it had got out that the medicine man was to be arrested. I do not [know] how that could be." Carr Inquiry.

8. During this period many soldiers did not wear their uniforms while in the field. John Finerty, a war correspondent for the *Chicago Times*, traveled with the

troops during the Cibecue aftermath. He wrote, "In the field, the United States army dresses nearly 'at will,' and there is no attempt whatever at producing a theatrical effect. So long as a soldier keeps his arms clean, he may dress about as he has a mind to." *Chicago Times*, Oct. 4, 1881.

9. When in the field with a military force the Indian scouts usually traveled on foot, one or two miles ahead of the force, looking for signs of danger. They normally spread out in a fan-shaped pattern. A white officer commanded each Indian scout company and traveled with the scouts, but on horseback.

While marching to the Cibecue the scouts mostly traveled single file. The trail was narrow and Carr did not want to provoke an isolated attack.

10. NA, M689, 5845AGO1881, Carr to AAG DAZ, Nov. 2, 1881.

11. Ibid., 5843AGO1881, Cochran to AAG DAZ, Oct. 6, 1881.

12. Ibid., 394AGO1883, Carr to AG Army, Jan. 6, 1883.

13. Carr Inquiry.

14. Ibid.

15. Carr reported that during his talk with Nock-ay-det-klinne at his village there were "fifteen or twenty male Indians around besides the scouts." NA, M689, 5845AGO1881, Carr to AAG DAZ, Nov. 2, 1881.

During the trials of the Indian scouts and Carr's court of inquiry, Carter's, Cruse's, McCreery's, and Stanton's recollections differed from Carr's. They said many Indian women were present, but only a few male Indians were in sight. During Carr's inquiry McCreery said, "I can only recollect of seeing three [Indian men] outside of the Indian scouts and the medicine man. . . . There were quite a good many squaws." I have used the lesser number here.

16. NA, M689, 5845AGO1881, Carr to AAG DAZ, Nov. 2, 1881.

Chapter 3. The Battle on the Cibecue

1. NA, M689, 394AGO1883, Carr to AG Army, Jan. 6, 1883.

2. Trial of Dead Shot.

3. Carr Inquiry.

4. Ibid.

5. Ibid.

6. NA, M689, 5845AGO1881, Carr to AAG DAZ, Nov. 2, 1881.

7. During Carr's inquiry, Carr asked Major Cochran, "At the last time you heard the officers talking [prior to leaving Apache to arrest Nock-ay-det-klinne], Captain Hentig volunteered to go for him by himself [to make the arrest], with his company?" Cochran replied, "I suppose with his company. He said—I think his remark was in substance this: General, If you think best, I will go for him, but I don't think it is much use; he will probably get out of the way, or something of that sort."

Most officers in Carr's command were surprised that Nock-ay-det-klinne had not taken to the hills before their arrival at his village. In fact, Carr had the command take ten days rations on the trip in anticipation of having to hunt for him.

8. Carr Inquiry.

9. Carter posted thirty-four soldiers for the guard details; however, only about half were at the campsite. The others were to be detailed from Troop E when it arrived.

10. Carr Inquiry.

11. Ibid.

12. Trial of Dead Shot.

13. Ibid.

14. Trial of Pvt. No. 15.

15. In November 1881 Cruse testified that after the Cibecue fight he learned that this Indian was Tobo-ka-sin, a brother of Sanchez.

16. Trial of Dead Shot.

17. Trial of Skippy.

18. Trial of Pvt. No. 15.

19. The version of the Cibecue fight presented in this chapter is based primarily on the accounts of white participants. Cruse's scouts gave a different version of the start of the fight. Their accounts are presented in a later chapter.

20. During Carr's inquiry Carter stated, "We always turn them [the horses] loose [when going into camp]." He was then asked, "Is it not practicable to picket them?" He replied, "It might be for two or three weeks but would not be practicable [if you want] to have anything to go on the next trip. I have served in this department over eight years and in three different regiments, and I have never known these California horses to be picketed out at night unless you were going to start during the night or some emergency of that sort. We habitually graze them from the time we go into camp until we get ready to start the next morning."

21. NA, M689, 5845AGO1881, Carr to AAG DAZ, Nov. 2, 1881.

22. Carr Inquiry.

23. Thomas Cruse, *Apache Days and After*, 116.

24. In May 1883 Cruse wrote a letter to a friend describing the fight. He said, "At the first volley, the sergeant stepped up to the medicine-man and shot him, his son attempted to run in with a pony and was killed; and his squaw grabbed a revolver and attempted to shoot a soldier and was killed by another one." Arizona Historical Society, Gatewood Collection, Box 2, Folder 38, Cruse to Abbot, May 25, 1883.

Carter, in his memoir, *From Yorktown to Santiago with the Sixth U.S. Cavalry*, states that after Nock-ay-det-klinne was shot by the trumpeter, his wife was allowed to pass out of the camp and while doing so she was "chanting a weird death song." He does not mention Nock-ay-det-klinne's son.

Although much was written about the Cibecue battle before May 1883, there was no mention of Nock-ay-det-klinne's wife or son at the fight.

25. Whether Mose stayed loyal only because he was away from the scouts is unknown. During Carr's inquiry Cruse was asked if Mose was acting in good faith when he went ahead to Nock-ay-det-klinne's village before the command arrived. Cruse said he "did not know whether Mose was acting in good faith or not. . . . Taking it all together I felt that they were all most decidedly shaky."

The day after Carr's command returned to Fort Apache, Corydon Cooley, who was then at the fort, sent Mose to Pedro's camp to advise them regarding the troubles. Mose could have deserted at that time but did not.

26. Carr Inquiry.

27. Hentig was a handsome man, about six feet two inches tall. He and his family had moved to Camp Apache in 1875. In summer 1881 he received orders to go east in September for recruiting duty. He sent his family ahead. When Hentig left for the Cibecue (August 29, 1881), he was making his final preparations for his departure from Arizona. He planned to meet his family nine days later in Reading, Pennsylvania. The September 8, 1881, issue of the *Reading Times* said:

The news of the death of Capt. Hentig was concealed from his wife [Laura Hentig] until yesterday. The papers were withheld from her and everything in regard to the massacre was suppressed. Mrs. Hentig, who has relatives, by marriage, of Collector Valentine, of this city, arrived in this city yesterday, when the sad intelligence was for the first time imparted. Up to that time she had been in the best of spirits and expected her husband's arrival in this city that evening. The news of the terrible tragedy, so unexpected, which robbed her of her dear husband, was of course shocking in the extreme. (*Army and Navy Journal*, Sept. 17, 1881)

Hentig turned thirty-nine years old six days before he died. On January 9, 1882, Sen. Samuel B. Maxey of Texas introduced a bill to increase Laura Hentig's monthly pension from $20 (then "the full rate allowed to widows" of captains) to $50. Biddle, Willcox, and Maj. Gen. Irvin McDowell (Willcox's superior) wrote favorably for the increase. Willcox said,

The present legal allowance is entirely inadequate to the support of Mrs. Hentig, who is an invalid and physically and mentally unable to provide for her own support. She has been in hospital at Philadelphia some months for treatment.

It is known that her husband left her nothing. His devotion to his country sealed by his death in the Cibicu massacre presents a peculiar claim on the government and the example of providing for her would stimulate all soldiers in the consecration of life to their country. NA, RG 98, CS, DAZ, 1882, no. 141, Willcox to AG Army through Hq. Div. of Pacific (DP), Jan. 23, 1882

The bill was referred to the Committee on Pensions, which recommended against it. It did not pass.

28. NA, RG 153, Trial of Sgt. Dandy Jim, 1881. Hereafter cited as Trial of Dandy Jim.

29. Condon said several shots were fired by the Indian followers about when Dandy Jim fired. In fact, he could not tell if Dandy Jim fired the first shot of the battle. Condon was no more than 15 feet from Hentig when he was killed. Sgt. Daniel Conn, Troop E, who was detailed on the guard over the pack train, was about fifteen yards from Dandy Jim when he fired at Hentig. His testimony agreed with Condon's, except he said that after Dandy Jim fired at Hentig, "he [Hentig] dropped dead. He never opened his mouth at all." Trial of Dandy Jim.

30. During the trials of the four scouts three members of Carr's command testified that Dead Shot fired at Livingston when he was killed. Two members testified that Dandy Jim shot his rifle toward Sullivan at the instant he was killed.

31. Trial of Dandy Jim.

32. Two weeks after the battle Carr told Tiffany that Sanchez or his men killed Miller.

33. Cruse, *Apache Days and After*, 115.

34. Three soldiers received the Medal of Honor for deeds during the Cibecue battle. Both Carter and Heartery were awarded the medal for their heroism in retrieving Hentig's body and assisting Bird back to cover. The third Medal of Honor was earned by Sgt. Alonzo Bowman for "conspicuous and extraordinary bravery in attacking mutinous scouts." Before the fight Bowman was in charge of

the detail erecting the officer's tents. When the Indian scouts opened fire on the troops he advanced to the edge of the mesa where the scouts had taken position. He helped clear them from the camp, then joined Stanton's troop in the charge to the creek bottom to clear it of hostiles.

35. Trial of Dead Shot. Burton probably mistook Dead Shot for another Indian. Cruse testified that Dead Shot came into camp with him from the opposite direction.

36. NA, M689, 5845AGO1881, Carr to AAG DAZ, Nov. 2, 1881.

37. Carr Inquiry.

38. NA, M689, 5845AGO1881, Carr to AAG DAZ, Nov. 2, 1881.

39. *Army and Navy Journal*, Oct. 8, 1881, 213.

40. Carter, *From Yorktown to Santiago with the Sixth U.S. Cavalry*, 219.

John A. Smith was a sergeant in Troop D at the Cibecue fight. He told Anton Mazzanovich that he killed Nock-ay-det-klinne with the ax. Mazzanovich retold Smith's story in his memoir, *Trailing Geronimo*.

The official reports of the fight do not mention this incident, nor is it mentioned in any of the testimony during the trials of the Indian scouts or Carr's inquiry. However, in mid-September 1881, 2d Lt. Wallis O. Clark, who was not at the fight but was with the participants shortly thereafter, told a newspaper reporter the soldiers found Nock-ay-det-klinne alive after firing the shots into him. He said they then killed him by crushing in his skull with rifles. *New York Herald*, Sept. 21, 1881.

41. Cruse, *Apache Days and After*, 122.

42. Foran was wounded after the initial shooting, while the Indians were firing into Carr's campsite from long range.

43. Carr Inquiry.

44. NA, M689, 5845AGO1881, Carr to AAG DAZ, Nov. 2, 1881.

45. *Chicago Times*, Oct. 4, 1881.

46. Carr Inquiry.

47. Gracias Severiano was born to Mexican parents in Sonora, Mexico. He was captured by Apaches while a child. He grew up with the Apaches and married a Carrizo band Cibecue Apache woman. Since he knew Spanish well and was fluent in the Apache tongue, he sometimes served as an interpreter for the army. He was one of two interpreters Crook took on his expedition into the Sierra Madres of Mexico in 1883.

Charles B. Gatewood was a lieutenant who commanded Indian scouts during the latter years of the Apache Wars. He knew Severiano well. He said Severiano was excitable and nervous and had a lively imagination. See Thrapp, *Encyclopedia of Frontier Biography*, Severiano, 1289.

48. The two wounded soldiers were discharged for disability (Baege on Feb. 4, 1882, and McDonald on Apr. 14, 1882).

49. Carr Inquiry.

50. The Indians were enlisted in scout companies for a six-month period. The "greater part" of the scouts in Company A reenlisted each time. By the time of the Cibecue affair the sergeants and corporals in the company were the older scouts—the scouts who had shown their loyalty over the years.

During Carr's inquiry the court recorder questioned Carter about their loyalty:

> Did you use them against kindred Apaches? Yes, sir, they will kill one another.

In operating against a hostile tribe of Indians, you would select scouts which would be naturally hostile towards them also? I would if I knew the whole tribe was hostile. But I have ordinarily used these same scouts for operating against every body. They have operated against their own people continuously. Some of these scouts had been operating for six years, and I had known some of these scouts as far back as 1877. [I] knew them several years before. They scouted all through New Mexico.

Did you ever know of Indian scouts operating effectively against their own kindred? Yes, sir, on one occasion they killed their mothers and sisters who happened to be out. I asked why they did it, and how they come to do it. And the man who was the head one of them said they had no business to be out there; they ought to be on the reservation drawing their flour and rations, and that they could not stop to see who was in it when they jumped the village.

51. Carter, *From Yorktown to Santiago with the Sixth U.S. Cavalry*, 218.
52. *Chicago Times*, Oct. 4, 1881.

Chapter 4. The Hostilities Continue

1. NA, M689, 5843AGO1881, Cochran to AAG DAZ, Oct. 6, 1881.
2. Ibid.
3. There were three main routes between the Camp Thomas–San Carlos area and Fort Apache at this time. Two were trails; the other was a road. The road was called the Apache Road. From the Gila River valley, it departed from the Camp Thomas–San Carlos Road five miles east of the subagency, crossed the Gila River, ran through the Gila Mountains (in this area the road is now called the Yellow Jacket Road), across the Natanes Plateau, through the Natanes Mountains via a narrow rocky canyon (then known as Rocky Canyon), and then across a plain to the Black River. It crossed the river at the Black River Crossing, then ran across another flat, through Turkey Creek, over Seven-Mile Hill, and through Seven-Mile Canyon to Fort Apache. All wagon traffic to Fort Apache from the south (Camp Thomas and the San Carlos Agency) traveled over it since it was of sufficient width and was maintained for such traffic.

One of the two trails, Paymaster Trail, headed directly north from Camp Thomas. It cut through the Gila Mountains, passed by Paymaster Tank, then turned northwest until it joined the Apache Road. Finerty described it as an "old Indian trail." The cavalry usually used it when moving between Camp Thomas and Fort Apache.

The second trail ran between the agency and Fort Apache. From the agency, it followed the San Carlos River for about eighteen miles and then headed to Rock Spring. Past the spring, it crossed the Black River and then ran to the White River, which it followed to the fort. People traveling between the agency and Fort Apache usually used this trail—unless they were traveling with wagons.

There were no official or proper names for the roads or trails. Most had several names. For instance, the trail that ran from the agency to Fort Apache was called the Apache trail if one was at the agency—or the San Carlos trail if one was at Fort Apache. Sometimes it was referred to as the Apache–San Carlos trail or vice versa. Most other trails in the region were called similarly.

4. NA, M689, 5843AGO1881, Cochran to AAG DAZ, Oct. 6, 1881, App. C, Cochran to CO Thomas, Aug. 31, 1881.

5. NA, M689, 5843AGO1881, Cochran to AAG DAZ, Oct. 6, 1881.

6. Ibid., App. D, Cochran to CO Thomas, Aug. 31, 1881.

7. Barnes was awarded the Medal of Honor for climbing to the top of the mesa and observing and signaling the approach of the troops under such dangerous conditions.

8. NA, M689, 5845AGO1881, Carr to AAG DAZ, Nov. 2, 1881.

9. Gordon was promoted to the rank of captain on the death of Hentig.

10. MacGowan was breveted a major for his gallant service during the attack on the fort.

11. Forty-five civilians were at Fort Apache assisting in its defense.

12. There are no reliable estimates of the number of hostiles that attacked Fort Apache. Hurrle, the interpreter, guessed more than sixty or seventy Indians were engaged in the attack.

13. *Chicago Times*, Oct. 4, 1881.

14. Most of the Indians in Clark's scout company were Eastern White Mountain Apaches.

15. *New York Herald*, Sept. 21, 1881.

16. *Arizona Citizen*, Oct. 30, 1881.

17. It was believed that the Seven-Mile Hill victims who were shot in the head received that shot after they were dead.

18. *Chicago Times*, Oct. 4, 1881.

19. See Thrapp, *Encyclopedia of Frontier Biography*, Eugene through William Middleton, 981–83, for biographies of several members of the Middleton family.

20. *Arizona Gazette*, Sept. 10, 1881.

Chapter 5. Rumors Abound

1. NA, M689, 5216AGO1881, Willcox to McDowell, Sept. 1, 1881.

2. Robert Lincoln was the son of Abraham Lincoln, U.S. president from March 1861 to April 1865.

3. Mickey Free was captured by Apaches at a ranch in southern Arizona when he was a child. He was raised by them, married an Apache woman, and continued to live among them for the rest of his life. During the Apache Wars he served as scout, interpreter, and spy for the military. See Thrapp, *Encyclopedia of Frontier Biography*, Mickey Free, 518.

4. NA, M689, 5843AGO1881, Biddle to AAG DAZ, Sept. 2, 1881.

5. NA, RG 98, Communications Sent (CS), DAZ, 1881, No. 1421, Willcox to AG DP, Sept. 2, 1881.

6. NA, RG 393, Register of Letters Received (RLR), DAZ, 1881, No. 3160, Haskell to HQ DAZ, Sept. 2, 1881.

7. NA, RG 393, LR, DAZ, 1881, No. 3211, Haskell to Willcox, Sept. 3, 1881.

8. *New York Times*, Sept. 4, 1881.

9. NA, BIA, LR, 1881, No. 15869.

10. San Carlos Agency officials learned of the Cibecue fight at 8:00 P.M. on August 31 (an hour before the military learned of it) when "two Indians came across the river" with the news.

11. NA, M689, 5843AGO1881, Biddle to AAG DAZ, Sept. 2, 1881.

12. Several days later a military scouting party moved through Seven-Mile Canyon. It reported that hostiles had been in the canyon and left it well fortified.

13. NA, M689, 5843AGO1881, Biddle to AAG DAZ, Sept. 2, 1881.

14. While Carr was sending Stanton to Camp Thomas with his report on the events in the northern part of the reservation, Haskell, at Camp Thomas, was trying to quickly learn what had happened there. On September 3 he asked Tiffany to send a runner to Fort Apache with a message that told about the troops being sent to the fort and to return with a message containing the particulars of the fight and the state of the soldiers at the fort. Haskell asked that the messenger be instructed to make the round-trip as quickly as possible. Thinking there would be two messengers, he asked Tiffany to "make them fly." NA, BIA, LR, 1881, No. 16849, Incl. 1, Haskell to Tiffany, Sept. 3, 1881.

Tiffany sent only one messenger, and, indeed, he did fly. His journey covered approximately 132 miles through rugged, mountainous country. He left the agency at 9:00 P.M. on September 3 and returned on "the third day" with the dispatches from Apache (probably at 4:00 P.M. on the sixth). Although the Indian runner's feat was incredible, the effort was in vain, since Haskell had received Carr's report via Stanton on August 4.

15. Wilna was twenty-nine miles southeast of Lordsburg, New Mexico, on the Southern Pacific Railroad track.

16. During this period the Atlantic and Pacific Railroad Company was constructing a railroad line from A&P Junction, at present-day Isleta, New Mexico (15 miles south of Albuquerque), to California. On September 10, 1881, its terminus was north of Fort Apache at Sanders, Arizona, and was operational from that point eastward. The line, however, was complete to Navajo, Arizona, thirteen miles farther west, and the terminus was expected to be there within two weeks. It was then partially graded to Bill Williams Mountain, near present-day Williams, Arizona (162 miles west of Navajo).

17. Stein Pass is in the Peloncillo mountain range near the Arizona–New Mexico border, at present-day Stein, New Mexico.

18. NA, M689, 5264AGO1881, McDowell to AG Army, Sept. 5, 1881.

19. The issue of arms and ammunition by the military required the approval of the secretary of war. His approval was limited to arms that were superseded and no longer issued to the army. In this instance, on the application of General Willcox, Lincoln authorized the sale of fifty .50-caliber Sharps or Springfields, with 10,000 cartridges, at each of the following locations: Forts McDowell, Bowie, Grant, and Lowell and Willcox Station. The arms were to be sold to settlers for $15 each and the ammunition at $30 per 1,000 rounds.

20. The military tried to form a scout company composed of Chiricahua Apaches. At first they agreed to serve; however, before they enlisted they changed their minds, saying they were afraid to leave their families. See NA, RG 393, DAZ, HQ in the Field, Telegrams Sent, Sept.–Nov. 1881 (hereafter cited as TS Field HQ), Nos. 163, 164; and NA, RG 393, DAZ, HQ in the Field, Register of Telegrams and Reports Received, Sept.–Oct. 1881 (hereafter cited as RTRR Field HQ), Nos. 120, 139, 176.

21. During the 1880s in Arizona, the infantry usually performed garrison duties and protected the posts while the cavalry was in the field after Indians. General Willcox did not have many infantry companies to spare; Whipple Barracks and Fort Yuma were the only posts garrisoned by two companies. On September 3 he

ordered one of the companies at Whipple Barracks to the reservation (Company F, 12th Infantry). Since Fort Yuma was distant from the Cibecue troubles, both its companies (Company H, 12th Infantry, and Company I, 8th Infantry) were ordered to the front on September 2.

On September 12 McDowell sent 1st Lt. Joseph Garrard with a detachment of ten enlisted men of Battery A, 4th Artillery, to man Fort Yuma until some of its permanent men returned. Battery A was from Fort Point in San Francisco harbor.

Camp Huachuca was placed in a similar situation. Troop G, 6th Cavalry; Company K, 12th Infantry; and Company D, Indian scouts, were stationed at the post. The scout company had left there on August 10 on an extended mission. On September 3 the cavalry troop left for Camp Thomas. On that same day 1st Lt. Joseph Henry Hurst, commander of the infantry company, received orders from General Willcox to leave a guard at the post and take his company to Grant. Hurst left on the fourth; however, before he departed he notified Departmental Head-quarters that he was leaving and that he was the last officer at Huachuca. On the same day he reached Grant, September 6, Departmental Headquarters ordered him to return to Huachuca with his company. Hurst arrived back at the post on the thir-teenth. W. E. Camin, a corporal in Troop G, commanded Huachuca in the interim.

22. NA, RG 98, CS, DAZ, 1881, No. 1434, Willcox to AAG DP, Sept. 2, 1881.

23. Companies B and K, 8th Infantry, from Benicia Barracks and Companies C, D, and F, 8th Infantry, from Angel Island (both installations were in California, close to San Francisco) left for Arizona under the command of Wilkins on September 5. The force, composed of 12 officers and 137 enlisted men, traveled on the same train. Companies C and F debarked at Casa Grande on September 7 and marched to Globe, Arizona. That night the train reached Willcox with the three remaining companies. They were assigned to stations in the area.

Capt. Reuben Frank Bernard and Troop G, 1st Cavalry, left their station, Fort McDermit, Nevada, on September 4. Two days later Capt. Camillo Casatti Cadmus Carr and Troop I, 1st Cavalry, departed from their home post, Fort Halleck, Nevada, under the command of Major Sanford. Sanford's train stopped at Winnemucca, Nevada, and picked up Bernard's troop. The two troops rode to Lathrop, California, and then to Willcox, arriving there on September 10. Sanford's battalion was composed of 6 officers and 83 enlisted men.

24. The Military Department of Arizona included southern California. There-fore, San Diego Barracks was General Willcox's responsibility and the soldiers stationed there were under his command.

Company A, 8th Infantry (2 officers and 31 enlisted men strong), left San Diego Barracks on September 8. It arrived at Fort Lowell two days later.

25. NA, RG 98, CS, DAZ, 1881, No. 1419, Willcox to Sheridan, Sept. 2, 1881.

26. NA, M689, 5843AGO1881, Biddle to AAG DAZ, Sept. 2, 1881.

27. NA, RG 98, CS, DAZ, 1881, No. 1424, AAG DAZ to Biddle, Sept. 2, 1881.

28. Ibid., No. 1418, AAG DAZ to Biddle, Sept. 2, 1881.

29. NA, M689, 5843AGO1881, Biddle to AAG DAZ, Sept. 2, 1881.

30. NA, RG 98, CS, DAZ, 1881, No. 1429, AAG DAZ to Biddle, Sept. 2, 1881.

31. Ibid., No. 1431, AAG DAZ to Biddle, Sept. 2, 1881.

32. NA, RG 98, RLR, DAZ, 1881, No. 3172, Haskell to HQ DAZ, Sept. 3, 1881.

33. NA, RG 98, CS, DAZ, 1881, No. 1461, AAG DAZ to Biddle, Sept. 3, 1881.

34. TS Field HQ, No. 17, Arnold to Biddle, Sept. 4, 1881.

35. Ibid., No. 9, Arnold to Biddle, Sept. 5, 1881.

36. RTRR Field HQ, No. 80, CO Thomas to Arnold, Sept. 6, 1881.

37. About four hours after Biddle left Camp Thomas Stanton and his troop arrived there with Carr's report on the Cibecue battle and the attack on Fort Apache. Stanton's and Biddle's commands did not meet en route since Stanton stayed on the Apache Road while Biddle took Paymaster Trail.

38. This thunderstorm began at Fort Apache shortly before Biddle left Camp Thomas to cross the Gila. Although the lightning quit during the night, the rain continued, with interruptions, until 11:00 A.M. the next day. The fort received 2.3 inches of precipitation from this storm.

39. NA, M689, 5843AGO1881, Biddle to Haskell, Sept. 9, 1881.

Starting on about July 1, 1881, most supplies for Fort Apache came from the south. They were sent to Willcox Station via the Southern Pacific Railroad, then freighted to the Gila River valley and over the Apache Road to the fort. The distance, by road, from Willcox to Fort Apache was one hundred fifty miles. (Previously they had been forwarded to the fort from the northwest—via Whipple Barracks and Fort Verde on the Verde Road.)

The recent storms had washed out portions of the road, making it impassable for the wagons carrying supplies to the fort. It was particularly bad in Rocky Canyon, about forty-one miles from Thomas. The military could have supplied Fort Apache using pack mules, but none were available in the department. Off and on four infantry companies repaired the road. The repair work was started on September 11 and completed on December 8, 1881.

Chapter 6. Confusion and Mystery Reign

1. NA, RG 393, LR, DAZ, 1881, No. 3129, Tiffany to Willcox, Sept. 1, 1881.

2. NA, BIA, LR, 1881, No. 16849, Incl. 1, Tiffany to Benjamin, Sept. 2, 1881. In early September Carr received a report similar to Tiffany's. However, his information placed the hostiles farther east. He sent his information to General Willcox on the fourth: "Hostiles are reported to be all ensconced in rough country north east of Phipps' place and will stay there and fight it out." Carr added, however, that he did not believe it. See TS Field HQ, No. 92, Willcox to Kelton and Pope, Sept. 8, 1881.

3. TS Field HQ, No. 165, Arnold to Tiffany, Sept. 11, 1881.

4. NA, M689, 5843AGO1881, Biddle to AAG DAZ, Sept. 2, 1881.

5. The two scouts, whose names are unknown, were nos. 10 and 14.

6. NA, RG 393, LR, DAZ, 1881, No. 3446, Willcox to Kelton, Sept. 7, 1881.

7. Mackenzie was assigned command of the 4th Regiment of Cavalry on December 15, 1870. In the following years his troops won many victories against hostiles in the western United States and Mexico. By the time of the Cibecue troubles he was highly regarded as a skillful and successful Indian fighter by Generals Sherman and Sheridan.

8. Fort Bayard was seven and a half miles east of Silver City, New Mexico.

9. TS Field HQ, No. 964, Willcox to Pope, Sept. 7, 1881.

10. Bradley was commanding Fort Wingate and the 13th Regiment of Infantry. The force from Wingate did not leave for Fort Apache until September 11—contrary to previous statements by Pope and Sheridan that it had.

11. NA, M689, 5275AGO1881, Sheridan to AG Army, Sept. 6, 1881.

12. Ibid., 5279AGO1881, Sheridan to AG Army, Sept. 6, 1881.

13. The White Mountain Indians are Apaches, not Utes. Although Sheridan mistakenly says they are Utes in this telegram, he had previously called them Apaches.

14. NA, M689, 5360AGO1881, Sheridan to AG Army, Sept. 10, 1881.

15. Ibid., 5364AGO1881, Sheridan to AG Army, Sept. 11, 1881.

16. Ibid., 5389AGO1881, Sheridan to AG Army, Sept. 12, 1881.

17. Ibid., 5274AGO1881, AG Army to McDowell and Sheridan, Sept. 7, 1881.

18. Ibid., 5350AGO1881, AG Army to McDowell, Sept. 10, 1881.

19. Ibid., 5361AGO1881, AG Army to McDowell, Sept. 11, 1881.

20. Fort Craig was on the west bank of the Rio Grande, about thirty miles south of Socorro, New Mexico.

21. NA, M689, 5367AGO1881, AG Army to McDowell, Sept. 12, 1881.

22. Ibid., 5366AGO1881, McDowell to AG Army, Sept. 12, 1881.

23. TS Field HQ, No. 185, Willcox to Mackenzie, Sept. 12, 1881; No. 172, Willcox to Carr, Sept. 11, 1881; and No. 178, Willcox to Price, Sept. 11, 1881.

24. During the six-day period that Willcox did not keep McDowell and Sherman apprised of the situation, Willcox continued to keep General Pope, his counterpart in the Department of New Mexico, informed.

Chapter 7. Anxiety in the High Command

1. During the trip to the front Arnold sent nearly 225 telegrams for Willcox. Most were in support of troop movements and the forthcoming campaign to punish the hostiles. Some directed officers to stations for field duty, ordered medical officers to join certain units, asked for more telegraph operators for the field and for additional Indian scouts, and directed that wagons be obtained for transporting certain supplies and moving infantry units. Others ordered that arrangements be made for shipment of rations, fuel, tents, horses, pack mules, aparejos, grain, and so on, for the soldiers.

2. Finerty wrote a lengthy article for the *Chicago Times*, published on October 4, 1881, that included a detailed description of the march from Camp Thomas to Fort Apache.

Finerty was a veteran war correspondent, having covered the campaign of General Crook against the Sioux in 1876, the campaign of Gen. Nelson Appleton Miles on the Canadian border in 1879, and the Ute uprising in 1879. He had been at the Battle of the Rosebud and on the Sibley Scout and Crook's Starvation March and had seen action at the Battle of Slim Buttes and the Battle of Milk River.

3. On September 29 the *Arizona Miner* reported that the Gila River was again fordable.

4. NA, M689, 5448AGO1881, Sherman to McDowell, Sept. 15, 1881.

5. Ibid., McDowell to Sherman, Sept. 15, 1881.

6. Ibid., Sherman to McDowell, Sept. 16, 1881.

7. Saxton was the chief quartermaster for the Division of the Pacific.

8. NA, M689, 5465AGO1881, McDowell to Sherman, Sept. 16, 1881.

9. NA, M689, 5447AGO1881, Sherman to Sheridan, Sept. 15, 1881.

10. Ibid., Sheridan to Sherman, Sept. 15, 1881.

11. Ibid., Aide-de-Camp Div. of the Missouri to Sherman, Sept. 15, 1881.

12. Ibid., Sherman to Sheridan, Sept. 16, 1881.

13. NA, M689, 5507AGO1881, Sheridan to Sherman, Sept. 16, 1881.

14. Ibid., Sherman to Sheridan, Sept. 17, 1881.

15. Nodeski was an Apache chief whose band was composed of seventy-nine Indians. He may have been a Cibecue Apache but was probably a Tonto. When the Cibecue battle occurred he and his band were living on Cherry Creek, south of the Moody Ranch. On September 4 the Middleton family passed through his camp while traveling to Globe with their rescuers after their ranch was attacked. They found his band friendly. Shortly thereafter Nodeski and his band came in to the agency.

16. During the Cibecue aftermath James Cook was employed by the military as a pack master.

17. NA, BIA, LR, 1881, No. 18075, Incl. 1, Tiffany to Willcox, Sept. 14, 1881.

18. Ibid., Tiffany to Willcox, Sept. 15, 1881.

19. Ibid., Tiffany to Willcox, Sept. 16, 1881.

20. Ibid., Carr to AAG DAZ and to Tiffany, Sept. 12, 1881.

21. NA, RG 393, DAZ, Troops in the District of the Apache, Letters Sent, Sept.–Oct. 1881 (hereafter cited as LS DoAP), No. 10, Carr to Haskell, Sept. 15, 1881.

22. TS Field HQ, Sept.–Nov. 1881, No. 213, Arnold to Pope, Sept. 15, 1881.

23. Both Bonito's and George's bands were from the subagency but were living near Fort Apache on expired passes during the Cibecue troubles. Bonito's band was camped within five miles east of Fort Apache, in Seven-Mile Canyon. George's band was camped about seven miles east of the post, on Turkey Creek.

George and his band were Eastern White Mountain Apaches. George was the principal White Mountain chief. Bonito was a White Mountain chief who, from all indications, married into the Chiricahua tribe.

On June 21, 1881, Bonito had obtained a sixty-day pass at the subagency for himself and his small band to plant corn with George along Eagle Creek, southeast of Fort Apache. A couple of days before the pass expired Carr sent the interpreter, Hurrle, to his camp to learn about him and his followers. Hurrle said his camp was composed of both White Mountain and Chiricahua Apaches. Of the 49 Indians then with him, 21 were Chiricahuas (4 men and 17 women and children).

24. A few days earlier, on September 13, Carr had informed Tiffany that Hurrle thought George's band participated in the killings south of Fort Apache and in the attack on the post.

25. LS DoAP, Carr to Tiffany with copy to Willcox, Sept. 16, 1881.

26. As a result of the Cibecue affair a heliograph network was set up. It was the first such system in Arizona. Its establishment was first suggested on September 4, a few days after the military received word of the Cibecue battle, when Col. John C. Kelton, McDowell's AAG, wrote Willcox, "The mountain-plateau country within which Indian operations are now confined is peculiarly suited to sun-signalling." Kelton strongly suggested "that stations be established to carry on communications by flashes with reflectors." NA, RG 98, RLR, DAZ, 1881, No. 3338, Kelton to HQ DAZ, Sept. 4, 1881.

On September 16, 1st Lt. Frederick King Ward, the acting signal officer for the Department of Arizona, asked Willcox if he should get heliographs and give instructions in them and flags. Arnold replied, "At present no time to arrange for heliograph. Will talk the matter over when you arrive [at Camp Thomas]." TS Field HQ, No. 218, Arnold to Ward, Sept. 16, 1881. After the Cibecue troubles were over Willcox began work on its establishment. In spring and early summer 1882 soldiers in the department were trained in its use. That summer, the system was set up in the field. First Lt. Marion Perry Maus headed the effort. By August 31 the heliograph system connected Forts Grant and Bowie and the military camps on the upper Gila.

About mid-July of that year, however, Willcox had received official notification that he and his regiment (the 12th Infantry) were being transferred out of Arizona. Nevertheless, he proceeded with his plans to add Camp Price, on the south side of the Chiricahua Mountains near the mouth of a canyon now named Price Canyon, to the system. His plan was for a signal party to accompany each moving column of troops. Whenever possible the party would communicate with the heliograph operators on the mountains near the posts and camps.

Crook assumed command of the Department of Arizona on September 4, 1882. Two things caused a quick demise of the system: (1) about two-thirds of the heliograph operators, who had undergone extensive training at Whipple Barracks in its use, were with the 12th Infantry, which had left the department with Willcox; (2) Crook did not wholeheartedly support the heliograph system. After his arrival he notified Maus that he "prefer[red] not to transact any business [by heliograph] except such as relates to Indians and is of an urgent nature." NA, RG 98, CS, DAZ, 1882, No. 2930, Bourke to Maus, Oct. 15, 1882.

27. NA, BIA, LR, 1881, No. 18075, Incl. 1, Tiffany to Sterling, Sept. 17, 1881. Captain Stacey's Company H, 12th Infantry, had arrived at the agency on September 14 replacing 2d Lt. John Nelson Glass's Troop A, 6th Cavalry, which was stationed there September 2.

28. NA, M689, 5488AGO1881, McDowell to Sherman, Sept. 17, 1881.

29. TS Field HQ, No. 233, Willcox to McDowell, Sept. 17, 1881.

30. NA, RG 393, LR, DAZ, 1881, No. 3555, Willcox to Pope, Sept. 17, 1881.

31. TS Field HQ, No. 235, Willcox to Pope, Sept. 17, 1881.

32. NA, M689, 5465AGO1881, Sherman to McDowell, Sept. 17, 1881.

33. NA, RG 393, LR, DAZ, 1881, No. 3555, Willcox to McDowell, Sept. 17, 1881.

34. TS Field HQ, No. 259, Arnold to Carr, Sept. 17, 1881.

35. LS DoAP, Sept.–Oct. 1881, Carr to Arnold, Sept. 17, 1881.

36. TS Field HQ, Sept.–Nov. 1881, No. 239, Arnold to Carr, Sept. 17, 1881.

37. Ibid., No. 237, Willcox to Pope, Sept. 17, 1881.

38. Ibid., No. 238, Willcox to McDowell, Sept. 17, 1881.

39. Ibid., No. 251, Willcox to McDowell, Sept. 18, 1881.

40. NA, M689, 5488AGO1881, Sherman to McDowell, Sept. 19, 1881.

41. Ibid., 5507AGO1881, McDowell to Sherman, Sept. 19, 1881.

42. Ibid., 5507AGO1881, Sherman to McDowell, Sept. 20, 1881.

43. Ibid., 5488AGO1881, Sherman to Sheridan, Sept. 19, 1881.

44. Ibid., 5508AGO1881, Sherman to Sheridan, Sept. 20, 1881.

45. RTRR Field HQ, No. 377, McDowell to Willcox, Sept. 21, 1881.

Chapter 8. The Hostiles Surrender

1. Carr's command was composed of 12 officers, 182 enlisted men, 54 Indians, and 20 civilian employees (packers and guides). Because of a lack of "serviceable horses" he left four troopers at Fort Apache.

Fifty of the Indians, from the Mojave and Yuma tribes, belonged to Gatewood's company; the others were Mose and three other Apaches (probably of Pedro's band).

2. TS Field HQ, No. 265, Carr to Arnold, Sept. 18, 1881.

3. Finerty described the place where Sanchez's village was located: "It is a fine valley, planted to a great extent with Indian corn. . . . The valley is deep and somewhat narrow, the bluffs well wooded, and the water slightly alkaline." *Chicago Times*, Oct. 4, 1881. The village was twelve miles north of the Verde Trail.

4. *Chicago Times*, Oct. 4, 1881.

5. While Carr was at the Cibecue battleground a party of civilians arrived. They were also hunting hostiles. On October 9, 1881, the *Arizona Citizen* reported,

> Frank Middleton, who wet out on an Indian hunt two weeks ago last Tuesday [September 13] with twelve men, returned to Globe on Thursday morning [September 29]. He went to Cherry Creek, the scene of the murder, then to Pleasant Valley, and then to the Cibicu, scouting the country thoroughly as he went. . . . He did not see an Indian or any fresh signs. He found some deserted rancherias, the houses, in which gave evidence of the expectation of the Indians to have a protracted trouble. All the utensils for cooking, working their fields, etc., were piled upon the top of the houses, and covered with rawhides. He found some troops there, who that morning had buried Hentig and the soldiers killed in the fight at that place. . . . The place gave every indication of a hasty retreat on the part of Carr, as cartridge boxes, boxes of horseshoe nails, and the usual supplies of a camp were scattered about in all directions.

6. Finerty went with Tupper's detachment. The region near the junction of the Cibecue and the Black River is so rugged that they could not reach the Black River. Finerty's description of this scouting trip is in the October 4, 1881, *Chicago Times*.

7. LS DoAP, Carr to Arnold, Sept. 24, 1881.

In December 1882 a detachment composed of 1st Lt. William Baird, Acting Assistant Surgeon C. H. Allen, and ten enlisted men went to the Cibecue and disinterred the remains of the soldiers who were killed in the battle. They placed their bones in gunnysacks and brought them back to Fort Apache on pack mules. Their remains were interred in the cemetery at Fort Apache with full military honors. Later Private Livingston's body was taken to Ohio and reburied there.

The military abandoned Fort Apache in the fall of 1922. On February 2, 1932, the remains of the six remaining Cibecue fatalities were disinterred and taken to the Santa Fe National Cemetery for reburial on March 14, 1932. They are located in Section P of the cemetery: Grave 55, Sonderegger; 56, Sullivan; 57, Miller; 58, Hentig; 59, Bird; and 61, Foran.

8. On September 11 Willcox ordered Kerr to bring the 6th Cavalry non-commissioned staff, clerks, and regimental band from Lowell to Apache. Three days later Kerr left Lowell with 33 enlisted men. When he reached Apache on September 20 only 23 of the men were with him. On the night of September 24 he and 18 men joined Carr at his campsite on Cedar Creek, mounted and equipped as troopers (the other five were left at Fort Apache because there were not enough horses). These men remained in the field with Carr until October 13, when Carr arrived back at Fort Apache after completing his field duties.

9. LS DoAP, No. 18, Carr to Arnold, Sept. 24, 1881.

10. NA, M689, 5843AGO1881, Price to AAAG DAZ, Oct. 23, 1881.

11. Ibid.

12. Ibid.

13. While Mills was traveling from Camp Thomas to the agency he was involved in an accident:

> I came down in an ambulance and everything went all right, tho' very dusty until we crossed the Gila River about two miles from here [the agency]. The river was high and very rapid, the driver got about half way over all right, then lost his head, swerving his team to the left and the next minute, ambulance mules and men were up side down in deep water. I jumped clear of it as it went over and had to swim for a minute or two. It looked squally for a time, but we finally struck bottom and by cutting away the harness saved all the mules. Everything I had was of course, wet thro'; but nothing hurt. Letter from Lt. Mills to his mother, Sept. 26, 1881.

14. TS Field HQ, No. 315, Sanford to Arnold, Sept. 21, 1881.

15. NA, RG 393, DAZ, Troops in the District of the Apache, Letters and Telegrams Received (hereafter cited as LTR DoAP), No. 13, Cooley to Carr, Sept. 18, 1881.

16. On September 22 Esketeshelaw and 7 men and 20 women and children came in to Fort Apache from Cooley's Ranch. Three days later another group, 5 men and 22 women and children, arrived at the post. Cochran immediately disarmed this second group and put them in camp with the first.

The second group had left the hostiles' camp on the Black River at the same time as the first. All these Indians, except one, claimed to have not been involved in any of the hostilities. Cochran could not obtain any evidence of their participation. The one Indian who said he had engaged in hostilities was placed in irons and confined in the guardhouse at the fort. The others were soon released.

17. NA, BIA, LR, 1881, No. 18075, Incl. 1, Tiffany to Willcox, Sept. 20, 1881.

18. The five men were chiefs of small Cibecue Apache bands living on Cibecue and Carrizo creeks when the Cibecue battle occurred. Ne-big-ja-gy was Nock-ay-det-klinne's brother. Na-ti-o-tish was certainly at the battle; he came up to Hurrle and talked with him while Carr's column was moving down the Cibecue toward their campsite after arresting Nock-ay-det-klinne.

19. TS Field HQ, No. 297, Arnold to Tiffany, Sept. 21, 1881.

20. NA, M689, 5542AGO1881, McDowell to Sherman, Sept. 21, 1881.

21. TS Field HQ, Willcox to McDowell, Sept. 21, 1881.

22. NA, M689, 5524AGO1881, McDowell to AG Army, Sept. 22, 1881.

23. TS Field HQ, No. 302, Willcox to McDowell, Sept. 21, 1881.

24. The mail copy of the telegram reached Sherman's headquarters two weeks later, on October 5—too late to help Willcox.

25. NA, BIA, LR, 1881, No. 18075, Incl. 2, Tiffany to Willcox, Sept. 24, 1881.

26. Ibid., Sept. 25, 1881.

27. NA, RG 393, LR, DAZ, 1881, No. 3666, Sanford to Arnold, Sept. 27, 1881.

Chapter 9. George and Bonito Are Accused

1. TS Field HQ, No. 287, Arnold to Cochran, Sept. 21, 1881.

2. Of course, the Natchez of Bonito's band was not the Natchez who was a Chiricahua chief and a son of Cochise.

3. TS Field HQ, No. 299, Cochran to Arnold, Sept. 21, 1881.

4. Ibid., Arnold to Tiffany, Sept. 21, 1881.

5. NA, BIA, LR, 1881, No. 18075, Incl. 1, Tiffany to Arnold, Sept. 21, 1881.

6. Ibid., Incl. 2, Tiffany to Hoag, Sept. 23, 1881.

7. NA, M689, 5843AGO1881, Tiffany to Price, Sept. 25, 1881.

8. NA, BIA, LR, 1881, No. 18075, Incl. 2, Tiffany to Willcox, Sept. 24, 1881.

9. NA, RG 393, Letters and Endorsements Sent and Field Orders Issued, Dist. of the Gila, 1881 (hereafter cited as LESFOI), Biddle to Smith, Sept. 24, 1881.

10. TS Field HQ, No. 371, Arnold to Cochran, Sept. 25, 1881.

11. RTRR Field HQ, No. 456, Cochran to Arnold, Sept. 25, 1881.

12. NA, M689, 5843AGO1881.

Chapter 10. Colonel Mackenzie Arrives

1. The first force left Fort Wingate for Fort Apache under the command of Capt. Emory White Clift, 13th Infantry. It reached Zuni, New Mexico, 43 miles from Wingate, on September 14 and was retained there for several days. On the night of the seventeenth, Major Van Horn arrived and assumed command under orders from Mackenzie dated the previous day. On the nineteenth the force resumed its march to Fort Apache, 124 miles away.

2. RTRR Field HQ, No. 389 Mackenzie to Arnold, Sept. 22, 1881.

3. TS Field HQ, No. 318, Arnold to Mackenzie, Sept. 22, 1881.

4. Ibid., No. 332, Willcox to Pope, Sept. 23, 1881.

5. NA, LR, DAZ, 1881, No. 3635, Arnold to Van Horn, Sept. 24, 1881.

6. Ibid., Arnold to Mackenzie, Sept. 25, 1881.

7. *Chicago Times*, Sept. 28, 1881.

8. RTRR Field HQ, No. 468, Mackenzie to Arnold, Sept. 25, 1881.

9. NA, LR, DAZ, 1881, No. 3656, Willcox to Mackenzie, Sept. 25, 1881.

10. RTRR Field HQ, No. 465, Mackenzie to Arnold, Sept. 26, 1881.

11. Ibid., No. 467, Mackenzie to Arnold, Sept. 26, 1881.

12. NA, LR, DAZ, 1881, No. 3665, Arnold to Mackenzie, Sept. 26, 1881.

13. Ibid., Willcox to McDowell, Sept. 26, 1881.

14. NA, M 689, 5600AGO1881, McDowell to AG Army, Sept. 28, 1881.

15. On September 24, 1881, General Willcox had ordered Carr to move his force to the point on the San Carlos–Apache Trail "within thirteen miles [north] of San Carlos, where all trails unite." Carr arrived there on September 27.

16. NA, RG 393, LR, DAZ, 1881, No. 3672, Arnold to Mackenzie, Sept. 28, 1881.

17. RTRR Field HQ, No. 494, Mackenzie to Arnold, Sept. 28, 1881.

18. TS Field HQ, No. 412, Arnold to Mackenzie, Sept. 28, 1881.

19. RTRR Field HQ, No. 513, Mackenzie to Arnold, Sept. 29, 1881.
Mackenzie sent Company H, 13th Infantry, and Troops I and K, 9th Cavalry, to guard the Apache Road.

20. TS Field HQ, No. 417, Arnold to Mackenzie, Sept. 28, 1881.

21. NA, M689, 970AGO1883, Carr to AAAG HQ DAZ in the Field, Nov. 4, 1881.

22. RTRR Field HQ, No. 511, Mackenzie to Arnold, Sept. 29, 1881.

23. TS Field HQ, No. 419, Arnold to Mackenzie, Sept. 29, 1881.

24. RTRR Field HQ, No. 521, Mackenzie to Arnold, Sept. 29, 1881.

25. NA, M689, 5590AGO1881, Sheridan to Drum, Sept. 27, 1881.
26. Ibid., AAG Army to McDowell, Sept. 28, 1881.
27. Ibid.
28. NA, M689, 5640AGO1881, McDowell to Sherman, Sept. 29, 1881.
29. TS Field HQ, No. 432, Arnold to Mackenzie, Sept. 29, 1881.
30. Ibid., No. 428, Mackenzie to Arnold, Sept. 29, 1881.
31. Bernard was appointed provost marshal over the prisoners at the agency on September 27, 1881.
32. NA, RG 393, LR, DAZ, 1881, No. 3714, Arnold to Bernard, Sept. 29, 1881.
33. LTR DoAP, No. 28, Sanford to Carr, Sept. 29, 1881.
34. NA, BIA, LR, 1881, No. 18075, Incl. 2, Tiffany to Willcox, Sept. 29, 1881.
35. TS Field HQ, No. 443, Arnold to Mackenzie, Sept. 29, 1881.
36. NA, M689, 5597AGO1881, Sherman to McDowell, Sept. 29, 1881.

Chapter 11. More Problems for General Willcox

1. NA, M689, 970AGO1883, Carr to AAAG DAZ in the Field, Nov. 4, 1881.
2. NA, BIA, LR, 1881, No. 18075, Incl. 2, Tiffany to Sanford, Sept. 30, 1881.
3. Dandy Jim was a sergeant; Mucheco was a private in Cruse's company.
4. *Weekly Arizona Citizen*, Oct. 9, 1881.
5. The Chiricahua outbreak is thoroughly described in Charles Collins, *The Great Escape: The Apache Outbreak of 1881*.
6. After fleeing the reservation with the Chiricahuas Bonito stayed with them until General Crook traveled to their stronghold in the Sierra Madres in May 1883. Bonito returned to the reservation with Crook and remained peaceful thereafter. He was not sent to Florida in 1886 with the Chiricahuas, probably because he had lived on the reservation for a number of years as a White Mountain Apache.
7. NA, M689, 5725AGO1881, McDowell to AG Army, Oct. 4, 1881.
8. NA, RG 393, LR, DAZ, 1881, No. 3715, Arnold to Mackenzie, Sept. 30, 1881.
9. NA, M689, 5843AGO1881, AAG DAZ to Carr, Oct. 1, 1881.
10. NA, M689, 970AGO1883, Carr to AAAG DAZ in the Field, Nov. 4, 1881.
11. NA, RG 393, LR, DAZ, 1881, No. 3753, Mackenzie to Arnold, Oct. 1, 1881.
Mackenzie sent two copies of this message to Carr. One was wired direct to Carr at the agency. The other was sent to Arnold to be forwarded to Carr. Carr received both copies during the evening of October 1.
12. See Collins, *The Great Escape*, for a detailed discussion of General Willcox's dissatisfaction with Carr's slow response to his order to send troops at once after the Indians who had broken out.
13. TS Field HQ, No. 463, Arnold to Mackenzie, Oct. 1, 1881.
14. RTRR Field HQ, No. 562, Mackenzie to Arnold, Oct. 1, 1881.
15. NA, RG 393, LR, DAZ, 1881, No. 3753, Arnold to Mackenzie, Oct. 1, 1881.
16. RTRR Field HQ, No. 554, Mackenzie to Arnold, Oct. 1, 1881.
17. TS Field HQ, No. 471, Arnold to Mackenzie, Oct. 1, 1881.
18. Ibid., No. 465, Arnold to Mackenzie, Oct. 1, 1881.
19. LESFOI, Biddle to Mackenzie, Oct. 1, 1881.

20. NA, RG 393, LR, DAZ, 1881, No. 3753, Arnold to Mackenzie, Oct. 1, 1881.

21. NA, M689, 5676AGO1881, Willcox to AG Army, Oct. 1, 1881.

22. TS Field HQ, No. 985, Arnold to Mackenzie, Oct. 1, 1881.

23. NA, M689, 5676AGO1881, Willcox to AG Army, Oct. 1, 1881.

24. Ibid., 5675AGO1881, Willcox to AG Army, Oct. 2, 1881.

25. Ibid.

26. LESFOI, Biddle to Mackenzie, Oct. 1, 1881.

27. NA, RG 393, Misc. Records, 1875–89, Telegrams Received, Dist. of the Gila, 1881, Mackenzie to Biddle, Oct. 1, 1881.

28. RTRR Field HQ, No. 576, Mackenzie to Arnold, Oct. 1, 1881.

29. NA, RG 393, LR, DAZ, 1881, No. 3753, Arnold to Mackenzie, Oct. 1, 1881.

30. RTRR Field HQ, No. 564, Mackenzie to Arnold, Oct. 1, 1881.

31. Ibid., No. 3754, Arnold to Hodges, Oct. 2, 1881.

32. Correspondence from Willcox's field headquarters on September 30, two days before Willcox left Camp Thomas, hints that he was then thinking about leaving Thomas. Probably Willcox planned to leave after McDowell told him Mackenzie was in charge of his troops but delayed his departure until troops were sent after the Chiricahuas.

33. Juh was the principal Apache leader during this Chiricahua breakout. See Dan L. Thrapp, *Juh: An Incredible Indian*, and *Encyclopedia of Frontier Biography*, Juh, 753, for biographies.

34. Ibid., No. 3697, Willcox to McDowell, Oct. 3, 1881.

35. TS Field HQ, No. 496, Willcox to Kelton, Oct. 3, 1881.

36. NA, M689, 5676AGO1881, AAG Army to Willcox, Oct. 2, 1881.

37. TS Field HQ, No. 495, Willcox to Burke, Oct. 3, 1881.

38. RTRR Field HQ, No. 581, McDowell to Willcox, Oct. 3, 1881.

39. The scout at the agency was named Dead Shot. He had surrendered on October 1—less than an hour after Sanford had left there with the forty-seven prisoners.

40. TS Field HQ, No. 498, Willcox to Kelton, Oct. 3, 1881.

41. Brayton's Company A, 8th Infantry, was from San Diego Barracks, California. The company had been stationed at Fort Lowell since its arrival there on September 10. On October 3 Brayton brought a detachment of his company to Willcox to help escort the prisoners to Lowell.

Bailey's Company D, 8th Infantry, from Angel Island, California, was stationed at Willcox on arriving there on September 8. The company guarded trains between Willcox and Deming, New Mexico, before escorting the prisoners to Fort Lowell.

Chapter 12. The General Leaves the Field

1. NA, RG 393, LR, DAZ, 1881, No. 3755, Arnold to Mackenzie, Oct. 3, 1881.

2. NA, M689, 5734AGO1881, McDowell to AG Army, Oct. 5, 1881.

3. NA, RG 393, LR, DAZ, 1881, No. 3756, Willcox to Kelton, Oct. 4, 1881.

4. TS Field HQ, No. 509, Arnold to Mackenzie, Oct. 4, 1881.

5. RTRR Field HQ, No. 602, Mackenzie to Arnold, Oct. 4, 1881.

6. NA, M689, 970AGO1883, Carr to AAAG HQ DAZ, Nov. 4, 1881.

7. Ibid.

8. LTR DoAP, No. 54, Mackenzie to Carr, Oct. 4, 1881.

9. NA, RG 393, LR, DAZ, 1881, No. 3756, Arnold to Mackenzie, Oct. 4, 1881.

10. NA, M689, 5675AGO1881, AAG Army to Willcox, Oct. 3, 1881.

11. Mackenzie's views were, in fact, taken after Willcox received McDowell's telegram of September 30.

12. NA, M689, 5725AGO1881, McDowell to AG Army, Oct. 4, 1881.

13. Ibid., 5734AGO1881, McDowell to AG Army, Oct. 5, 1881.

14. TS Field HQ, No. 533, Willcox to AAG DP, Oct. 5, 1881.

15. Ibid., No. 552, Arnold to Mackenzie, Oct. 5, 1881.

16. NA, M689, 5725AGO1881, Sherman to McDowell, Oct. 5, 1881.

17. NA, RG 393, LR, DAZ, 1881, No. 3786, Willcox to President of United States, Oct. 6, 1881.

18. NA, M689, 5778AGO1881, Sherman to President of United States, Oct. 7, 1881.

19. Ibid., 5887AGO1881, AG War Dept. to Willcox, Oct. 17, 1881.

20. Ibid., 5756AGO1881, Mackenzie to AG Army, Oct. 6, 1881.

21. Ibid., 5789AGO1881, AAG Army to McDowell, Oct. 10, 1881.

22. RTRR Field HQ, No. 668, AAG DP to Willcox, Oct. 7, 1881.

23. TS Field HQ, No. 563, McDowell to AAG DP, Oct. 7, 1881.

24. NA, M689, 5916AGO1881, McDowell to AG Army, Oct. 17, 1881.

25. *Weekly Arizona Citizen*, Oct. 30, 1881.

26. NA, RG 393, Letters, Telegrams & Endorsements Sent by the Hq. for U.S. Troops Operating Against the Chiricahua Indians at Willcox, Arizona Territory, Oct. 1881, Haskell to Wagner, Oct. 6, 1881.

27. TS Field HQ, No. 731, Mackenzie to Arnold, Oct 12, 1881.

28. NA, M689, 4327AGO1881, Field Orders No. 32.

29. Pope issued Standing Order 216 on October 22, 1881. The order exchanged the stations of the regiments of the 4th Cavalry (headquartered at Fort Riley, Kan.) and the 9th Cavalry (stationed at Santa Fe, New Mex.). Pope had been planning to transfer the 9th Cavalry, as well as the 15th Infantry. A month before he issued the order, he said,

> These two regiments have for several years been almost continuously in the field, the greater part of the time in harassing and wearisome pursuit of small bands of Indians who infest the mountains of Southern New Mexico and Mexico, and are, therefore, much run down in every way. They need rest and recuperation, and I trust it will be in my power this autumn to replace them at their stations by fresh troops, and bring them into posts where they can have the opportunity not only to rest, but to re-establish discipline and tactical knowledge, which they have been considerably impaired by the service they have had to perform for a number of years past. Report of the Secretary of War, 1881, Report of Brigadier General Pope, Sept. 22, 1881, 453.

Mackenzie assumed command of the District of New Mexico on October 30, 1881—an assignment that was not unexpected. Col. Edward Hatch, commander of the 9th Cavalry, was the preceding commander of the district.

30. NA, M 1088, 4914DNM1881, Lieutenant Willcox to General Willcox, Dec. 1, 1881.

Chapter 13. Find the "Guilty" Apaches!

1. Scouts 8, 10, and 14 belonged to Not-chi-clish's band. All his band, except four men, had come into the subagency shortly after learning of the Cibecue fight. Scout 8 was a corporal and Scouts 10 and 14 were privates in Cruse's mutinous company.

2. The two scouts were enlisted in Company C, Indian scouts, per Orders No. 15, Field Hq. DAZ, Sept. 20, 1881.

3. During Skippy's court-martial Biddle was asked if Skippy was sent on any duty while at Camp Thomas. He replied, "I believe he was sent out to carry a message. Performed it very well and came back." A couple of Carr's men, including one who said he knew Skippy well, testified that they saw Skippy firing at the troops with the other scouts at the start of the Cibecue battle. Cruse said, "He [Skippy] crossed the creek [going into Carr's campsite] with me. I noticed him especially because he is always getting off laughable things and in crossing made several remarks which drew my attention and he came on into camp following me." Skippy testified that he was sick the day of the battle and did not come into Carr's camp. Trial of Skippy.

4. The military paid a reward of $30 for Dead Shot's apprehension.

5. RTRR Field HQ, No. 680, Mackenzie to Arnold, Oct. 9, 1881.

6. LS DoAP, No. 35, Carr to Gatewood, Oct. 1, 1881.

7. LESFOI, Field Orders No. 3, Oct. 6, 1881.

8. RTTR Field HQ, No. 574, Mackenzie to Arnold, Sept. 30, 1881.

9. LTR DoAP, No. 126, Mackenzie to Carr, Oct. 13, 1881.

10. Esketeshelaw was the old man who was the former chief of George's band and had come in to Cooley's Ranch from the hostiles' camp on the Black River. He was arrested for being with the hostiles at the Black River.

11. NA, BIA, LR, 1881, No. 21916, Tiffany to CIA, Dec. 6, 1881.

12. NA, RG 98, RLR, DAZ, 1881, No. 4581, Carr to HQ DAZ, Dec. 7, 1881.

13. NA, M689, 5592AGO1881, AAG War Dept. to McDowell, Sept. 28, 1881.

14. NA, BIA, LR, 1881, No. 21407, Tiffany to CIA, Nov. 28, 1881.

15. TS Field HQ, No. 907, Willcox to AAG DP, Nov. 9, 1881.

16. NA, RG 98, CS, DAZ, 1881, No. 1989, Willcox to AG DP, Nov. 17, 1881.

17. NA, M689, 5843AGO1881, Stacey to AAG DAZ, Dec. 4, 1881.

18. Ibid., Brayton to AAG DAZ, Dec. 14, 1881.

19. NA, RG 98, CS, DAZ, 1881, No. 2215, Willcox to AG DP, Dec. 20, 1881.

20. See NA, M689, 5843AGO1881, Egbert to AAG DAZ, Dec. 10, 1881.

21. Egbert listed the names of the twenty-one Indians and their bands in his report.

22. Egbert also gave the names of most these Indians and their bands in his report. He said the small band of outlaws was composed of Mosby, Mazill, Oohell, Skippy, Gar, and Johnson. During Carr's inquiry Egbert questioned Carter about the White Mountain Apaches. They briefly discussed a few of these outlaws:

> You say you have known them [the scouts] to go against their own people. Did you ever know the White Mountain Indians to break out before this time? They have not broken out as a band that I know of since I have been down here, but they have had a great many bad Indians amongst them, and they have always helped to capture and bring them in, and frequently have been paid to kill and bring their heads in.

Were they not looked upon as outlaws? Yes, sir, but they all live together and the others will work like dogs to feed them.

Were they not looked upon as outlaws by the rest of the tribe? You can't get them to tell on them. When an Indian kills another in camp, they will generally kill him if they don't run away, and they generally return in a year and live with them. That was the way with Mosby and Gar, both of whom were outlaws and murderers. Gar having engaged in the killing of Mazill, one of his own confederates who had been with him in all his difficulties.

Don't you understand that Gar, Mazill and one or two others were looked upon by the tribe as being outlaws and did not belong to any of the other small tribes? They are generally looked upon as the young bloods. Drink all the tiswin [*sic*] they can get.

Many years later Cruse said Mosby was a sergeant in his scout company from December 1880 to May 1881. Cruse said, "I thought I would have to shoot him several times. I busted him." Regarding Gar, he said, "Gar died true to character. Great woman's man, always running off some squaw or girl. Indian police finally sent good looking girl out where he was supposed to be, he appeared promptly and proceeded to cohabit—the police find while in the act and killed him. He was a corker." Gar had threatened to kill Lieutenants Gatewood and Cruse and others. Arizona Historical Society, MS 282, Box 10, Folder 162, Letter 179.

23. In August 1882 Cochran described several members of Pedro's band. He said Pedro "was very much respected by the garrison people and by the white people—settlers in the country and by the Indians. He was quite an old man and quite infirm, very hard to hear, almost deaf." Uclenny was described as "a young man who had been a scout formerly but considered peaceable. . . . He was a very popular man with the tribe." He was a sub-chief. Cochran thought "he was next to Pedro" and that he was Pedro's "natural successor." And he described Bottalish as "a very quiet Indian [who] seemed to desire to remain at peace with everybody [and] expressed himself that way often." He thought Bottalish was popular with everyone. Carr Inquiry.

In 1871 Bourke found Alchesay was "as faithful as an Irish hound." Thrapp, *Encyclopedia of Frontier Biography*, Alchisay, 12. Ten years later, in August 1881, he described him as "a tall, handsome and finely formed Indian, formerly the fastest runner in the tribe, and one of General Crook's scouts [during the early 1870's]." Bourke Diary, Vol. 45, 2069.

Alchesay earned the Medal of Honor while serving as a scout in Crook's 1872–73 campaign to drive the Indians living in the wilderness of central Arizona onto reservations. As the 1st sergeant of Company A, Indian scouts, he participated in the grueling 1879–80 campaign against Victorio. When the company returned to Fort Apache from the campaign Alchesay did not reenlist. During the Geronimo campaign, several years after the Cibecue affair, he again served faithfully under Crook. Alchesay was a son or nephew of Pedro (present-day historians do not know which).

24. Carr Inquiry, Letter of Captain MacGowan, Dec. 11, 1881.

25. NA, M689, 5843AGO1881, Egbert to AAG DAZ, Dec. 10, 1881.

26. The Dry Tortugas are a small group of islands of Florida. They are seventy-one miles, by boat, west of Key West, the westernmost island of the Florida Keys. The Dry Tortugas served as a Union military prison during the U.S. Civil War.

27. NA, M689, 5843AGO1881, Egbert to AAG DAZ, Dec. 10, 1881.

28. Ibid., Kirkwood to Lincoln, Oct. 10, 1881, 3d Endorsement, Willcox, Dec. 13, 1881.

29. NA, RG 98, RLR, DAZ, 1881, No. 4858, Force to HQ DAZ, Dec. 20, 1881.

30. NA, M689, 5843AGO1881, AAG DP to Willcox, Dec. 25, 1881.

31. NA, RG 98, CS, DAZ, 1881, No. 2257, Willcox to AG DP, Dec. 26, 1881.

32. NA, M689, 5843AGO1881, Kirkwood to Lincoln, Oct. 10, 1881, 4th Endorsement, McDowell, Dec. 26, 1881.

33. Ibid., 406AGO1882, Egbert to AAG DAZ, Jan. 10, 1882.

34. NA, RG 98, CS, DAZ, 1882, No. 73, Willcox to AG DP, Jan. 11, 1882.

35. NA, BIA, LR, 1881, No. 20507, Carr to AAAG DAZ, Nov. 5, 1881. Tiffany was upset about the expedition. On November 10 he reported, "Gatewood's scouts killed two old men, one a cripple, one boy and one man in Cibicu while scouting, they were peaceable and gathering remnant of corn raised this year." About a month later he said, "The scouts tell me today, that they killed the old cripple, one boy fourteen years old and four old women and took one women and one child into Fort Apache." NA, BIA, LR, 1881, No. 20507, Tiffany to Willcox, Nov. 10, 1881; and No. 21916, Tiffany to CIA, Dec. 6, 1881.

During this period Willcox kept the peace lines in effect. He said they would be removed the moment the renegade scouts, who he believed were in the White Mountains, were secured. Tiffany was sure the scouts were being harbored by Pedro's band; hence he thought the peace lines were useless. Citing Dravo's and Gatewood's scout, he said, "As my peaceable Indians are killed when across that line, I cannot let any of my Indians cross it." NA, BIA, LR, 1881, No. 21916, Tiffany to Willcox, Dec. 5, 1881.

Tiffany pleaded with Willcox to discontinue the lines. He even brought the matter to the attention of the commissioner of Indian affairs. On December 15, 1881, they were removed.

36. RTRR Field HQ, No. 854, Chaffee to Arnold, Oct. 27, 1881.

37. Ibid., No. 978, Chaffee to Arnold, Nov. 10, 1881.

38. Ibid., No. 982, Willcox to Arnold, Nov. 11, 1881.

39. Ibid., No. 1006, Carr to Arnold, Nov. 13, 1881.

40. NA, RG 98, RLR, DAZ, 1881, No. 4333, Carr to HQ DAZ, Nov. 19, 1881.

41. NA, RG 98, CS, DAZ, 1881, No. 2164, Smith to Carr, Nov. 22, 1881.

42. NA, BIA, LR, 1881, No. 21916, Tiffany to CIA, Dec. 6, 1881.

43. Ibid., No. 4581, Carr to HQ DAZ, Dec. 7, 1881.

44. NA, RG 98, RLR, DAZ, 1881, No. 4941, Tiffany to HQ DAZ, Dec. 9, 1881.

Chapter 14. General Willcox Is Transferred

1. NA, M689, 853AGO1882, Tiffany to Price, Jan. 20, 1882.

2. Ibid., Price to Kirkwood, Jan. 25, 1882.

3. NA, RG 98, CS, DAZ, 1882, No. 219, Willcox to AG DP, Feb. 3, 1882.

4. NA, M689, 1665AGO1882, Foulk to AAG DAZ, Mar. 20, 1882.

5. *Arizona Daily Star*, Mar. 3, 1882.

6. Ibid., Mar. 4, 1881.

7. NA, M689, 1665AGO1882, Foulk to AAG DAZ, Mar. 20, 1882.

8. Cruse, *Apache Days and After*, 139.

9. During this period Tiffany was on a trip to the East Coast. Dr. Pangburn had been the White Mountain Reservation physician since 1876.

10. NA, RG 98, CS, DAZ, 1882, No. 273, Pangburn to Madden, Feb. 7, 1882.

11. Willcox offered to pay Scout 11's captors the standing reward of $30. It was probably paid.

12. General Court-Martial Orders No. 9, Series 1882, Dept. of Ariz.

13. *Arizona Daily Star*, Apr. 4, 1882.

14. Tiffany was never a colonel in the military. Sherman was using the rank as an honorary, nonmilitary title.

15. NA, M348, C12527, 1882, Sherman to Kirkwood, Apr. 4, 1882.

16. Ibid., Kirkwood to Price, Apr. 6, 1882.

17. The four prisoners who escaped from the San Carlos guardhouse were Gar, Choclan, Arshay, and Inda Beshashe. George was one of the eleven who did not escape.

18. About five months before the Chiricahua's 1882 raid, on November 28, 1881, Chaffee reported that Dravo's scouts had killed Na-ti-o-tish, his two brothers, and a man of Indaschin's band. The report was incorrect. Neither Na-ti-o-tish nor his brothers had been killed.

19. Sherman had been at the agency visiting Tiffany two weeks before the Chiricahuas raided it (on April 4 and 5).

20. NA, RG 98, CS, DAZ, 1882, No. 1739, Willcox to AG Army through Hq. DP, May 30, 1882.

21. An Indian policeman recognized four of the hostiles who attacked Colvig and the policemen. They were Na-ti-o-tish, his two brothers, and Arshay.

22. Davis, *The Truth about Geronimo*, 10.

23. NA, RG 393, LR, DAZ, 1882, No. 4043, Biddle to Brackett, July 25, 1882.

24. Ibid., No. 4205, Evans to Brackett, Aug. 1, 1882.

25. NA, M711, 3351AGO1882, General Orders No. 78, 1882.

26. NA, RG 98, CS, DAZ, 1882, No. 2152, Willcox through Hq. DP to AG Army, July 21, 1882.

27. Ibid.

28. NA, M689, 3432AGO1882, Sherman to Secretary of War, Aug. 2, 1882. Although the Cibecue troubles and the troubles thereafter assured Willcox's transfer out of Arizona, he and his regiment were expected to rotate out of the territory, as a routine, planned action, during 1882. The transfer took place about when expected—early in the fiscal year (which started July 1).

29. General Orders No. 105, Aug. 29, 1882.

Willcox's new position was of lesser stature. In his old position he had commanded the Department of Arizona according to his brevet rank of major general; in his new job he reverted to commanding the 12th Infantry in accordance with his actual rank of colonel.

In the Department of the East Colonel Willcox was stationed at Madison Barracks, New York. About four years later, on October 13, 1886, he was promoted to brigadier general and assumed command of the Department of the Missouri. He retired six months later, on April 16, 1887.

30. Report of Secretary of War, 1882, Report of Brevet Major General O. B. Willcox, Aug. 31, 1882, 146.

Chapter 15. General Crook Takes Over

1. Crook had previously served as commander of the Department of Arizona (from June 4, 1871, to March 22, 1875).

2. Bourke described Pedro at the meeting. He said, "Pedro, who had always been a firm friend of the whites, was now old and decrepit, and so deaf that he had to employ an ear-trumpet." Bourke, *On the Border with Crook*, 435.

3. Captain Randall was stationed at Camp Apache during Crook's first assignment as commander of the Department of Arizona. The Apaches liked and respected Randall.

4. Crook's report of his trip, including the minutes of his meetings with the Indians, is at NA, BIA, LR, 1882, No. 19337, Crook to AG DP, Sept. 28, 1882. Only the Indian testimony concerning the Cibecue affair is quoted herein.

5. About a month before Crook assumed command of the Department of Arizona Willcox had reported there was a "strong probability of peace [in the territory] with good management on the reservation which Agent Pangburn reports all quiet." NA, RG 98, CS, DAZ, 1882, No. 2232, Willcox to AG DP, July 31, 1882.

6. NA, RG 98, CS, DAZ, 1882, No. 2780, Crook to AG DP, Sept. 28, 1882. A few days after Crook submitted his report on his visit to the Apaches he had his AAAG issue General Orders No. 43. In the orders he said, "The commanding general, after making a thorough and exhaustive examination among the Indians of the eastern and southern part of this Territory, regrets to say that he finds among them a general feeling of distrust and want of confidence in the whites, especially the soldiery; and also that much dissatisfaction, dangerous to the peace of the country, exists among them." (General Orders No. 43, Hq. Dept. of AZ, Whipple Barracks, Oct. 5, 1882).

Of course "the soldiery" was the 6th Cavalry and 12th Infantry. Many years later Thomas Cruse wrote to Charles Gatewood's son, "General Crook did not have any use whatsoever for any of our regiment [the 6th Cavalry]—Gatewood included" (Arizona Historical Society, MS 282, Box 10, Folder 162, Letter 179).

7. *Arizona Daily Star*, Oct. 7, 1882.

8. Z. L. Tidball was the U.S. marshal for Arizona.

9. NA, RG 98, CS, DAZ, 1882, No. 3277, Crook to Zabriskie, Oct. 8, 1882.

10. A memorandum of Crook's meeting is in the Report of the Secretary of War, 1883, Report of Brigadier General George Crook, Sept. 27, 1883, App. C.

11. NA, RG 98, CS, DAZ, 1883, No. 1318, Crook to AAG DP, Nov. 3, 1883.

12. NA, RG 98, CS, DAZ, 1884, No. 656, Crook to AAAG DP, May 24, 1884.

13. W. H. Wharfield, *Cibicu Creek Fight in Arizona: 1881*, 33 fn. 3.

14. NA, RG 393, DAZ, Misc. Records, Gatewood to Crawford, Mar. 1, 1884.

15. For a biography of Alchesay, see Thrapp, *Encyclopedia of Frontier Biography*, Alchisay, 12–13.

Chapter 16. Conclusion

1. NA, RG 98, CS, DAZ, 1881, No. 2195, Willcox to AAG DP, Oct. 12, 1881.

2. Report of the Secretary of War, 1881, Report of Major General McDowell, Oct. 14, 1881, 140.

3. Several period messages and reports and one memoir mention a trouble-maker. Carr Inquiry, Exhibit 24, contains several documents that discuss malicious rumors being spread among the Cibecue and White Mountain Indians. See also NA, M689, 5843AGO1881, Tiffany to Biddle, Aug. 20, 1881; and Thomas E. Farish, *History of Arizona*, 3:336–37.

4. See Thrapp, *General Crook and the Sierra Madre Adventure*, 20–22; and NA, M689, 5845AGO1881, Carr to AAG DAZ, Nov. 2, 1881.

5. Interview of Seiber by a reporter for the *Solomonville Bulletin* as quoted in the *Arizona Enterprise*, May 12, 1892.

6. NA, M689, 5843AGO1881, Tiffany to Biddle, Aug. 20, 1881.

7. Ibid., 394AGO1883, Carr to AG Army, Jan. 6, 1883.

8. Hurrle made $13 a month as a private in the army. Initially, he received $75 a month as interpreter at Fort Apache. On September 24, 1881, his salary was increased to $100 per month.

9. NA, RG 98, CS, DAZ, 1882, No. 2770, Bourke to CO Fort Apache, Sept. 25, 1882.

10. NA, RG 393, LR, DAZ, 1882, No. 5639, Schofield to Bourke, Sept. 25, 1882.

11. Ibid., No. 5640, Hurrle to Crook, Sept. 26, 1882.

12. NA, RG 98, CS, DAZ, 1882, No. 2771, Crook to CO Fort Apache, Sept. 26, 1882.

13. During the trial of Dead Shot Carter was asked, "From your knowledge do you consider this outbreak spontaneous on the arrest of the medicine man or preconcerted?" He answered, "I do not think it was spontaneous on the arrest of the medicine man as it was some time subsequent to his arrest that the outbreak took place. The medicine man surrendered in the most peaceable manner. My opinion of the outbreak is that after having failed to get us into the cañon below the camp their next plan was to get into the midst of our camp by following the guard in and jump us while the men were scattered about preparing the camp. General Carr had only given permission for the medicine man's family to accompany him and the others knew they had no right in the camp. I believe the fight was immediately precipitated by ordering them out, but think that the order being given at the time was all that kept a great many more from being killed."

14. Report of the Secretary of War, 1881. Report of Brigadier General Pope, Sept. 22, 1881, 121.

15. The *San Francisco Examiner* as quoted in the *Tombstone Epitaph*, Nov. 3, 1881.

16. Carr Inquiry.

17. NA, M689, 5843AGO1881, Kirkwood to Lincoln, Oct. 10, 1881, 4th Endorsement, McDowell, Dec. 26, 1881.

BIBLIOGRAPHY

Archives

NATIONAL ARCHIVES AND RECORDS ADMINISTRATION, WASHINGTON, D.C.

Letters Sent by the Office of Indian Affairs, 1824–81, M21, Roll 159, Letters Relating to Misc. Subjects, October 16, 1880–January 5, 1882.

Report Books of the Office of Indian Affairs, 1838–85: M348, Roll 42, Vol. 42, April 13–July 24, 1882.

Returns from U.S. Military Posts, 1800–1916, M617: Forts Apache, Ariz., May 1870–December 1887, Roll 33; Bidwell, Calif., January 1880–October 1893, Roll 113; Bowie, Ariz., July 1862–December 1882, Roll 129, Grant, Ariz., January 1875–December 1894, Roll 415; Halleck, Nev., January 1876–December 1886, Roll 440; Huachuca, Ariz., March 1877–December 1888, Roll 490; Lowell, Ariz., January 1878–March 1891, Roll 654; McDermit, Nev., January 1876–July 1889, Roll 667; Thomas, Ariz., August 1876–January 1891, Roll 1265; Whipple Barracks, Ariz., January 1875–December 1886, Roll 1426; Wingate, New Mex., January 1872–December 1882, Roll 1449; Yuma, Calif., January 1877–May 1885, Roll 1490.

Returns from Regular Army Infantry Units, June 1821–December 1916, M665: 8th Infantry, January 1874–December 1882, Roll 94; 12th Infantry, January 1876–December 1885, Roll 137; 13th Infantry, January 1877–December 1886, Roll 146; 15th Infantry, January 1881–December 1889, Roll 167.

Letters Received by the Office of the AG, Main Series, 1881–89, M689: 4327AGO1881, Rolls 36–39; 3432AGO1882, Roll 117.

Registers of Letters Received by the Office of the AG, Main Series, 1881–89, M711: 1881, Vol. 57(pt.) (3700–6888), Roll 72; 1882, Vol. 58(pt.) (1–3100), Roll 73; 1882, Vol. 58(pt.) (3101–5969), Roll 74.

Returns of Regular Cavalry Regiments, 1833–1916, M744: 1st Cavalry, 1877–86, Roll 7; 4th Cavalry, 1877–83, Roll 43; 6th Cavalry, 1875–80, Roll 63, and 1881–85, Roll 64; 9th Cavalry, 1881–87, Roll 89.

Indexes to Letters Received by the Office of the AG, Main Series, 1846, 1861–89, M725, Vols. 24–26, Name Indexes, 1881–83, Roll 7.

Letters Received by Hq. Dist. of New Mexico, September 1865–August 1890, M1088: July–December 1880, 2103–4519, Roll 41; January–April 1881, 5–1544, Roll 42; May–October 1881, 1568–4364, Roll 43; November–December 1881, 4368–5690, Roll 44; January–February 1882, 1–1037, Roll 45; March–April 1882, 1044–1895, Roll 46.

Records of the Office of the Secretary of the Interior, RG 48, Selected Documents Relating to the San Carlos Indian Agency 1881–86, Indian Division, Letters Received, 1881, 1882, 1883.

Records of the Bureau of Indian Affairs, RG 75, Selected Documents Relating to the San Carlos Indian Agency 1881–86, Indian Division, Letters Received, 1881, 1882, 1883.

Records of the AG's Office, RG 94, Document File 4327–1881, Papers Relating to Apache Outbreak of 1881 and Subsequent Events, Including Skirmishes, Cibicu Fight, Trial of Indian Deserters; Document File 1066–1883, Indian Activities; Muster Rolls, Company A, Apache Indian Scouts, 1881, June 30–August 31 and August 31–September 30.

Records of the War Department, U.S. Army Commands, RG 98, Dept. of Arizona, Communications Sent, 1879–86, January 2, 1879–December 31, 1880, Roll 1; January 1, 1881–December 31, 1881, Roll 2; January 1, 1882–December 31, 1882, Roll 3; January 1, 1883–December 31, 1883, Roll 4.

Records of the Judge Advocate General's Office, RG 153, Court-Martial Case Files, Trial of Enlisted Men at Fort Grant, A.T., 1881; Court of Inquiry of Col. Eugene A. Carr at Whipple Barracks, A.T., 1882.

Records of the U.S. Regular Mobile Units, 1821–1942, RG 391, Ninth Cavalry, Entries 921–23.

Records of U.S. Army Continental Commands, 1821–1920, RG 393, Pt. 1, Dept. of Arizona, 1870–93, Entry 180, Register of Letters Received, 1881; Entry 181, Letters Received, 1881 and 1882; Entry 187, Manuscript Reports, 1880–85; Entry 203, Misc. Routine Reports Received, 1880–88; Entry 204, Misc. Records, 1875–89; Entry 208, Hq. in the Field, Telegrams Sent, September 1881–November 1881; Entry 209, Hq. in the Field, Register of Telegrams and Reports Received, September–October 1881; Entry 241, Troops in the Dist. of the Apache, 1881, Letters Sent, September–October 1881; Entry 242, Troops in the Dist. of the Apache, 1881, Orders Issued and Endorsements Sent, September–October 1881; Entry 243, Troops in the Dist. of the Apache, 1881, Register of Letters and Telegrams Received, September–October 1881; Entry 244, Troops in the Dist. of the Apache, 1881, Letters and Telegrams Received, 1881; Entry 245, Troops in the Dist. of the Verde, 1881, Letters, Telegrams, and Endorsements Sent, September–October 1881 and March–October 1882; Entry 249, Letters, Telegrams, and Endorsements Sent by the Hq. for U.S. Troops Operating Against the Chiricahua Indians at Willcox, Arizona Territory, October 1881; Entry 250, Battalion Repairing Road Between Camp Thomas and Fort Apache, 1881, Letters and Telegrams Sent, October–December 1881. Pt. 1, Dept. of the Missouri, Entry 2601, Letters Received, 1881. Pt. 3, Entry 171,

Dist. of the Gila, Letters and Endorsements Sent and Field Orders Issued, 1881. Vol. 41, Camp Grant, Ariz., Letters, Endorsements and Telegrams Sent, October 1881. Vol. 69, Camp Grant, Ariz., Orders Issued, October 1881. Unnumbered vol., Camp Grant, Ariz., Letters and Telegrams Received, October 1881. Unnumbered vol., Fort Thomas, Ariz., Orders Issued, October 1881.

Bureau of the Census, 10th Census, 1880, Arizona, Vol. 1.

U.S. Weather Bureau, Climatological Records, 1819–92, Arizona, Reel 9.

ARIZONA HISTORICAL SOCIETY, TUCSON

MS 282, Gatewood Collection. Box 5, Folder 70. Extracts of a letter by William Baird printed in *Winners of the West*, April 1925.

———. Box 2, Folder 38. Letter from Thomas Cruse to Abbot, May 25, 1883.

———. Box 10, Folder 162, Letter 179. Letter from Thomas Cruse to Charles Gatewood, January 19, 1926.

U.S. ARMY MILITARY HISTORY INSTITUTE, CARLISLE BARRACKS, PA.

Letters of Lt. Stephen C. Mills.

OTHER ARCHIVAL MATERIAL

Annual Reports of the Secretary of War, 1880–83. Washington, D.C.: GPO, respective years.

Annual Reports of the Commissioner of Indian Affairs to the Secretary of the Interior, 1875, 1876, 1880, 1881, 1883. Washington, D.C.: GPO, respective years.

Bourke, John G. "The Medicine-Men of the Apache." Bureau of American Ethnology Ninth Annual Report (1892), 443–603.

Chronological List of Actions, &c., with Indians, from January 15, 1837, to January 1891. Washington, D.C.: Adjutant General's Office; reprint ed., 1979.

Diary of John Gregory Bourke, 1872–96. Vols. 45–47.

Heitman, Francis B. "Historical Register and Dictionary of the U.S. Army from Its Organization." September 29, 1789–March 2, 1903. 2 vols. Washington, D.C.: GPO, 1903.

Journal of the Senate of the United States of America, Session Specially called Monday, October 10, 1881, and 1st sess., 47th Cong. Washington, D.C.: GPO, 1881.

Medal of Honor of the United States Army. Washington, D.C.: GPO, 1948.

Register of Graduates and Former Cadets of the United States Military Academy, 1964 Thayer Memorial Edition, 1802–1964. West Point Alumni Foundation, Inc.

Reports of the Committees of the Senate of the United States for 1st sess., 47th Cong., 1881–82. Washington, D.C.: GPO, 1882.

Maps

Official Map of the Territory of Arizona. E. A. Eckhoff and P. Riecker. 1880.

Outline Map of the Field Operations Against Hostile Chiricahua Indians Showing Operations from April 12, 1886, through September 4, 1886. Corps of Engineers.

Southern Arizona in the Late 1870s. Paul Riecker. Modification of a map dated 1879.

Southwestern New Mexico. Office of the Chief Engineer, Dept. of the Missouri, 1883.

Territory of Arizona. Department of the Interior, General Land Office, 1883.

Territory and Department of Arizona Commanded by Brig. Gen. George Crook. Compiled and drawn by 1st Lt. T. A. Bingham, Corps of Engineers, U.S.A., 1885.

Territories of New Mexico and Arizona. Prepared in the Office of the Chief of Engineers, U.S.A., 1879.

Untitled Map of the San Carlos Reservation and Vicinity, Lt. C. F. Palfrey, Engr. Office, Hq. Dept. of Arizona, ca. 1881.

Eastern Arizona and western New Mexico, 1886–1987, U.S. Geological Survey.

Books and Articles

Agnew, S. C. *Garrisons of the Regular U.S. Army: Arizona, 1851–1899.* Arlington, Va.: Council on Abandoned Military Posts, 1974.

Altshuler, Constance. *Cavalry Yellow and Infantry Blue: Army Officers in Arizona Between 1851 and 1886.* Tucson: Arizona Historical Society, 1991.

Aye, Tom. "History of Fort Huachuca." *Bisbee Daily Review* 34, no. 185, sect. 6, August 3, 1931.

Ball, Eve. *Indeh, an Apache Odyssey:* Norman: University of Oklahoma Press, 1988.

Barnes, William C. *Apaches and Longhorns: The Reminiscences of Will C. Barnes.* Los Angeles, Calif.: Ward Ritchie Press, 1941; reprint ed., 1982.

———. *Arizona Place Names.* 1st ed. Tucson: University of Arizona, General Bulletin no. 2, 1935.

———. *Arizona Place Names.* Tucson: University of Arizona Press, 1935. 2d ed. revised and enlarged by Byrd H. Granger, 1960.

Basso, Keith H. *The Cibicu Apache.* New York: Holt, Rinehart and Winston, 1970.

———, ed. *Western Apache Raiding and Warfare: From the Notes of Grenville Goodwin.* Tucson: University of Arizona Press, 1971.

Bourke, John G. *On the Border with Crook.* New York: Charles Scribner's Sons, 1891; reprint ed., 1971.

Brandes, Ray. *Frontier Military Posts of Arizona.* Globe, Ariz.: Dale Stuart King, 1960.

Brinckerhoff, Sidney B. "Aftermath of Cibecue: Court Martial of the Apache Scouts, 1881." *Smoke Signal,* Tucson Corral of the Westerners, no. 36 (Fall 1978).

———. Book review. *Journal of Arizona History* 9, no. 1 (Spring 1968).

Carter, W. H. *From Yorktown to Santiago with the Sixth U.S. Cavalry.* Baltimore: Lord Baltimore Press, 1900.

Clum, John P. "Apache Misrule." *New Mexico Historical Review* 5, no. 2 (April 1930), and no. 3 (July 1930).

Collins, Charles. *The Great Escape: The Apache Outbreak of 1881.* Tucson, Ariz.: Westernlore Press, 1994.

Croxen, Fred W., Sr. "Dark Days in Central Arizona." *Smoke Signal,* Tucson Corral of the Westerners, no. 34, Fall 1977.

Cruse, Thomas. *Apache Days and After.* Caldwell, Ida.: Caxton Press, 1941.

Davis, Britton. *The Truth about Geronimo.* New Haven: Yale University Press, 1929.

Davisson, Lori. "New Light on the Cibecue Fight: Untangling Apache Identities." *Journal of Arizona History* 20, no. 4 (Winter 1979).

Farish, Thomas E. *History of Arizona*. Vol. 3. San Francisco, Calif.: Filmer Brothers Electrotype Co., 1918.

Finerty, John F. *War-path and Bivouac or the Conquest of the Sioux*. Chicago: Donohue and Henneberry, 1890.

Goodwin, Grenville. *The Social Organization of the Western Apache*. Chicago: University of Chicago Press, 1942; reprint ed., 1969.

Hart, Herbert M. *Tour Guide to Old Western Forts*. Fort Collins, Colo.: Old Army Press, 1980.

Harte, John B. "The Strange Case of Joseph C. Tiffany: Indian Agent in Disgrace." *Journal of Arizona History* 16, no. 4 (Winter 1975).

Horn, Tom. *Life of Tom Horn: A Vindication*. Denver: Louthan Co., 1904.

Kessel, William B. "The Battle of Cibecue and Its Aftermath: A White Mountain Apache's Account." *Ethnohistory* 21, no. 2 (Spring 1974).

King, James T. *War Eagle: A Life of General Eugene A. Carr*. Lincoln: University of Nebraska Press, 1963.

Lekson, Stephen H. *Nana's Raid: Apache Warfare in Southern New Mexico, 1881*. El Paso: Texas Western Press, 1987.

Mazzanovich, Anton. *Trailing Geronimo*. Los Angeles: Gem, 1926.

Myrick, David F. *New Mexico's Railroads*. Albuquerque: University of New Mexico Press, 1990.

―――. *Railroads of Arizona: The Southern Roads*. Vol. 1. San Diego: Howell-North Books, 1975.

Ogle, Ralph H. *Federal Control of the Western Apaches, 1848–1886*. Albuquerque: University of New Mexico Press, 1940.

Porter, Joseph C. *Paper Medicine Man: John Gregory Bourke and His American West*. Norman: University of Oklahoma Press, 1986.

Roberts, David. *Once They Moved Like the Wind*. New York: Simon and Schuster, 1993.

Smith, Cornelius C. "The Fight at Cibicu." *Arizona Highways* 32, no. 5 (May 1956).

Thrapp, Dan L. *Al Sieber: Chief of Scouts*. Norman: University of Oklahoma Press, 1964.

―――. *The Conquest of Apacheria*. Norman: University of Oklahoma Press, 1967.

―――. *Encyclopedia of Frontier Biography*. Glendale, Calif.: A. H. Clark, 1988.

―――. *General Crook and the Sierra Madre Adventure*. Norman: University of Oklahoma Press, 1972.

―――. *Juh: An Incredible Indian*. Southwestern Studies, Monograph no. 39. El Paso: Texas Western Press, 1973.

―――. *Victorio and the Mimbres Apaches*. Norman: University of Oklahoma Press, 1974.

Wellman, Paul I. *Death in the Desert: The Fifty Years' War for the Great Southwest*. New York: Macmillan, 1935.

Wharfield, H. B. *Cibicu Creek Fight in Arizona: 1881*. El Cajon, Calif., privately printed, 1971.

Wheeler, Cadet Brian. "The Mackenzie Syndrome." *Assembly*, Association of Graduates, United States Military Academy (March 1990).

Newspapers and Periodicals

Arizona Citizen
Arizona Gazette
Arizona Miner
Arizona Silver Belt
Arizona Star
Army and Navy Journal
Chicago Times
New York Herald
New York Times

INDEX